Bradshaw'S Illustr

Through Paris And Its Environs

Exhibiting In A Comprehensive Form All That Can Be Seen And How To See It With The Least Fatigue, Time And Expense ; With A Map Of Paris And Its Environs, And A Bird'S-Eye View Of The City ; And Other Executed Steel Engravings Illustrative Of The French Metropolis

Unknown

Alpha Editions

This edition published in 2021

ISBN : 9789354488177

Design and Setting By
Alpha Editions
www.alphaedis.com
Email - info@alphaedis.com

BRADSHAW'S

ILLUSTRATED

GUIDE THROUGH PARIS

AND ITS ENVIRONS:

EXHIBITING IN A COMPREHENSIVE FORM

ALL THAT CAN BE SEEN

AND

HOW TO SEE IT

WITH THE LEAST FATIGUE, TIME, AND EXPENSE;

WITH A

MAP OF PARIS AND ITS ENVIRONS,

AND

A BIRD'S-EYE VIEW OF THE CITY.

AND OTHER WELL EXECUTED STEEL

ENGRAVINGS ILLUSTRATIVE OF THE FRENCH METROPOLIS.

LONDON:
W. J. ADAMS & SONS (BRADSHAW'S GUIDE OFFICE), 59, FLEET STREET, E.C.;
MANCHESTER:—HENRY BLACKLOCK & Co., ALBERT SQUARE;
And SHEFFIELD:—FARGATE;
LIVERPOOL:—T. FAIRBROTHER, 40, LORD STREET; BIRMINGHAM:—GUEST & BARTON, 82, BULL STREET;
BRIGHTON:—H. & C. TREACHER, 1, NORTH STREET;
SOUTHAMPTON:—E. & M. PHILLIPS, 1, PENINSULAR AND ORIENTAL BUILDINGS; W. SHARLAND, HIGH STREET;
EDINBURGH:—JOHN MENZIES & Co., 12, HANOVER STREET; GLASGOW:—JAMES REID, 144, ARGYLE STREET;
DUBLIN:—CARSON BROTHERS, 7, GRAFTON STREET (CORNER OF STEPHEN'S GREEN);
LISBON:—MATHEUS LEWTAS, BOOKSELLER, 26, RUA NOVA DO GARMO;
PARIS:—THE GALIGNANI LIBRARY, 224, RUE DE RIVOLI; F. CLAVEY, AGENT FOR ADVERTISEMENTS, 4, RUE
BELLEFOND; K. NILSSON, 212, RUE DE RIVOLI;
BRUSSELS:—M. J. BIL (BRADSHAW'S GUIDE OFFICE), 2, PLACE ROYALE;
ZURICH:—H. F. LEUTHOLD, RUE DES POSTES A COTÉ L'DE HOTEL BAUR;
MALTA:—MR. MUIR, 220, STRADA REALE;
ALEXANDRIA AND CAIRO.—THE ALEXANDRIA STATIONERS AND BOOKSELLERS' COMPANY
SAINT MARK'S BUILDINGS;
UNITED STATES:—W. N. HARRISON & SON, 26, SECOND STREET, EXCHANGE BUILDINGS, BALTIMORE;
And Sold by all Booksellers, and at all Railway Stations throughout Great Britain, Ireland, and the Continent.
(80)

PLANS AND ILLUSTRATIONS.

GRAND HOTEL

DU

PAVILLON DE ROHAN,

172, RUE DE RIVOLI,

OPPOSITE THE LOUVRE AND THE AVENUE DE L'OPERA.

LARGE AND SMALL APARTMENTS. ROOMS FROM 3 FRANCS.

FIRST-CLASS TABLE D'HOTE. READING ROOM.

BOARD and **LODGING**, at **8 SHILLINGS** per **DAY.**

DINNERS À LA CARTE AND IN THE APARTMENTS.

BATHS IN THE HOTEL.

SEVERAL LANGUAGES SPOKEN.

This Hotel is strongly recommended for the luxury and the comfort of the Apartments, as well as for moderate charges. It is, besides, admirably situated in the centre of Paris, and in the healthiest quarter. From the windows of the Hotel there is a view of the whole length of the magnificent Avenue de l'Opera, and of the new Opera itself.

PATENT SAFETY LIFT.   [Lo-.3,

PREFACE.

The rapid and extensive sale of the first editions of this popular Guide has induced the proprietors to publish a new edition annually.

The work is in the form of an Itinerary, and is divided into such portions, or routes through Paris, as the Visitor will be able to accomplish in a given time. Everything specially worthy of attention is noticed, and the plan for each day is so arranged, that the trouble and confusion generally arising from the indiscriminate view of numerous objects are avoided. Many useful hints respecting the journey, hotels, lodgings, &c., have been added to the present edition, and the whole has been carefully revised, so as to render it a complete Guide to the objects of attraction in the French capital and its environs.

The injuries done to the buildings and localities in and around Paris, during the Franco-German war of 1870-1, and under the ferocious rule of the Commune, especially in the dark days of 20th-28th May, 1871, will be found noticed in their respective places, in this revised edition of the Guide to Paris.

[1880.]

CONTENTS.

INTRODUCTION.

INDEX.

INTRODUCTION.

GENERAL REMARKS FOR TRAVELLERS.

In drawing up the following instructions, it has been presumed that the traveller will have provided himself with *Bradshaw's Continental Railway Guide*, as indispensable to railway travelling on the Continent.

WHAT SHOULD BE DONE IN LONDON.—PASSPORTS—MONEY—LETTERS. Under the present arrangements British subjects are now admitted into France *without passports*, by simply declaring their nationality. But to travel in France is one thing, and to visit the interior of its public buildings is another, and those who desire to be on the safe side, for the latter purpose, should procure a passport; or, at least, they should have their visiting cards stamped by the Special Agent, at the port of landing, or on the frontier; or, otherwise their cards can be stamped upon application to the Prefect of Police, at Paris, near the Palais de Justice; open 9 to 4. It may be added, however, that frequently the theory of demanding a passport is not carried out in practice.

MONEY.—See *Bradshaw's Continental Guide*. Bank-notes are negotiable in Paris, but sovereigns are the best coins to take to Paris, as they are readily changed, and generally at a premium. Do not change your money in London, or you will lose the premium which English gold or notes bring in Paris. An English sovereign will exchange for 25 francs and a few centimes, which vary according to the rate of exchange, at any respectable money changer's in Paris. Bank of England notes about the same rate; but they are looked upon with suspicion, unless the person presenting them is known. Circular notes from a respectable London bank are the safest; but a commission is charged *if changed at an hotel*. As to expenses, 10s. to 20s. per head per day may be allowed; or you may live much cheaper, *cela dépend*. The latter sum will cover all charges of living in the best hotels, and travelling by first class railway, with the best places in the coach.

LETTERS.—The traveller will find it convenient to have his letters addressed to him to the "Poste Restante." (See Post Office, p. xix.) They will be delivered on the passport or name-card being shown at the General Post Office. There are now two posts daily (one in the morning and the other in the evening) leaving London for France. All letters for France go through the London post-office, and for the morning mail must be in the London chief office before 7 45 mrn., and the evening mail before 6 aft.

GENERAL POSTAL UNION.—This Union (Union Générale des Postes), according to the Convention of Berne, 1875, includes every country in Europe, with Egypt, Asiatic Russia, Turkey, Morocco, the United States, Canada, &c. Under this Convention, which has been in force from January, 1876, the Postage on all *Letters* from any country in the Union to any other, is at the rate of 2½d. under ½ oz. (15 grammes). *Post Cards* are 1d. *Newspapers* are 1d. per 4 oz. *Books*, are ½d. per 2 oz.; Commercial Papers, 2½d. per 4 oz.; Patterns, 1d. per 2 oz. These are the rates from England; and the return postage from every other country in the Union is the same, or as near as the currency and weights will allow. From France, for instance. Letters are 25 cents. for 15 grammes; Post cards are 15 cents; Newspapers are 5 cents. for 50 grammes. Within the Union, prepayment is compulsory by stamps of the country from which the letter is sent; that is. French stamps, &c., can be used only in France; German stamps, in Germany; and so on. If a letter be insufficiently prepaid, the extra charge is 2½d. per ½ oz. Registered Letters, 2d. extra. Telegrams to the United Kingdom, 2½d. a word. Money Orders—under £2, for 9d.; £5, for 1s. 6d.; £7, for 2s. 3d.; £10, for 3s.

Under the term "Printed Matter" are included periodical works other than registered newspapers, stitched or bound books, pamphlets, sheets of music, catalogues, prospectuses, announcements, and notices of every kind, whether printed, engraved, or lithographed.

The following regulations must be strictly observed:—1. Every packet must be sent without a cover, or in a cover open at the ends or sides. 2. There must be no enclosure, except newspapers or other printed papers. 3. There must be no other writing or marks upon the newspapers or printed papers than the name and address of the person to whom they are sent, nor anything upon the cover but such name and address, the printed title of the papers, and the printed name and address of the publisher or vender who sends them. If any of the above regulations be disregarded, or if the whole postage be not paid in advance, the packets will either be detained or forwarded charged as unpaid letters.

Newspapers addressed to the Mediterranean or the East Indies, and intended to be sent in the closed mails by way of Marseilles, will continue liable to the existing regulations, including the present rates of postage.

The time required for conveying Letters, &c., to any part of France, can be ascertained by reference to *Bradshaw's Continental Railway Guide*, and in very little more than this time the traveller may expect them at their appointed place.

WAY TO GET TO FRANCE AND LANDING THERE.—The following are the

ROUTES TO PARIS.

[As the Railway Trains are subject to change every month, the information given here respecting them had better be compared with *Bradshaw's General Railway Guide*.]

CALAIS ROUTE.—London to Paris, direct, *viâ* Dover and Calais, 283 miles (sea passage, 21½ miles), in 9¼ hours. Trains leave *South Eastern Stations* at Charing Cross (West End Terminus) at 7 40 mrn. (1 & 2 class) and 8 25 aft. (1st class), and Cannon Street (City Terminus) five minutes later. Or the *London, Chatham, and Dover Stations* at Victoria (West End Terminus) and Ludgate Hill (City Terminus), at 7 35 mrn. (1 & 2 class exp.) and 8 15 aft. (1st class exp.) They arrive at Dover at 9 30 mrn. and 10 20 aft.; proceed by Steamer from Dover at 9 35 mrn. and 10 20 aft.; and by train from Calais at 12 35 aft. and 1 20 mrn.; and reach Paris at 6-5 aft. and 6 20 mrn. Through Fares. 1st class, 60s.; 2nd, 45s. Return Tickets, available for a month, 95s. and 75s. There is also a Special Fixed Night Service, 1,2,3 class, viz.:—From Victoria at 6 25 aft., Ludgate Hill, 6 22 aft., Charing Cross 6 35 aft., Cannon Street 6 48 aft., arriving at Dover at 9 45 aft.,

B

leaving Dover at 10 20 aft., arriving at Calais at 12 10 mrn., leaving Calais at 7 20 mrn., and arriving at Paris at 4 30 aft. Fares, 31s. 6d. and 21s. Return Tickets, available for 14 days, 47s. and 31s. 6d.

Or by *General Steam Navigation Company's* Boats (occasional—for departures see advertisements in daily papers) from Iron Gate Wharf to Calais. Fares, 12s. chief cabin, 8s. fore cabin (steward's fee included).

This route in the old coach days took 58 to 60 hours between London and Paris. By the direct trains registered luggage is examined only on arrival at Paris. The station, refreshment room, and douane, at Calais, are close to the quay. Three departures from Calais for Dover daily. The companies employ officers to pass baggage at Dover without charge, when free of duty. The holders of through tickets are allowed 56lbs. of registered baggage, free of charge, and without any registration fee, except from Dover to Paris, when a charge of 5d. per package additional is made. All foreign articles must be declared to the customs' officers. Tobacco, cigars, and any article registered, being merchandise, are liable to seizure. The registered luggage of passengers who desire to stop at Dover can be had there by giving the baggage ticket at the station.

On returning, passengers by *South Eastern* route should register their baggage to Charing Cross, and by the *London, Chatham and Dover* route to Victoria Station or Ludgate Hill, and on arrival at Dover should proceed to the Custom House, at the station, to pass the customs' examination of their baggage, without which it will not be put into the train for London. On the out journey registered baggage is examined at Paris ; on the return journey by *South Eastern* route at Charing Cross, and by *London, Chatham, and Dover* route at Dover. Passengers are booked and their luggage registered from Calais to Charing Cross or Victoria, at the Company's office, in the *Northern of France Railway Station* at Calais. The registration of baggage saves the trouble and expense of landing and shipping it, and conveying it between the train and the boat, as well as harbour dues and other imposts hitherto made. Luggage should be at the station at least a quarter of an hour before starting.

BOULOGNE ROUTE.—London to Paris, direct, *via* Folkestone and Boulogne, 255 miles (sea passage, 25½ miles) in about 10 hours. Trains leave the *South Eastern Station* at Charing Cross (West End Terminus) and Cannon Street (City Terminus), twice daily; and Packets run from Folkestone according to tide. Through Tickets, 56s. and 42s.. Return Tickets, available for a month, £4 15s. and £3 15s. By Cheap Night Service, 31s. 6d. and 21s. Return Tickets, 47s.; 31s. 6d. Baggage can be registered from London and Falkestone, respectively, every day, and from Paris and Boulogne every day but Sunday, when it is examined at Folkestone. On the return, passengers should order their luggage to be registered to Charing Cross, which obviates the examination *en route.*

Or by *General Steam Navigation Company's* Boats, almost daily, direct from St. Katherine's Wharf in 8 hours. Fares to Boulogne, 12s. and 8s. 6d. (steward's fee included).

DIEPPE ROUTE.—London to Paris, direct, *via* Newhaven and Dieppe, 246 miles (sea passage, 64 miles). Tidal Trains leave the *London, Brighton, and South Coast Stations* at 7 50 to 8 0 p.m. at London Bridge (City Terminus), and Victoria (West End Terminus) ; and Packets start from Newhaven to Dieppe, according to tide. Buffet at the Harbour Station. Through Fares, 1st class, 33s.; 2nd class, 24s.; 3rd class (by Night Service only), 17s. Return Tickets, 55s.; 39s.; 30s. Luggage should be registered before leaving England (at London or Newhaven) in order to avoid examination at Dieppe ; and on the return journey it should be registered through to London; but the Customs examination takes place at Newhaven. *See Bradshaw's Continental Guide.*

HAVRE ROUTE.—London to Paris, *viâ* Southampton and Havre, 341¾ miles (sea passage, 120 miles). Trains leave the *London and South Western Station* at Waterloo Bridge at 9 aft. (1 & 2 class), every Monday, Wednesday, and Friday, arriving at Southampton at 11 35 aft.; proceed by Steamer from Southampton at 11 45 aft.; by train from Havre at 12 10 (1st class) and 9 35 and 12 24 (2nd class); arrive at Paris at 4 35 aft. (1st class) and 5 5 and 7 35 aft. (2nd class). Through Fares, 33s.; 24s. Return Tickets, 55s.; 39s.

Also by the *General Steam Navigation Company's* Vessels, every Sunday, in about 20 hours, to Havre. Fares, 13s.; 9s. *See Bradshaw's Continental Guide.*

CHERBOURG ROUTE.—By the Great Western Company's Steamers from Weymouth at 11 30 p.m. every day, except Sunday; in about six hours to Cherbourg (65 sea miles), where the Western of France may be taken at 8 3 a.m. for Paris, and trains for Normandy, Brittany, &c. Fares, Weymouth and Cherbourg, 17s. 6d., and 12s. 6d.

DUNKIRK ROUTE.—From London, direct, Steamers from Butler's or Fenning's Wharf, twice a week, in about 11 hours. Fares, 10s.; 7s.

Once on board on the return you cannot go ashore again without special permission. You may bring back, free of duty, a pint of spirits, and half-a-pint of Eau-de-Cologne.

LUGGAGE.—On alighting from the train in Paris, the passenger need give himself no anxiety about his luggage. What he has to do is quietly to follow the others, and he will enter a spacious room where he will find his trunk and boxes, as well as those of his fellow voyagers arranged on a long platform. Selecting his own, he will give up the keys to the nearest officers, who are the *Customs' Officers* for Paris. They will proceed to unlock, open, and examine his various packages, or most likely mark them without examination; and when they have satisfied themselves, re-deliver him his keys, with permission to pass. The passenger will then ask a porter *(facteur)*, who can easily be distinguished by his special dress, to take his trunks, &c., for him to a conveyance. Charge, 10c. a package.

CALL A CAB.—By all means call for a cab, as you will find a variety of omnibuses waiting at the station, ready to seize upon you and carry you to what they call a good Hotel, professedly for less than a cab. But their object is to drive you to one of *their* Hotels; we say *their* Hotels because either the driver or conductor is invariably paid for each passenger he brings to the Hotel. This, of course, is made up for by the exorbitant charges which the keeper of the hotel, to which you are conducted, manages to make.

CHOICE OF A LOCALITY.—There are many parts of Paris in which a person intending to reside for some time, would find very commodious and cheap lodgings, which, however, would be perfectly unsuited for a traveller who wishes to spend only a few days, and to see as much in that limited time as he can. We, therefore, recommend him to take up his quarters *somewhere near* the Madeleine. This is the centre from which nearly all the principal monuments may be visited. In the neighbourhood are the Tuileries, the Champs Elysées, the Rue de la Paix, the Boulevards, the Louvre, the Place de la Concorde, the Place Vendôme, the Palais Royal, Rue de Rivoli, the principal Embassies, &c.; and a few moments' walk will take him to either of the Operas or the principal French theatres. If the traveller intend to remain for some time, he will find suitable accommodation, either *pensions* or private lodgings, in the neighbourhood. The "English Quarter," as it is called by the Parisians, is perhaps the most delightful place of residence in Paris, but it is not central; however, omnibuses continually traverse it for all parts of the town. Fare: inside, 3d.; outside, 1½d.

Hotels.—Having made a choice of your locality, the next thing is the choice of your hotel. This we might observe should be made before arriving at the station, that you may at once order the cabman where to drive you, and being decided upon this point you will not suffer interruption from the importunities of the conductors of the omnibus. As it may be difficult for the traveller to determine where to put up on his arrival in Paris, without some idea of the hotels in this metropolis, we subjoin a list of the best.

Grand Hotel, 12, Boulevard des Capucines. Re-opened. New Managers have reduced the tariffs.

Grand Hôtel du Louvre. Reduced Tariff.

Hôtel des Deux Mondes et d'Angleterre, 22, Avenue de l'Opera, and 5, Rue Thérèse.

Hôtel Continental, 3, Rue Castiglione, overlooking the Tuileries Gardens; 600 rooms: great comfort and moderate charges.

Hôtel du Rhin, 4, Place Vendôme; excellent first-class hotel. Well situated.

Grand Hôtel Mirabeau, 8, Rue de la Paix, the finest part of Paris; table d'hôte at 6 fr.

Grand Hôtel de la Bourse et des Ambassadeurs, 17, Rue Notre Dame des Victoires, corner of the Place de la Bourse.

Hôtel Meurice, 228, Rue de Rivoli; fine situation; conducted by H. Scheurich.

St. James's Hotel, 211, Rue Saint Honoré; excellent. The *Hôtel Bergere*, Rue Bergere, belongs to the same proprietor.

Hôtel de Lille et d'Albion, 223, Rue St. Honoré, a well-conducted good house.

Hôtel de Wagram 208, Rue de Rivoli, overlooking the Tuileries Gardens. J. Boeck, proprietor.

Hôtel de la Place du Palais Royal. 170, Rue de Rivoli; deservedly recommended for its comfort and good Table d'Hôte.

Metropolitan Hotel, 8, Rue de Luxembourg, overlooking the "Jardins des Tuileries."

Grand Hôtel de l'Athenée, 15, Rue Scribe. Conducted with great care by Mr. Vautier, manager. Lift; two Bath Rooms on each floor.

Hôtel de la Grand Bretagne, 14, Rue Caumartin; very quiet; recommended.

Grand Hôtel de Londres, 5, Rue Castiglione. Well situated and well frequented.

Grand Hôtel de Normandie, 266, Rue St. Honoré, good and moderate.

Hôtel Vauillemont, 15, Rue Boissy d'Anglas, near the Madeleine, good situation and quiet.

Hôtel de Rivoli, 202, Rue de Rivoli, J. Stolle, proprietor; very good, opposite the Tuileries: charges moderate.

Hôtel Bedford, 17 and 19, Rue de l'Arcade, near the Madeleine, excellent in every respect.

Hôtel du Danube and Glasgow, 11, Rue Richepanse; finest situation in Paris, C. Brunel, proprietor.

Hôtel d'Albe, 71 and 73, Avenue de l'Alma, Champs Elysées. Kept by Messrs. Henry de la Blanchetais and Co.

Hôtel Meyerbeer, at the Rond point of the Champs Elysées, facing the Palais de l'Industrie. Entirely newly furnished.

Hôtel Malesherbes, 26, Boulevard Malesherbes, between the Madeleine and the Opera. Recommended for its good attendance and very moderate charges.

Hôtel Belle Vue, 39, Avenue de l'Opera, and Rue d'Antin, comfortable, and reasonable prices.

Hôtel Buckingham, 32, Rue Pasquier (ex Rue de la Madeleine). The proprietor speaks English.

Family Hotel, 6, Rue Castiglione, near the Tuileries Gardens.

London and New York Hotel, conveniently situated, near the Madeleine and Champs Elysées.

Hôtel du Prince Albert, 5, Rue St. Hyacinthe, St. Honoré, near the Tuileries: recommended.

Stohr's Hotel, Rue de Provence, No. 55, very good English Establishment; moderate charges.

Hôtel du Palais (Family Hotel), 28, Avenue cours la Reine.

Hôtel de St. Petersbourg, 35, Rue Caumartin; entirely refitted up by the new proprietor, M. Motte.

English Family Boarding-House, 3, Cité Retiro. Entrance, Rue Boissy d'Anglas, and 30, Faubourg St. Honoré.

Hôtel Violet, Passage Violet, very quiet; recommended.

Hotel de l'Univers, 46, Rue de Châlons, second class hotel, opposite the Lyons railway station.

Hôtel Castiglione, Rue Castiglione. Kept by Mrs. and Mr. Vitet.

Hôtel du Pavillon de Rohan, 172, Rue de Rivoli, facing the Louvre and the Avenue du Grand Opera.

Hôtel du Chemin de fer du Nord, Place du Chemin du fer du Nord, very good hotel for families and gentlemen. Piet, proprietor.

Hôtel de Bruxelles, 33, Rue du Mall, near the Boulevards.

Hôtel du Globe, 4, Rue Croix des Petits Champs.

Boarding House, or Private Hotel, 9, Rue Castiglione; Dominici, proprietor.

Grand Hotel Anglo Americain, 113, Rue St. Lazare, opposite the St. Lazare station.

Hôtel Rastadt 44, Rue Neuve St. Augustin, near the Rue de la Paix and the Grand Opera.

Hôtel Byron, 30 and 22, Rue Laffitte, Boulevard des Italians.

Hôtel de Calais, 5, Rue Neuve des Capucines, a comfortable and reasonable house.

Grand Hotel de Choiseul et d'Egypte, 15, Rue Neuve St. Augustin, corner of the Avenue de l'Opera.

Hôtel Therese, 13, Rue Ste. Anne, near the Avenue de l'Opera.

Grand Hotel d'Orleans, 17, Rue Richelieu, near the Avenue de l'Opera and the Palais Royal.

Hotel Binda (formerly Prince Albert), 11, Rue de l'Echelle. Recommended.

Hôtel Richepanse, 14, Rue Richepanse, near the Madeleine.

Grand Hotel Jules Cesar, Avenue Lacuée, corner of the Rue de Lyon, 20.

Hotel d'Oxford et de Cambridge, 13, Rue d'Alger, near the Jardin des Tuileries.

Grand Hotel Mirabeau, 8, Rue de la Paix, the finest part of Paris; table d'hôte at 6 fr.

Hôtel d'Espagne et de Hongrie—Mr. List, proprietor, 4 and 5, Rue Taitbout (Boulevard des Italians), near Tortoni.

Grand Hotel de Nice, Place de la Bourse, in the centre of commerce and public walks.

Hôtel Coquillière, 21, Rue Coquillière, near the Exchange, Chief Post Office, Louvre, and Palais Royal.

Hôtel des Etats Unis, 16, Rue d'Antin, Avenue de l'Opera, finest and most central situation.

Hôtel d'Alexandrie, 344, Rue Laffitte, near the Boulevard des Italians: very comfortable Hotel.

The English Hotel, 24, Rue d'Amsterdam; very conveniently situated, moderate charges.

Hôtel de l'Amirauté, 20, Rue Duphot, Boulevard de la Madeline.

Hôtel Liverpool, 11, Rue Castiglione, Place Vendôme, an excellent Family Hotel.

Hôtel de la Terrasse Jouffroy, 10, Boulevard Montmartre; Renceray, junr., proprietor.

Hôtel de l'Empire, 57, Rue Neuve St. Augustin, corner of the Rue de la Paix.

Constantinople Hotel, 7, Rue de Constantinople; close to railway station of St. Lazare, and Omnibus Office.

Hotel and Boarding House, 29, Rue Caumartin; Demailly, proprietor.

Villa-Dorée, 5, Rue Lord Byron, Champs Elysees; family Hotel, in the centre of fashionable walks. Garnier-Knop, proprietor.

Pension de Famille, 7, Rue Lauriston, Champs Elysées, Miss Baker.

Furnished Apartments, 36, Rue du Colisée, Champs Elysées, Mr. Brodhurst

APARTMENTS AND BOARDING HOUSES.—Persons visiting Paris are recommended to apply to Messrs. John Arthur & Co., 10, Rue Castiglione, Agent to the British Embassy, and Wine Merchant, where every information will be given gratis; or, to Messrs. Sprent & Phipps, 240, Rue de Rivoli; or, Mr. Largier, 32, Boulevard Malesherbes.

The principal Restaurants are sumptuous establishments, and a good dinner at any of them would be found an expensive affair. The Etablissements de Bouillon Duval are, however, good cheap Restaurants, known chiefly to the French, found on the Boulevards, in the Rue de Rivoli, Rue Montmartre, &c., &c., and offering a good dinner for about 2 francs, wine included. Visitors should endeavour to make a party of three or four, and then, by ordering one dish for two persons, or two dishes for four, they can then have a considerable variety of particular dishes at a moderate price. The best houses in the Palais Royal are Salon Français, La Rotonde, &c. The Maison Dorée, the Café de Paris, the Café Anglais, Café Foy, Grand Hotel, and Café Cardinal, on the Boulevards, are also excellent Restaurants. As a general rule, however, it is better for the traveller to dine at his hotel, if there is a table d'hôte, as these dinners are very good, and the wines better than those to be had at the Restaurants. The Parisians do not sit long over their wine, but adjourn to a Café to take a cup of Coffee, with a glass of Cognac. It is agreeable enough to sit in front of one of the magnificent Cafés on the Boulevards, in the Palais Royal, or Champs Elysées, and sip a cup of this refreshing beverage as they make it in France, and at the same time watch the motley crowd of passers by who throng the streets and Boulevards in the evening. Those who wish to vary their experience of Paris dinners, without exceeding the limits of economy, can go to the Diners à Prix Fixe: Passage Jouffroy; at No. 11, Le Diner de Paris, the price is 5 francs; at No. 16, le Diner du Rocher, it is 3½ francs. Again, at le Diner du Commerce, No. 24 Passage des Panoramas, you dine for 3 francs; and at Rue de Mail, No. 3, you have a good Table d'Hôte for 1 franc 80 cents.

Besides the Etablissements Bouillon Duval noticed above, there are others of the same kind in Boulevard St. Michel, at No. 34, Rue Lafayette; No. 52 (very crowded, 6 aft.), near Faubourg Montmartre; another (the largest) is Rue Montesquieu, No. 6, near the Louvre. Best, but most crowded time, 11 mrn. to 1 aft., or 5 to 7 aft.

Conveyances.—One of the best features of Paris is the order, regularity, and civility with which the public conveyance system is arranged. The drivers of all hired carriages are under the strict surveillance of the police; and the penalties of the law are very severe against any who infringe the comfort of a Parisian, either by ill conduct or extortion. In every respect the system in England might be improved by adopting a few of the regulations that affect the French management. To a Londoner the prices will appear very economical. The **Cab** is not taken by the mile, but by the course or by the hour. The *Course* is any distance between the Barrières of Paris, or to the Bois de Boulogne, but it should be observed that any stoppage, however slight, by order of the "fare," completes a course, and a new one is commenced. It will be therefore best for a person having many sights to see, to take a cab by the hour; the difference is very trifling. There are two sorts of Cabs, those which stand under sheds, and those which stand in the open street. The former will be met with in nearly every street, not more than two or three together in the same place; they are called *voitures sous remise*—remise signifying a coach-house; and they are numbered in *red figures*. Many remise cabs are to be met on the stands. The latter remain in long file in some open place or street, and are called *voitures de place* or *fiacres*. The numbers on the *voitures de place* are *yellow*.

For Cabs, plying in the streets, whether *voitures de place* or *voitures de remise*, the following are the

DAY CHARGES WITHIN THE FORTIFICATIONS:—

For 2 persons, 1 fr. 50 ct. to 1 fr. 80 ct. the course ; 2 fr. to 2 fr. 25 ct. the hour.
For 4 persons, 2 fr. to 2 fr. 25 ct. the course ; 2 fr. 50 ct. to 2 fr. 75 ct. the hour.
Landaus with 4 places, and Voitures with 6, are 2 fr. 50 ct. to 3 fr. per hour.

The day begins at 6 in summer (1st April to 1st October), and 7 in winter ; and ends at 12 30 at night.

Night Cabs, or rides beyond the Fortifications, or Cabs called from a remise (stable), are liable to extra charges, for which see the Regulations.

When the traveller leaves the Cab beyond the fortifications, *i.e.*, does not return with it, he has to pay an extra franc, whether he has engaged a *voiture de place* or a *remise.* Trunks or packages outside, 25 cents each ; but no more than three are to be paid for. No charge for articles inside. The driver is bound to load and unload the luggage ; and to give a ticket, with his number, when you take your seat. Going to a theatre, or concert, you pay in advance. Though fees are prohibited, it is usual to give 15 to 20 cents extra for the course ; 25 cents by the hour.

When hiring by time, the whole first hour is paid for, and the time beyond is paid in proportion.

In visiting places, and going by the hour, it is always cheaper to take a *voiture de remise*, because the horses are kept in better condition and go over the ground faster. The drivers expect always a few sous, "*pour boire*," additional.

Most of the Cabs now belong to two Companies, some of the drivers being distinguished by white hats and coats.

Some Cabs (*Voitures de grande remise*) have no number, and may charge what they please if no agreement be made. Their drivers wear black glazed hats and brass buttons. They may be hired by the day (20 to 30 francs) or month.

Always ask for the ticket before sitting down in the Cab, and do not say whether you take it by the hour or course (trip) till you have got the ticket.

Besides the Cabs there are nearly 700 *Omnibuses* (all under one Company), by which the visitor may traverse Paris in any direction — thirty-two different lines. It frequently happens that he will, however, require two omnibuses to get to a particular point, and he will then have to ask for a ticket of correspondence, by which, when he leaves the first omnibus, he can get into another going in his direction. The charges are 15 cents outside, and 30 cents inside, repeated, of course, outside only, when taking a correspondence ticket. Children above four years of age must be paid for. See page xliii. for a list.

STEAMERS.—Small Steamers (called *Bateaux Omnibus*), comfortable and well fitted up, run up and down the Seine within the fortifications every ten minutes, from Pont National. near Bercy, to Pont du Tour, near Bois de Boulogne. Fares, 1½d.; 2½d. on Sunday. They also run up the river to Charenton and down the river (in summer) from Pont Royal to Sèvres, St. Cloud, and Suresnes,

Shops.—The visitor cannot be too much on his guard against taking the advice of his *maitre d'hôtel* as to the shops where he might wish to make purchases. In some instances the shop-keeper and the hotel-keeper play into one another's hands, and a per centage is allowed for every customer thus introduced. To enable the visitor to rely upon himself as much as possible, and select his own shop for making purchases, we will subjoin some of the shops as well as a few of the streets where the best and most reasonable business may be transacted. See *Bradshaw's Continental Railway Guide.*

First, there are the Boulevards, Rue de la Paix, Rue Castiglione, Rue St. Honoré, Rue du Faubourg St Honoré. Rue Vivienne, Rue Richelieu, Rue Neuve des Petits Champs, Rue de Rivoli, the Palais Royal, and the Rue Montmartre, where goods are cheaper than in the "West End." But the visitor should avoid, if possible, shops where they speak English, as this accomplishment, generally very imperfect, has to be paid for. See List of Shops, &c., page xxxviii.

Post Office.—The General Post Office is in the Rue Jean Jacques Rousseau. A new one is building in Rue Aux Ours. Letters for England should be posted before 5 aft. in the boxes at the shops; there are certain principal offices where they can be posted till 5 30, or at the head office till 7, with an extra fee. The Poste Restante is opened daily from 8 mrn. to 7 aft., except on Sundays, when it closes at 5 aft. There are seven deliveries of letters daily in Paris. Letters from England arrive at the chief office at 9 mrn. and 7 aft. Postage on letters throughout France and Algiers, 15 cents under 15 grammes. (N.B.—5 cents=½d. or a sou; and 5 grammes=the weight of a silver franc; 10 grammes=¼ ounce 15 grammes=½ ounce). Postal cards, 10 cents. A Registered (recommandée) letter for any part of France pays 25 cents extra. Money Orders (Mandats de poste) for France, 1 per cent. For England and the Postal Union, see p. xiii.

Telegraphs.—There are 50 to 55 offices, including the railway stations. Charge, to any part of France, 5 cents. per word, with a minimum charge of 50 cents. Money Orders up to 5,000 francs may be sent by telegraph through France, by making a deposit at the station. Telegraph to the United Kingdom, see p. xiii.

District Post Offices.—There are 60 branch offices or bureaux, and above 700 district offices or *boîtes*, at the tobacconists' and pillar boxes. Stamps are to be had at the tobacconists' shops.

Money.—The following is the relative value of English and French coins, subject to the rate of Exchange:—

5 Centimes	1 Sou, equal to about	1 half-penny, English.
20 Sous, or 100 Centimes	1 Franc	,, nearly 10 pence, ,,
100 Sous	5 Franc-piece ,,	4 shillings ,,
20 Francs	1 Napoleon ,,	16 ,, ,,

There are also gold pieces valued at forty and a hundred francs; and Notes of 1, 2, and 5 francs are now issued; as well as notes for 20, 50, 100, 500, 1,000 and 5,000 francs.

Money accounts in France are kept in francs and centimes, or hundredths; the décimes or tenths, which come between, being seldom mentioned.

COMPARISON OF FRENCH AND ENGLISH MONEY.

1 fra ns = 10 décimes = 100 (copper) centimes
20 sous or sols = 10d. English.
(1 sous therefore = 5 centimes = $\frac{1}{2}$d.)
24 francs = 1 Louis d'or (gold) = 19s.
20 francs = 1 Napoleon (gold) = 16s.
100 francs = £4
The franc exceeds the old livre by $1\frac{1}{4}$ per cent. ($1\frac{1}{4}$ centime.)

£1 = 25 francs, or 25 francs 5 cents, or a trifle more, according to the rate of Exchange.
1s. = $1\frac{1}{4}$ franc or 25 sous.
1d. = $10\frac{1}{2}$ centimes or 2 sous.
The modern French *Gold* coins are pieces of 5 fr., 10 fr., 20 fr., 40 fr., 50 fr., and 100 fr. The *Silver* coins are pieces of 20 centimes, 50 cents. or $\frac{1}{2}$ franc, 1 franc, 2 franc, and 5 franc pieces. *Copper* coins are 2 sous, 1 sou, 2 centimes, and 1 centime.

To turn English Money into French.—Make it into shillings, add three noughts, divide by 8, cut off two figures, and you get francs and cents. Thus £3 5s. = 65s.; $\frac{65000}{8}$ = 8125, or 81f. 25c. *To turn French Money into English.*—Multiply francs and cents by 8; cut off two figures; and you get shillings and decimals.

Weights and Measures (in round numbers).—A Mètre, which is the basis of all French measures and weights, is equal to $1\frac{1}{10}$ of an English yard nearly (3 feet 3·37 inches); and 1,000 mètres (or a kilomètre) are equal to about $\frac{5}{8}$ of a mile (4 furlongs, 213 yards).

Gramme	= $15\frac{1}{2}$ grains troy	10 Kilomètres	= 6 miles, 1 furlong, 156 yards
Hectare	= $2\frac{1}{2}$ acres = 10,000 square mètres	Litre	= $1\frac{3}{4}$ pint = $\frac{1}{4}$ gallon
10 Hectares	= $22\frac{3}{4}$ acres	10 Litres	= $2\frac{1}{5}$ gallons
Hectolitre	= 22 gallons	Mètre square	= $1\frac{1}{5}$ square yard
Kilogramme, or "kilo"	= $2\frac{1}{5}$ lbs. avoirdupois	Metric Quintal	= 2 cwt.
10 Kilogrammes	= 22 lbs.	Toise	= 6 French feet = $6\frac{2}{3}$ English feet
Kilomètre, or "kilom"	= $\frac{5}{8}$ mile = 1000 mètres		

Form of Application to a Minister.—For the benefit of those who may wish to obtain an order of admission into the public buildings, we subjoin the following model; the title of address will require to be changed according to the person addressed. For example: if to a minister, *à Monsieur le Ministre de*————; if to a general, *à Monsieur le Genéral de*————

A MONSIEUR LE MINISTRE DE————

Monsieur le Ministre,

En ma qualité d'étranger, en passant par cette ville, je prends la liberté de m'adresser à votre Excellence, pour solliciter l'extrême faveur d'une autorisation qui me permette de visiter——— (name of place) le ——— (date).

En accédant à ma demande vous rendrez une véritable service à celui qui a l'honneur d'être, avec le plus profond respect,

Monsieur le Ministre,

Votre très humble et très obéissant,

————

HOW TO SEE PARIS FOR ABOUT £4 4s.

1. Buy *Bradshaw's Illustrated Hand-Book to Paris*, and consult it for the particulars of all the places hereinafter mentioned, 1s. 6d.

2. Return Ticket, Second Class, London to Paris *viâ* Newhaven and Dieppe, or one of the Thames routes, £1 19s.

3. Three days' bed, breakfast, dinner, wine, &c., at a first-class hôtel, 12 fr. 50 cents. per day, £1 10s.

For hotels see handbook, page xvi., choose one in, or near to, Rue de Rivoli.

FIRST DAY.—Breakfast at eight ; walk down Rue de Rivoli, Avenue des Champs Elysées to the Arc de Triomphe, climb to the top and look at the magnificent view all round ; Montmartre, Bois de Boulogne, Meudon, windings of the Seine the Champs de Mars, Paris with its Churches and streets of Palaces, stretching away to Charenton and Vincennes ; Villette, Batignolles, and the Park of Monceau. Come down and walk to the corner of the Rue Chaillot. Take an omnibus to the Madeleine. See it, inside and out. Walk down Rue Royale and turn eastward down the Rue St. Honoré to the Church of St. Roch. See it. Walk still eastward down the Rue St. Honoré to the Palais Royal. Walk round the gardens and take a cup of coffee or an ice and a biscuit. Come out at the south entrance, cross the Rue de Rivoli, and enter the Louvre. See the pictures (consult the hand-book) till four o'clock. Call a *voiture de place*, tell the driver to take you one hour round the Boulevards, or by the tower of St. Jacques de la Boucherie, Boulevards de Sebastopol, Poissonniere, des Italiens. Home to dinner.

Cost of day :—

	F.	C.
Arc de Triomphe	0	50
Omnibus	0	30
Ice, or Coffee	0	60
Voiture (Cab)	1	90
Driver	0	10
	3	40

Or in English money about 2s. 9d.

SECOND DAY.—Breakfast at eight. Take a voiture to Notre Dame. See it. Thence walk to the Jardin des Plantes. See the wild beasts. Take a voiture to the Panthéon (church of St. Geneviève). Walk to the Palais de Luxembourg. See the pictures there. Take a voiture to the Hôtel des Invalides, or walk. See it, and if the right day, the tomb of Napoleon. Walk to the Ecole Militaire and the Champ de Mars, both very near, and to the Trocadérô. Then cross the bridge, Pont de Jena, take the rail omnibus to the Place de la Concorde. It will now be time for dinner.

Cost of day :—	F.	C.
Voiture to Notre Dame	1	50
Driver	0	20
Voiture to Panthéon	1	50
Driver	0	20
Coffee or ice at the Jardin	0	60
Guide at Invalides	0	50
Omnibus	0	30
	4	80

Or in English money, 4s.

THIRD DAY.—Breakfast at eight. Take voiture to the Palais de Justice. See the Sainte Chapelle close by. Then to the remains of the Palace of the Tuileries. At eleven or twelve take the rail omnibus from the Place de la Concorde to St. Cloud, and its ruined Palace. See it, and return in time to start by an afternoon train for the night boat across the Channel, reaching London in the forenoon of the next day.

Cost of the day :—	F.	C
Voiture	1	50
Driver	0	10
Voiture	1	50
Driver	0	10
To St. Cloud and back	1	50
Guide	0	50
Voiture to Station	1	50
Food, &c., on road	4	20
Porters at landing	1	40
	12	30

Or in English money, 10s.

SUMMARY OF EXPENSES.

	£	s.	d.
Hand-Book	0	2	6
Return Ticket	1	19	0
Three days' lodging and food	1	10	0
First day's expenses	0	2	9
Second ditto	0	3	1
Third ditto	0	9	8
Total	£4	7	0

OBSERVATIONS.

I.—Take no luggage but a small carpet bag. This you can carry in your hand, and the custom house officers will "visité" it while you hold it, both at landing and in the station in Paris. Thus you will have no delay.

II.—In the evenings you may walk out and see the Place Vendôme, the Column of July (on the site of the Bastile), the ruined Hôtel de Ville, the Bourse, the gardens of the Tuileries, and any other near objects. Or you may hear good music at the Concert à la Musard, near the Champs Elysées; entrance one franc.

III.—Instead of boarding altogether at your hotel, you can take a bed there, 3 fr. or 3 fr. 50 cent.; service, 1 fr. or 1 fr. 50 cent.; breakfast, 1 fr. 25 cent. or 1 fr. 50 cent.; and dine where you please. A good dinner and a pint of ordinary wine can be had at many good restaurants for 2 fr.; coffee and roll and butter, 1 fr. French coffee is good; but they do not yet know how to make tea. As to purchases, the English visitor will often find that he can get better things in London at less price.

HINTS FOR VISITORS MAKING ONLY
A SHORT STAY IN PARIS.

1. *To Visitors passing only One day at Paris.*—Take up your abode at one of the Hotels which you will find mentioned at page XVII., but let it be, if possible, near the Boulevards, or the Rue St. Honoré. Breakfast at 8 o'clock, walk along the Boulevards, from the Boulevard des Italiens to the Madeleine, one of the most beautiful and modern churches of Paris. Here you may take a *voiture de remise* (a superior kind of cab, something like an English brougham), for which you will have to pay 2fr. 25c. an hour. Thus you gain your money in having a better horse, and going over your ground in less time. The coachman expects about 25 cents the hour, although legally he is not allowed to demand it. If you give the driver to understand that your object is to see all you can of Paris, he will take you by the most public streets, and point out the principal public buildings that lie in your route. It should be observed that you will find *remises* in nearly every street. They stand always under some shed or building, and not, as the cabs, in the open air. They are always ready, and you will find the coachmen generally civil and obliging.

Drive then to *Notre Dame,* visit the *Palais de Justice* and the *Sainte Chapelle,* which adjoins it. Then proceed to the *Gardens and the Palace of the Luxembourg.* You will only have time to view the exterior, and take a momentary glance at the *Picture Gallery,* filled with the works of living artists, which it contains. Direct your course next to the *Hôtel des Invalides,* where your passport or stamped card will gain you admission to see the church and tomb of Napoleon, one of the sights of Paris. Thursdays, from 12 till 3. The entrance is at the rear, in the Place Vauban. The Trocadérō and in Champ de Mars is near at hand. After seeing the tomb, you may pass into the Chapel of the Invalides, decorated with the flags and standards taken in various battles. From the Invalides drive to the *Place de la Concorde,* and (here discharging your remise) walk through the *Gardens of the Tuileries,* to view their beauties, and the ruined Palace, whose principal front faces them. Go out by one of the gates on the left, into the Rue de Rivoli, and cross over to the *Palais Royal,* which, with its shops, cafés, and restaurants, is always interesting. The southern extremity, facing the Louvre, formerly inhabited by Prince Napoléon, burnt 1871, is now restored. In the Palais Royal you will find a luncheon at any price you desire, from 1 franc 25 centimes (1s. 0d.), upwards. After lunch a few minutes' walk will take you to the *Louvre* and the *Place*

de Carrousel. In this Place you will do well to pause to reconnoitre the extensive pile of buildings that surround you on every side, and the two united palaces, the palaces of the Louvre and the Tuileries, that are on the right and left of you, as well as the triumphal arch which rises before the entrance into the chateau. After this, you will be able to spare a little time to inspect some of the galleries of paintings and curiosities which the Louvre contains. The Louvre may be entered any day of the week, except Monday. On Sundays it is open to the public without restriction, and always closes at four in the afternoon.

When you leave the Louvre, you would do well to take another remise by the hour, drive through the Place de la Concorde, and the Champs Elysées to the Arc de Triomphe, which it will well repay you to mount. Should you like it you can prolong your drive to the Bois de Boulogne, remembering to visit the *Chapel of St. Ferdinand* (commemorating the death of the Duke of Orleans, 1842), which is situated a hundred yards or so to the right, in the avenue opposite the Porte Maillot. The *Bois de Boulogne,* in which two lakes and a handsome cascade have lately been constructed, is a most fashionable resort between the hours of 4 and 6 in winter, and from 7 to 9 in summer. The charge for the remise for coming outside the Barrière, is three francs per hour, instead of 2fr. 25c. ; but if you engage the remise for a drive to the Bois de Boulogne only, or to and from (the Bois being an exception), the fare is no more than for a drive of equal time *within* the Barrières.

On your return to the city, you will find good dinners at any of the Restaurants named in the Introduction, particularly the excellent and cheap Etablissements de Bouillon Duval. Good dinner, wine included, 2fr. (1s. 8d.), after which amusement of every description will be at hand for the next three or four hours. The Theatres, or the Circus, or one of the Operas, or some other diverting spectacle are always open ; but should none of these gay sights attract you, you will be much amused by walking along the Boulevards, taking your coffee or an ice on the outside of one of the Cafés, and watching the curious stream of human beings that rolls by you.

2. *Should your stay be prolonged for Two days*—you would do well to take a run down and see the Château and Gardens of *Versailles.* This is an occupation that will fill up the whole day. In the evening you will again be at liberty to select which of the many places of amusement you may like best. There are many gardens open after sunset, brilliantly lighted up with variegated lamps, where dancing and other gay scenes of delight take place ; such as the *Jardin Mabille,* the *Château des Fleurs,* the *Closerie des Lilas, Casino, &c.* There are also in the *Champs Elysées,* the *Boulevard de Strasbourg, Palais Royal,* &c., many *Cafés chantants,* where you may hear pretty good singing and sip your coffee, or have an ice, or indulge in brandy and water, or beer, at your leisure. The best among these are the Casino,

Palais Royal; l'Eldorado, Boulevard de Strasbourg; l'Alcazar, Rue du Faubourg
Poissonnière ; the Jardin Les Fleurs, Champs Elysées, &c. The *Jardins* alluded
to above are not visited by the *élite* of the Parisian society, but they give to a
foreigner a good insight into the habits and amusements of the French people.
Admittance, one franc ; good music from 8 to 11 p.m.

3. *Should your stay extend over Three days*—a visit to *Père la Chaise*, the *Jardin
des Plantes*, the *Gobelins Manufactory* (should it be on a Wednesday or Saturday,
from 2 to 4), the *Panthéon*, and the ruined *Hôtel Cluny* is recommended. An examination of these places will fully occupy your day until five or six o'clock, when the
evening attractions of Paris are again open to your choice.

4. *Should your visit extend over Four days*—you will find the ruined Château **and**
Park of *St. Cloud*, a short distance out of town, and the Museums of the porcelain
manufactory at *Sèvres*, very interesting, You may go to St. Cloud by the railway
(Banlieue) to Auteuil, where an omnibus will be waiting to take you for two sous,
by a pleasant drive through the Bois de Boulogne, the village, and across the
Seine to the park gates, or by rail direct from the Place du Havre. From Sèvres to
St. Cloud is only a short walk through the park. If you are a good walker, you
should visit the ruined *Château and Terrace of Meudon*, about a mile and a half
beyond Sèvres on the hill. This spot commands a magnificent view of Paris and
the river. Cabs may be obtained at St. Cloud to take you to Sèvres and Meudon,
should you prefer to ride.

5. *Should it be your intention to remain Five days*—on your return from Meudon,
or Sèvres, if your stay be over a Sunday, you will find Protestant services at the
various Churches and Chapels mentioned at the end of the book, or you might
witness mass at any of the principal Catholic Churches. The Churches of the
Madeleine, St. Clotilde, St. Eustache, and Notre Dame (the Metropolitan Church),
are the best, on account of the music and singing. The service commences exactly
at ten o'clock.

6. *Should your visit extend over Six days*—the *Musée des Beaux Arts*, and the **Musée**
d'Artillerie should be visited ; also *St. Germain* and the *Abbey of St. Denis*, which,
though on different lines of railway, may easily be accomplished in a day. St. Denis
should be seen first.

7. *Should you remain Seven days*—a trip to *Fontainebleau*, will be highly interesting; and should you have more days than these, you would do wisely to go over some
of those public places which the visitor for one day is invited to go to, and which
he had scarcely time to inspect, as for example the *Louvre*, the *Luxembourg*, **the**
Hôtel des Invalides, the *Champs de Mars*, &c.

COMMON FRENCH WORDS AND PHRASES.

A few of the commonest phrases are better than nothing to the inexperienced traveller, and we therefore add a short list for his benefit. When the knowledge of the language is limited, it is of course advisable not to attempt too much. Especial care should be taken to be distinct as to the principal substantive. The French are very quick in apprehension, and one word often gives them the cue to the wants of the stranger. The waiter is called "garçon"; the bill, "l'addition."

Des Repas.	Of Meals.
Le Déjeûner	Breakfast
Le goûter, le déjeûner à la fourchette	Luncheon (after 10 30)
Le diner	Dinner (5 to 7)
Le thé	Tea
Le souper	Supper

Le Manger.	Of Eating.
Un pain, du pain	A loaf, bread
Un petit pain	A roll
Du pain blanc	White bread
Du pain de ménage	Household bread
Du pain bis	Brown bread
Du pain frais	New bread
Du pain rassis	Stale bread
Du pain rôti	Toast
Des biscuits	Biscuits

La Carte.	The Bill of Fare.
Du bouillon	Broth
Un consommé	Jelly soup
De la soupe	Soup
Soupe au vermicelle	Vermicelli soup
Soupe au riz	Rice soup
Soupe à la purée	Peas soup
Soupe à l'oseille	Sorrel soup
De la viande	Meat
Des côtelettes de mouton	Mutton chops
Un gigot	A leg of mutton
Des rognons	Kidneys
De l'agneau	Lamb
Du lard	Bacon
Du jambon	Ham
Petit salé	Salt beef and cabbage
Du gibier	Game
Un pâté	A pie
De la volaille	Poultry
Un poulet	A fowl
Un dindon	Turkey
Du poisson	Fish

Du saumon	Salmon
Des soles	Soles
Des huîtres	Oysters
Des légumes.	Vegetables
Un chou	A cabbage
Un choufleur	A cauliflower
Des artichauts	Artichokes
Des pommes de terre	Potatoes
Des carrottes	Carrots
Des petits pois	Green peas
Des œufs	Eggs
Un œuf	An egg
Des œufs frais	New laid eggs
Des œufs à la coque	Boiled eggs
Une omelette	An omelet
Une salade	A salad
Une salade aux homards	Lobster salad
Du sel	Salt
Du poivre	Pepper
De la moutarde	Mustard
De l'huile	Oil
Du vinaigre	Vinegar
Des biscuits	Sponge Cakes
Des gâteaux	Cakes
Du fruit	Fruit
Du fromage	Cheese
Du beurre frais	Butter
Du sucre	Sugar
Du thé	Tea
Du café	Coffee
Du lait	Milk
Du chocolat	Chocolate

De la Boisson.	Of Drink.
De l'eau	Water
De l'eau rougie	Wine and water
Du vin	Wine
Du vin blanc	White wine
Du vin rouge	Red wine
Du vin ordinaire, ou vin de Bordeaux	Country wine, claret
Du vin du Rhin	Rhine wine

Du vin de champagne	Champagne
Du vin de Bourgogne	Burgundy
Du vin d'Oporto	Port wine
Du vin de Xérès	Sherry
De la bière	Beer

(Beer at the cafés, 30 to 40c. the glass or "boc.")
De l'eau de vie, ducognacBrandy—cognac

Un couteau	A knife
Une fourchette	A fork
Une cuiller	A spoon
Une assiette	A plate
Une serviette	A napkin
Une nappe	A tablecloth
Une salière	A saltcellar
Un huillier	A cruet frame

LES PLATS QU'ON TROUVE GÉNÉRALEMENT CHEZ LES RESTAURATEURS EN FRANCE.

THE DISHES GENERALLY FOUND AT THE FRENCH RESTAURATEURS.

LA CARTE. THE BILL OF FARE.

Potages. Soups.

Au macaroni	Macaroni soup
Au riz	Rice soup
Au vermicelle	Vermicelli soup
A la julienne	Soup with chopped carrots and herbs
A la purée	Peas Soup
Consommé	Jelly soup
À l'oseille	Sorrel soup

Bœuf. Beef.

Bœuf au naturel	Boiled beef
Bœuf à la sauce tomate	Beef with tomata sauce
Bœuf à la sauce piquante	Beef with savoury sauce
Bœuf aux choux	Beef with cabbage
Entrecôte	Ribs of beef
Filet sauté	Fillet of beef with gravy
Rosbif aux pommes	Roast beef with potatoes
Aloyau de bœuf	Sirloin of beef
Langue de bœuf	Neats' tongue
Palais de bœuf	Palate of beef
Bifteck à l'Anglaise	Beefsteak in the English manner
Bifteck aux pommes	Beefsteak with potatoes
Bœuf à la mode	A la mode beef

Veau. Veal.

Fricandeau au jus	Larded veal in gravy
Fricandeau aux épinards	Larded veal with spinage
Fricandeau à l'oseille	Larded veal with sorrel
Fricandeau à la chicorée	Larded veal with boiled endive
Foie de veau sauté	Stewed calf's liver
Côtelette de veau au naturel	Veal chops fried or boiled
Côtelette en papillote	Veal chops broiled in papers with sweet herbs
Côtelette au jambon	Veal chops with ham
Cervelle apprêtée de différentes manières	Calf's brains cooked in different ways
Tête de veau à la vinaigrette	Calf's head with oil and vinegar
Tête de veau d'autres manières	Calf's head in different ways
Langue à la sauce piquante	Calf's tongue with savoury sauce
Pieds de veau à la vinaigrette	Calf's feet with oil and vinegar
Blanquette de veau	Fricaseed veal with white sauce.
Ris de veau	Calf's sweet bread
Fraise de veau	Calf's fry

Mouton et Agneau. Mutton and Lamb.

Côtelettes panées	Chops fried in bread crumbs
Côtelettes en papillottes	Chops broiled in papers with sweet herbs
Côtelettes au naturel	Chops fried or broiled
Gigot aux haricots	Leg of mutton with gravy or French beans
Rognons au vin de champagne	Kidneys done in champagne
Pieds de mouton à la vinaigrette	Trotters with oil and vinegar
Rognons à la brochette	Kidneys broiled
Rognons aux truffes	Kidneys with truffles
Rognons sautés	Stewed kidney

Volaille. Poultry.

Chapon au gros sel	Capon (boiled)
Chapon au riz, &c.	Capon with rice
Poulet sauté	Chicken fried
Poulet à la tartare	Chicken devilled
Cuisse de poulet en papillote	Leg of a chicken in paper with sweet herbs
Dinde truffée	Turkey with truffles
Dindonneau	Young turkey
Poulet aux champignons	Chicken with mushroom sauce
Poulet au ris	Fowl and rice
Capilotade de poulet	Chicken hashed
Salade de volaille	Cold chicken in slices and vinegar

Salantine de volaille	Brawned fowl	**Légumes.**	**Vegetables.**
Poulet truffé	Chicken, with truffles	Asperges	Asparagus
Filets de poulet	Slices of chicken (breast)	Pointes d'asperges	Heads of asparagus
Canard aux navets	Duck and turnips	Choux de Bruxelles	Brussels sprouts
Canard aux pois	Duck and green peas.	Chou-fleur	Cauliflower
Caneton	Duckling	Pommes frites	Fried potatoes
Pigeon à la crapaudine	Broiled pigeon	Choux rouges	Red cabbage
Fricassée de poulet	Fricasseed chicken	Du raifort	Horseradish

Gibier.   **Game.**

Côtelette de chevreuil	Venison chops
Filet de chevreuil	Fillet of venison
Perdreau apprêté de différentes manières	{ Partridge dressed in different ways
Perdreau en salmis	Young partridge jugged
Manviettes de différentes manières	} Larks, variously dressed
Gibelotte de lapin	Rabbit smothered
Laperau sauté aux champignons	{ Young rabbit with mushroom sauce
Bécasse	{ Woodcock dressed in different ways
Bécassine	Snipes
Canard sauvage	Wild duck
Caille	Quails
Faisan	Pheasant
Ortolans	Ortolans
Grives	Thrushes
Des alouettes	Larks
Canard sauvage en salmis	} Wild duck jugged
Sarcelle en salmis	Teal jugged

Poisson.   **Fish.**

Saumon	Salmon
Turbot	Turbot
Raie	Skate
Morue	Cod
Truite	Trout
Sole	Soles
Merlans	Whiting
Maquereau	Mackerel
Éperlans	Smelts
Alose	Shad
Carrelet	Flounder
Homard	Lobster
Écrevisse	Cray-fish
Huîtres	Oysters
Brochet	Pike
Anguilles	Eels
Plie	Plaice
Carpe	Carp

c

Haricots blancs	French beans (shelled)
Haricots verts	French beans (green)
Chicorée	Endive
Pommes de terre à la maître d'hôtel	{ Potatoes sliced with parsley and butter
Petits pois	Green peas
Épinards	Spinage
Artichauts	Artichokes
Céleri	Celery
Salade	Salad
De Chicoree	Endive
Romaine	Roman or cos-lettuce
De mache	Corn salad
De la altue	Lettuce

Hors d'oeuvre.   **Extras.**

Omelette aux fines herbes	} Omelet with sweet herbs
Omelette au sucre	Omelet with sugar
Omelette au jambon	Omelet fried with ham
Œufs pochés	Poached eggs
Œufs sur le plat	Fried eggs
Beignets de pommes, etc	Apple fritters
Gâteau de riz	Rice pudding or cake
Charlotte russe	Syllabub in light paste
Tourte aux fruits	Tarts of various fruits
Plum pouding	Plum pudding
Fromage (différentes sortes)	} Cheese (different sorts)
Beurre frais, salé	Butter, fresh, salt
Petit pâtés	Savoury patties
Truffes au vin de champagne	{ Truffles done in champagne
Gelée de groseilles ou de framboises	{ Jellies (currant or raspberry)
Paté de foie gras	Strassburg patties
Sardines	Sardines
Anchois	Anchovies

Dessert.   **Dessert.**

Melon	Melon
Raisi de Fontainebleau	{ White grapes of Fontainbleau

Pêches	Peaches	Des cérises à l'eau de vie	Brandied cherries
Fraises au sucre	Strawberries with sugar	Des raisin à l'eau de vie	Grapes in brandy
Ananas	Pines	Bordeaux ou Mâcon ordinaire ou vieux	Claret, of Bordeaux, or Burgundy, ordinary or old
Figues	Figs	Bourgogne, ordinaire ou vieux	Burgundy, ordinary or old
Pruneaux cuits au sucre	Prunes cooked with sugar	Château Margaux	Claret, Château Margaux
Quatre mendiants	Raisins, almonds, nuts and figs (four beggars)	Chablis	Chablis
Cérises à l'eau de vie	Cherries preserved in brandy	Grave	Grave
Prunes de Monsieur	Orléans plums	Sauterne	Sauterne
Crevettes	Shrimps	Saint Péray	Saint Peray
Prunes de reine Claude	Green gages	Du Rhin	Rhenish
Pommes et poires	Apples and pears	Champagne	Champagne
Amandes vertes	Green almonds	Volnay	Volnay
Compote de différents fruits	Stewed fruits		

Gelée de groseilles, etc.	Currant jelly and others	**Habillements d'Hommes, &c.**	**Of Men's Clothes &c.**
Méringues	Trifle, cream-tarts	Une chemise (d'hommes)	A shirt
Abricots à l'eau de vie	Apricots with brandy	Un caleçon	Drawers
Biscuits de Rheims	Sponge cakes	Une camisole	An under-waistcoat
Macarons	Macaroons	Une robe de chambre	A morning-gown

Vins, Liqueurs, &c.   Wines, Liquors, &c.

Gingembre confit	Preserved ginger	Un pantalon	Trousers
Glace au chocolat	Chocolate ice	Une cravate	A neck cloth
Glace à la crème	Cream ice	Un col	A collar
Glace à la vanille	Vanilla ice	Un gilet	A waistcoat
Glace aux fraises	Strawberry	Des bas	Stockings
Glace aux framboises	Raspberry ice	Un cure-dents	A tooth pick
De l'eau sucrée à la fleur d'oranger	Sugar watered with extract of orange flower	Un tire botte	A boot jack
Sirop de groseilles	Currant syrup	Un peigne	A comb
Sirop de framboises	Raspberry syrup	Une brosseà cheveux	A hair brush
Limonade	Lemonade	Une brosse à habits	A clothes brush
Une bavaroise	Tea sweetened with syrup of capillaire	Se raser	To shave
Un verre d'orgeat	A liquor with extract of sweet almonds	Un nécessaire	A dressing case
De Noyau	Liquor flavoured with peach kernels	Des chaussettes	Socks
D'Eau de vie de Dantzic	Dantzic brandy	Des pantoufles	Slippers
De Maraschin	Maraschino	Des souliers	Shoes
De Curaçao	Curaçao	Des souliers vernis	Patent leather boots
D'Anisette de Bordeaux	Bourdeaux anisette	Des bottes	Boots
De sirop de ponch	Syrup of punch	Un chausse pieds	A shoe horn
De crème de Ceylan	Ceylan cream, sweetened		
De cassis	Black currants with brandy	**Habillement de Femmes.**	**Of Women's Clothes.**
Un chine	Greengage in Brandy	Une chemise	A chemise
		Un jupon	A petticoat
		Un corset	Stays
		Un lacet	Stay lace
		Une pélerine	A tippet
		Une robe	A gown or dress

Des volants	Flounces
Des manches	Sleeves
Un fichu	A neck handkerchief
Un mouchoir de poche	A pocket handkerchief
Des gants	Gloves
Un châle	A shawl
Une écharpe	A scarf
Un tablier	An apron
Un chapeau	A bonnet
Une voile	A veil
Un negligé	A morning gown
La coiffure	Head dress
Une robe d'enfant	A frock
Des papillotes	Curl papers
Une crinoline	Crinoline
Des bas	Stockings
Des chaussettes	Socks

Miscellanea.	Miscellaneous.
Du savon	Soap
Une éponge	A sponge
Une serviette, essuie-mains	A towel
encrier	An inkstand
De l'encre	Ink
Des épingles	Pins
De la soie	Silk
Du satin	Satin
Du velours	Velvet
De la dentelle	Lace
Un chambre à coucher	Bed room
Un petit salon	Sitting room
Un cabinet de toilette	A dressing closet
Le salon	The drawing room
La salle à manger	The dining room
Un rez de chaussée	A ground floor
Des appartements	The apartments
Un poêle	A stove
Un miroir—une glace	A looking glass
Un lit	A bed
Le cabinet d'aisance	Closet
Le vase de nuit	Bedchamber utensil
Le bois de lit	The bedstead
Un lit de plume	A feather bed
Un matelas	A mattress
Un oreiller	A pillow
Les draps	The sheets
Une couverture de laine	A blanket
Une courtepointe	A counterpane
Un bassinoire	A warm

Une table	A table
Une chaise	A chair
Une table de nuit	A night table
Une chandelle	A candle
Une bougie	A wax candle
Une lampe	A lamp
Une veilleuse	A night lamp
Les mouchettes	The snuffers
Un éteignoir	An extinguisher
Un bain (chaud)	A bath (warm)
Des allumettes	Matches
Du charbon	Coals
Du bois	Wood
Un acquit, une quittance	A receipt
Un billet de banque	A bank note
La cherté—cher	Dearness—dear
Bon marché	Cheap
La douane	The custom house
Le bureau de la poste	The post office
La grande poste	The general post office
Le facteur	The postman
La poste aux lettres	Post Office
Un banquier	A banker
Un changeur	A money changer
Un joaillier—un orfévre	A jeweller or goldsmith
Un marchand de soieries	A silk mercer
Un marchand de nouveautés	A linen draper
Un médecin	A doctor
Un pharmacien	An apothecary
Un dentiste	A dentist
Une marchande e modes	A milliner
Une couturière	A dress maker
Un coiffeur	A hair dresser
Un gantier	A glover
Un pâtissier	A pastry cook
Un boulanger	A baker
Un boucher	A butcher
Un fruitier	A fruiterer
Un épicier	A grocer
Chemin de fer	Railway
Voyageur	Traveller
Billet, ou coupon	Ticket
Bagage	Luggage
Franchise de port	Luggage allowed
Voiture	Carriage
La gare	Station
Salle d'attente	Waiting room
Facteur	Porter
Train, ou convoi	Train

Station, embarcadère, ou gare	Station, terminus
Chevaux	Horses
Chien	Dog
Moitié prix	Half-price
Matin (m.)	Morning
Soir (s.)	Evening
1re. cl. (première classe)	1st class
2e. cl. (seconde id)	2nd do.
3e. cl. (troisième id)	3rd do.
De grande vitesse, ou exp.	Fast train
Durée du trajet	Time taken
Prolongement	Extension
Service d'hiver	Winter service
Service d'été	Summer do.
Par tête	So much a head
Administration	Office
Billets d'aller et de retour	Return tickets
Voyage simple	Single journey
Trains mixtes (or 'bus)	Mixed trains
Trains directs	{Trains to 1st class stations only.
Bureau	Booking office
Impériale	{The seats on top of the carriages
Le Buffet	Refreshment room
La Buvette	Drinking room
Trains exprès	Express trains
Articles de messageries	Goods, &c. for luggage van
Le chef de gare	The station master
L'Interprète	Interpreter
Conducteur, mécanicien	Guard, engine driver
Chauffeur	Fireman, or stoker
Bulletin de baggage	Luggage ticket
Fumeurs	Smoking carriage
Dames seules	Ladies only
Changer de voiture	To change carriage
La wagon	Railway carriage
Montez en wagon	Take seat
Descendez	Get out
Bâteau à vapeur	Steam-boat
Bâteau à vapeur à hélice	Screw steamer
Bâteau de poste	Post-office packet
Paquebots	Packet boats
Matelots	Sailors
Bateau à voiles	Sailing vessel
Bateau à rames	Rowing boat
Deux fois par our	**Twice a day**

Deux départs par semaine	Twice a week
1re. Chambre	Chief cabin
2e. do.	Fore cabin
Pavillon (in Rhine Steamer)	1st cabin (one half more than saloon)
Salon do.)	2nd cabin
Chambre de devant (do)	3rd do. (half of saloon)
Nourriture	Living, or provisions
Une malle	A trunk
Un facteur	A porter
Télégraphe sous-marin	Submarine telegraph
Bains de mer	Sea baths
Douanier	Custom-house officer
Ville	Large town or city
Bourg	Town
Boulevards	{Site of old walls, or bulwarks.
Faubourg	Suburb
Rue	Street
Chaussée	Causeway
Chemin	Road
Pont	Bridge
Bac	Ferry
Montagne	Mountain
Valée	Valley
Rivière	River
Porte	Gate
Hôtel de ville, ou mairie	Town-hall
Place	Square
Église	Church
Cathédrale	Cathedral
Poste aux lettres	Post-office
Bibliothèque	Public library
Musée	Museum
Jardin des plantes	Botanic garden
Salle de spectacle	Theatre, &c.
Hôpital, ou Hôtel Dieu	Infirmary
Hospice	Asylum
La morgue	The dead house
Palais	Palace
Fonderie	Iron work
Verrerie	Glass work
Dimanche	Sunday
Lundi	Monday
Mardi	Tuesday
Mercredi	Wednesday
Jeudi	Thursday
Vendredi	**Friday**

Samedi	Saturday	Janvier	January
Le printemps	Spring	Février	February
Les semailles	Seed-time	Mars	March
L'été	Summer	Avril	April
L'automne	Autumn	Mai	May
La récolte	The harvest	Juin	June
Les vendanges	The vintage	Juillet	July
L'hiver	Winter	Août	August
La pluie	The rain	Septembre	September
Le temps	The weather	Octobre	October
La neige	The snow	Novembre	November
La tonnerre	The thunder	Décembre	December
L'éclair, la foudre	The lightning	Un mois	A month
La grêle	The hail	Un an, une année	A year
		Un siècle	A century

Une demi-douzaine.	Half a dozen.
Qu' est-ce que cela, Monsieur?	What is that, Sir?
Que dites-vous?	What do you say?
Monsieur, je ne vous comprends pas!	I do not understand you.
Où allez-vous?	Where are you going?
Que voulez-vous?	What do you want?
Quel est le chemin de Paris? ou Ayez la bonté de m'indiquer le chemin, &c.?	Which is the way to Paris? or, Have the goodness to tell me the way, &c.?
Allez tout droit.	Go straight on.
Tournez à gauche (ou, à droite).	Turn to the left (or, to the right)
Merci, ou, bien obligé.	Thank you.
Il fait beau temps.	It is fine weather.
Le temps est couvert; il va pleuvoir; prenez un parapluie.	It is cloudy weather, and going to rain; take an umbrella.
Il fait mauvais temps; nous aurons de l'orage.	It is bad weather; we shall have a storm.
Le soleil luit; il fait bien chaud.	The sun shines; it is very hot.
Le soleil est couché.	The sun is set.
Il fait clair de lune.	It is moonlight.
Il fait un brouillard épais.	There is a thick fog.
Le vent est changé.	The wind is changed.
Il fait beaucoup de poussière.	It is very dusty.
Il va neiger.	It is going to snow.
Quelle heure est-il, Monsieur?	What o'clock is it, sir?
Il est environ deux heures; ou, Deux heures vont sonner.	About two o'clock.
Il est deux heures un quart.	Quarter-past two.
Il est deux heures et demie.	Half-past two.
Il est deux heures moins un quart.	Quarter to two.
Il est deux heures moins cinq minutes.	Five minutes to two.
Il est midi.	It is twelve (noon).
Aujourd'hui.	To-day.
Ce matin; ce soir.	This morning; this evening.
Demain matin après demain,	To-morrow morning; day after to-morrow.

Hier ; avant ier.	Yesterday; day before yesterday.
Il y a deux jours.	Two days ago.
Dans huit jours; *ou*, d'aujourd'hui en huit.	In a week.
Tous les jours.	Every day.
Quinze jours.	A fortnight.
J'ai faim.	I am hungry.
J'ai soif	I am thirsty.
J'ai chaud.	I am warm.
J'ai froid.	I am cold.
Que voulez-vous manger ?	What will you eat.
Donnez-moi à boire.	Give me something to drink.
Donnez-moi un verre d'eau de vie.	Give me a glass of brandy.
Apportez le dîner.	Bring the dinner.
Donnez-moi des œufs.	Give me some eggs.
Voulez-vous une tasse de café (du vin, de la viande, du jambon, du thé, de l'eau de vie ?)	Will you take a cup of coffee (some wine, meat, ham, tea, brandy)?
Comment vous portez-vous ?	How do you do?
Fort bien ; *ou*, Très bien, je vous remercie.	Very well, I thank you
J'ai mal à la tete	I have headache
Je suis malade	I am ill.
Je suis Anglais (*ou* Anglaise).	I am English.
Parlez-vous Anglais?	Do you speak English?
Soyez le bien-venu, Monsieur.	Sir, you are welcome.
Où demeure Monsieur A ?	Where does Mr. A. live?
Il demeure dans la Rue B.	He lives in B. street.
Appelez-moi un fiacre (*ou* cabriolet)	Call a coach (or cab).
Conduisez moi à l' Hotel de ——.	Take me to the hotel ——.
Vous pouvez aller par la diligence, *ou* prendre une chaise de poste.	You may go by the stage coach, or take a post chaise.
A quelle heure la diligence part-elle d'ici ?	When does the coach start?
Combien prend-on par place? *ou*, Combien prenez-vous ?	What is the fare? or, what do you charge ?
Je désire une chambre à coucher.	I want a bed room.
Quel en est le prix ?	What is the price ?
Le service, est-il compris?	Is the service included ?
Combien de jours (*ou*, combien de tem s serons nous en route ?	How many days (or how long) will it take?
Quelle route prenez-vous ?	Which way do you go?
Voulez-vous avoir la bonté de m'indi'guer le chemin de ——?	Will you please to direct me to ——
Quel est le meilleur chemin?	Which is the best road ?
La route qui passe par B. est la plus courte.	The road through B. is the shortest.
Combien de —— à ——?	How far from —— to ——?
A qui est ce château ?	Whose seat is this ?
Quel est le nom de cet endroit ?	What is the name of this place?
Y-a-t-il des cabinets de tableaux ?	Are there any pictures to be seen ?
Quel est cet édifice	What building is this ?
Quel magnifique paysage !	What a beautiful country !
Comment appelle-t-on cette ville?	What town is this ?
Où nous arrètrons-nous ?	Where shall we stop?

Combien de temps d' arrêt ici ?	How long do we stop here ?
Quand partirez-vous ?	When do you depart ?
Au point du jour, or, à la marée.	At day break, or, high water.
Nous allons partir.	We are going directly.
Quand nous embarquons-nous ?	When do we go on board ?
Combien de temps serons-nous en mer ?	How long shall we be at sea ?
Je me sens mal, je puis à peine me tenir sur les jambes ; la tête me tourne.	I am very sick ; I can hardly stand on my legs, my head turns round.
Il fait du vent	There is wind out.
Je loge à l'hôtel de C.	I am staying at the Hotel de C.
Quel est le meilleur hôtel ; ou, la meilleure auberge ?	Which is the best inn ?
Un dîner à table d'hôte.	A dinner at the ordinary.
Un dîner seul.	Dinner alone.
A quelle heure voulez-vous dîner.	At what time do you wish to dine ?
On a servi.	Dinner is on the table.
Je suis prêt	I am ready.
Voulez-vous un peu de soupe, ou, de potage ?	Will you take soup ?
Non, je vous remercie, je commencerai par du poisson.	No, I thank you, I will take some fish.
Permettez que je vous presente du bœuf.	Allow me to offer you some beef.
De quel vin voulez-vous ?	What wine will you take ?
Garçon, donnez-nous une bouteille de vin de Bourgogne.	Waiter, bring us a bottle of Burgundy.
Apportez un tire-bouchon.	Bring a cork-screw.
Vous enverrai-je une tranche de ce gigot ?	Shall I send you a slice of mutton ?
Vou servirai-je des légumes ?	Will you take some vegetables ?
Vous servirai-je des pommes de terre ?	Will you take some potatoes ?
Pas davantage.	Not any more.
Garçon, changez cette assiette.	Waiter, change this plate.
Une cuiller, s'il vous plaît.	Give me a spoon.
Je vous remercie, c'est assez.	Thank you, that's enough.
Mettez les verres sur la table.	Put the glasses on the table.
Apportez-moi un verre d'eau.	Bring me a glass of water.
Garçon, une bouteille de vin ordinaire.	Waiter, a bottle of ordinary wine.
Donnez-nous le dessert.	Let us have the dessert.
Voulez-vous avoir la bonté de sonner ?	Be so good as to ring the bell.
J'ai bien dîné.	I have made a good dinner.
Lo thé est servi.	Tea is ready.
Combien vous devons-nous ?	What have we to pay ?
Je désire avoir la note.	I wish to have my bill.
Voici la note, monsieur.	Here is the bill, Sir.
Voici votre argent.	Here is your money.
Pouvons-nous coucher ici ?	Can we sleep here ?
Je n'aime pas à monter.	I don't like to go up stairs.
J'aimerais mieux une chambre au premier (ou, au second, au troisième).	I should like a room on the first floor (or, second floor, third floor).
Veuillez me donner du savon ?	I want a piece of soap ?
Les lits sont-ils bien bassinés ?	Are the beds well warmed ?
Les draps sont-ils bien secs ?	Are the sheets quite dry ?
Apportez-moi encore un oreiller.	Bring me another pillow.

A quelle heure voulez-vous que je vous appelle ? — When shall I call you ?

Monsieur, je vous souhaite une bonne nuit. — I wish you good night, Sir.

Dormez bien. — Sleep well.

Bon jour, Monsieur (ou Madame, ou Mademoiselle). — Good morning, sir, &c.

Apportez-moi de l'eau, ou de l'eau chaude. — Bring me some water, or hot water.

Faites cirer mes bottes (at an hotel); cirez mes bottes (in the street). — I want my boots cleaned.

Apportez-moi mes bottes. — Bring me my boots.

Le déjeûner est-il prêt ? — Is breakfast ready ?

Je prendrai du café, si vous voulez bien. — I will take coffee, if you please.

Du café noir s'il vous plait. — Coffee, without milk, if you please.

Il nous faut encore des tartines. — We want more slices of bread and butter.

Une tasse de thé. — A cup of tea.

Déjeûner à la fourchette. — A meat breakfast.

Voilà de la viande ; voici des saucisses, du jambon, de la volaille. — Here is meat; here are sausages, ham, fowl.

Avez-vous des chambres à louer? — Have you apartments to let ?

Meublées ou non meublées ? — Furnished or unfurnished ?

Quel est le prix du loyer ? — What are the terms.

C'est très cher. — It is very dear.

Voudriez-vous échanger ces souverains ? — Will you be so good as to give me French money for these sovereigns ?

Un banquier. — A banker.

Un négociant. — A merchant.

Où est le bureau de poste ? — Where is the post-office

Je voudrais acheter un chapeau. — I want to buy a hat.

Je voudrais acheter des souliers. — I want to buy a pair of shoes.

Je voudrais acheter une robe. — I want to buy a dress (ladies').

Voilà une jolie boutique. — Here is a fine shop.

Voulez-vous me raser ? — Will you shave me ?

Voulez-vous me couper les cheveux ? — Will you cut my hair?

J'ai du linge à laver ; lavez le avec soin. — I have some linen to wash ; wash it carefully.

Quand me le rapporterez-vous ? — When will you bring it home ?

Il faudra que vous rapportiez la note. — Bring the bill with you.

Voulez-vous que nous allions faire un tour de promenade ? — Shall we take a walk ?

De bien bon cœur, ou, très volontiers, ou, avec plaisir. — With great pleasure.

Peut-on passer à travers ce champ? — Is there a way across the fields ?

Quel est ce joli hameau ? — What pretty hamlet is that ?

Où peut-on lire les journaux? — Where can we see the newspapers?

On lit les ouvrages périodiques et les journaux aux cabinets de lecture au Palais Royal. — You may see the periodicals and papers, &c., at the reading rooms of the Palais Royal.

Je vous suis bien obligé. — I am obliged to you.

J'aime mieux une tasse de café et un verre de liqueur. — I prefer a cup of coffee and a glass of liquor.

Je suis à vos ordres ; allons nous en, ou, partons. — I am ready ; let us go.

Je n'ai pas le temps ce soir — I have no time this evening.

J'ai besoin d'un cheval de selle.	I want a horse to ride.
Donnez-lui une mesure d'avoine.	Give him a feed of oats.
Il me faut une belle voiture à quatre roues (ou, voiture de voyage).	I want a good four-wheeled carriage (or travelling carriage).
Combien en demandez-vous? ou quel en est le prix?	What is the price? If the reply is not understood, as English figures are used, it will be clear if written; therefore say "Ecrivez le si vous plait."
C'est trop cher.	It is too dear.
Au revoir.	Good bye for the present.
Bon jour.	Good day.
Bonne nuit.	Good night.
Bon soir.	Good evening.
Bon appétit	Good appetite.
Bonne santé.	Good health.

CARDINAL NUMBERS.

Un, une	1	Neuf	9	Dix-sept	17	Soixante	60
Deux	2	Dix	10	Dix-huit	18	Soixante-dix	70
Trois	3	Onze	11	Dix-neuf	19	Quatre-vingt	80
Quatre	4	Douze	12	Vingt	20	Quatre-vingt-dix	90
Cinq	5	Treize	13	Trente	30	Cent	100
Six	6	Quatorze	14	Quarante	40	Mille	1000
Sept	7	Quinze	15	Cinquante	50	Million	1,000,000
Huit	8	Seize	16				

ORDINAL NUMBERS.

Le premier / L'unième	the First	Le dixième	the Tenth
Le second / Le deuxième	the Second	L'onzième	the Eleventh
		Le douzième	the Twelfth
Le troisième	the Third	Le treizième	the Thirteenth
Le quatrième	the Fourth	Le quatorzième	the Fourteenth
Le cinquième	the Fifth	Le quinzième	the Fifteenth
Le sixième	the Sixth	Le seizième	the Sixteenth
Le septième	the Seventh	Le dix-septième	the Seventeenth
Le huitième	the Eighth	Le dix-huitième	the Eighteenth
Le neuvième	the Ninth	Le dix-neuvième	the Nineteenth
		Le vingtième	the Twentieth

One thousand eight hundred and eighty.   Mille huit cent quatre-vingt, 1880,

ENGLISH DIRECTORY OF FIRST-CLASS HOUSES IN PARIS, PROFESSIONAL GENTLEMEN, &c.

ENGLISH AND AMERICAN BOOKSELLERS (where Bradshaw's *Guides* and *Handbooks* may always be obtained).—Baudry, Jeancourt, and Co., 224, Rue de Rivoli; K. Nilsson, 212, Rue de Rivoli; Hautecœur and Richard, 12, Boulevard des Capucines; A. Hautecœur, 172, Rue de Rivoli.

APARTMENTS, FURNISHED AND UNFURNISHED; ALSO BOARDING HOUSES.—Persons visiting Paris are recommended to apply to Messrs. John Arthur and Co., 10, Rue Castiglione, Agent to the British Embassy, Wine Merchant, and Banker.

FURNISHED APARTMENTS.—Families can in confidence apply to Sprent-Sprent and Phipps. See page xvii.

FURNISHED APARTMENTS.—Agent, Henri Largier, 32, Boulevard Malesherbes, formerly Rue de la Paix.

ENGLISH BOARDING HOUSE.—Mrs. Cabarrus, 3, Cité du Retiro. See advertisement.

FURNISHED APARTMENTS.—26, Rue du Colisée, Champs Elysées.

NOVELTIES IN SILKS AND FANCY ARTICLES.—Au bon Marché, 135 and 137, Rue du Bac, corner of the Rue de Sèvres. This establishment, so beautifully enlarged that it is now one of the curiosities of Paris, is celebrated for its excellent qarticles and moderate prices. N.B.—All good that have ceased to please, will be exchanged or retaken.

KRAMER, JEWELLER, 350, Rue St. Honoré, recommended as having an unrivalled stock of Jewellery, Diamonds, &c.

PHYSICIAN.—Sir John Cormack, M.D., of Edinburgh and Paris; F.R.C.P. of London; Chevalier of the Legion of Honour; Physician to the Hertford British Hospital of Paris. Residence—7, Rue d' Aguesseau, next house to the English Church (at home from 2 to 4 o'clock).

ENGLISH PHYSICIAN.—Dr. H. E. Gantillons Accoucheur, M.C.P. of Savannah, U.S.; author of Treatise on Diseases of Women. Stomach diseases and Gout. From 2 till 3 o'clock, 12, Rue du Mont Thabor (3rd house from Rue Castiglione).

SURGEON DENTIST.—We particularly recommend as operating and mechanical dentist Mr. Barwis, No. 10, Rue d'Alger, near the gardens of the Tuileries, especially for a superior description of artificial teeth, for which he has just received a patent. He has published a pamphlet on the subject, which may be had on application.

OPTICIAN.—For all descriptions of optical glasses and instruments, there is comparatively no choice, as those of M. Chevallier, 15, Place du Pont Neuf, are exported all over the world.

OPTICIAN.—A. Chevalier, son and grandson of Messrs. V. and C. Chevalier. Oldest and most celebrated house, Palais Royal, 158.

TOBACCO.—W. D. & H. O. Willis' best Bird's Eye at the Bureau of the Regie, Grand Hotel.

WATCHES AND CHRONOMETERS.—A. H. Rodanet, 36, Rue Vivienne, Chronometer Makers to the French Navy, the Emperor of Brazil, and to the King of Portugal. Sole Agent for Watches of Patek Philippe & Co; sold at the same price as in Geneva. Jewellery. Travelling Clocks.

OPTICIAN.—G. Strope, 24, Palais Royal, Maison Derepas, founded 1814.

PERFUMER.—Guerlain, 7, Rue de la Paix. First-class old house of confidence.

BOOTMAKER.—Roche, 16, Rue Vivienne. English spoken.

FANCY CRYSTAL GLASS.—L. Boutigny, 1,3,5,7,9, Passage des Princes, Boulevard des Italiens.

CLOTHING.—At the Belle Jardinière, 2, Rue du Pont Neuf.

COPPER AND TIN SMITH.—Aubry, 3, Rue de la Visitation, Boulevard Malesherbes.

THEATRES AND PLACES OF AMUSEMENT.

[Open generally at 7-30 p.m.; a few from 7-45 to 8-30 p.m.—See *Galignani's Messenger*.]

THEATRES.

Opera, or Académie de Musique, Place de l'Opéra.
Français, Palais Royal (S.W. side).
Odéon, Place de l'Odéon.
Variétés, Boulevard Montmartre.
Gaîté, Place des Arts et Métiers.
Porte St. Martin, Boulevard St. Martin.
Opéra Comique, Place Boïeldieu.
Vaudeville, Boulevard des Capucines.
Palais Royal, Palais Royal (N.W. side).
Châtelet, Place du Châtelet.
Bouffes Parisiens, Passage Choiseul.
Cluny, 71, Boulevard St. Germain.
Folies Dramatiques, 40, Rue de Bondy.
Ambigu-Comique, Boulevard St. Martin.
Renaissance, Boulevard St. Martin.
Fantaisies Parisiennes, Boulevard Beaumarchais.
Château d'Eau, 50, Rue de Malta.
Gymnase Dramatique, Boulevard Bonne Nouvelle.
Des Arts, Boulevard de Strasbourg.
Nouveautés, Boulevard des Italiens.
Troisième Théâtre Francais, Boulevard du Temple.
Eldorado, 4, Boulevard de Strasbourg.

Other Theatres are—Athénée; Théâtre Historique or Des Nations; Folies Marigny; Rob. Houdin (conjuring); Délassemens Comiques;

Faubourg St. Martin; Folies Bergères, Rue Richer; Théâtre-Ecole des Jeunes Artistes, Rue de la Tour d'Auvergne; Théâtre Miniature, Boulevard Montmartre; Alcazar, Faubourg Poissonnière; Thomas Holden, 11, Faubourg Poissonnière.

CIRCUSES.

Cirque d'Eté, Champs Elysées.
Cirque d'Hiver, Boulevard des Filles du Calvaire.
Hippodrome, Avenue de l'Alma.
Cirque Fernando, Boulevard des Martyrs.
American Circus, Place du Château d'Eau.

CONCERTS.

Conservatoire du Musique, Rue Bergère.
Opéra Populaires, in Cirque d'Hiver.
Des Ambassadeurs.
De l'Horloge.
Mabille Ball.

SKATING.

Skating-Concert of Chaussée d'Antin, Rue de Clichy.
Skating-Theatre, Rue Blanché.
Skating Palace, 55, Avenue du Bois de Boulogne.

BALLS AND CONCERTS.

Frascati, 49, Rue Vivienne.
Valentino, 251, Rue St. Honoré.

PANORAMA.

Champs Elysées.

DAYS AND HOURS FOR VISITING PUBLIC BUILDINGS, PALACES, MUSEUMS, &c.

Admittance to the places marked with a star [*] can only be obtained by a special order, or by shewing the passport. For British subjects, it may suffice to show a card, stamped; and in some cases even this restriction is now relaxed, though it may at any time be enforced. Refer to *Galignani's Messenger* for latest particulars.

LIST OF THE MOST REMARKABLE BUILDINGS, PALACES, &c.	Open to the Public.		REMARKS.
	From	To	
Abattoir de la Villette	...	...	Fee.
Abbey of St. Denis—By rail..................	11 mrn	3 30	Fee.
Arc de Triomphe, Barrière de l' Etoile ...	until	dusk	Fee to the keeper.
Artesian Well of Grenelle......................			
Bank of France, Rue Croix des Petits Champs	...	...	By Government Order

DAYS AND HOURS FOR VISITING PUBLIC BUILDING, PALACES, MUSEUMS, &c.

LIST OF THE MOST REMARKABLE BUILDINGS, PALACES, &c.	Open to the Public.		REMARKS.
	From	To	
Bibliothèque Nationale	10mrn	4 aft.	To students, every day except Sun. and holidays. Coins & Antiquities, Tues. Closed 1st Sept. to 15th Oct.
Botanical Gardens	...	...	At Jardin des Plantes
Bourse, Place de la Bourse	9 ,,	6 ,,	Daily, free. Business hours 12 to 3.
*Cabinet of Architecture, Rue Bonaparte,16	10 ,,	4 ,,	Apply to the doorkeeper.
*Cabinet of Mineralogy, Rue d'Enfer, 30...	10 ,,	3 ,,	Daily, Holidays excepted.
*Catacombs	...	...	2nd and 3rd Saturdays, by ticket, from Prefect of Seine.
Cemetery of Père la Chaise	...	...	Open daily.
Chapelle Expiatoire	10 ,,	4 ,,	Fee to the keeper.
Church of St. Étienne du Mont	...	...	
Chapel of St. Ferdinand	10 ,,	5 ,,	Fee to the keepers } Churches open for Service; and 1 to 4 for Visitors.
Church of St. Germain des Prés	...	...	
Church of St. Sulpice	...	...	
Church of St Vincent de Paul	...	...	
Column of July, Place de la Bastille	10 ,,	4 ,,	Small fee to the keeper.
Column of the Place Vendôme	10 ,,	4 ,,	Fee to keeper, 25 cents.
Conservatoire des Arts et Métiers (Industrial Museum)	10 ,,	4 ,,	On Sundays, and Thursdays, gratis; other days, one franc.
*Dépôt de la Guerre (War), Rue de l'Université, 71	10 ,,	4 ,,	With permission of the director, 82 Rue St. Dominique.
École des Beaux Arts, Rue Bonaparte	10 ,,	4 ,,	Daily; Saturday, 10 to 2, Sunday, 12 to 4.
École des Beax Arts, Drawings of Old Masters	10 ,,	6 ,,	One franc.
École des Mines	11 ,,	3 ,,	
Flower Garden of the City	1 ,,	4 ,,	
Fontainebleau—By Rail	11 ..	4 ,,	Daily; Fee.
Gobelins Manufactory	1 aft.	3 ,,	By Passport or stamped card, Wed. & Fri.
Hammam (Turkish Bath)	8mrn	9 ,,	
Hôtel Cluny (Museum)	11 ,,	4 ,,	By Passport or stamped card, daily, except Monday; to the public on Sunday.
Hôtel de Ville	...	...	Re-building.
Hôtel des Invalides	12 non	3 ,,	Fees expected; daily (except Sundays).
Hôtel des Invalides	12 ,,	3 ,,	Napoleon's Tomb, Monday, Tuesday, Thursday, and Friday.
Imprimerie Nationale	...	2 ,,	By Passport, Thurs.; ticket from Director.
Jardin d'Acclimatation, Bois de Boulogne.	...	...	Daily, one franc; Sunday, half franc.
Jardin des Plantes, Museums	1 aft.	4 ,,	Tuesday, Thursday, Saturday.
Jardin des Plantes, Menagerie	11mrn	4 ,,	Daily.
Libraire Mazarin, Palais de l'Institut	10 ,,	4 ,,	Daily, except Sundays and Festivals.
Library of Sainte Geneviève, Place du Panthéon	10 ,, 6 aft.	3 ,, 10 ,,	Reading Room, daily, except Sundays and Festivals. Closed 1st Sept. to 15th Oct.
Library of the Arsenal, Rue de Sully	10mrn	3 ,,	Daily, except Sundays and Festivals.
Louvre, six different collections	9 ,,	5 ,,	To the public daily, except Mondays. Sundays, 10 to 4.
Luxembourg, Palace of	10 ,,	4 ,,	Gardens and Museum open. Daily, except Mondays.
Madeleine Church	...	...	After 1 p.m.
Mint, or La Monnaie, Museum of Coins	12 non	3 ,,	Tuesdays and Fridays.
Musée d'Artillerie and Armoury (Invalides)	12 ,,	3 ,,	Tuesdays, Thursdays and Sundays.
Museum of Decorative Art	10mrn	4 ,,	Daily, 1 fr.
*Museum Dupuytren, 15, Rue de l'École de Médecin }	11 ,,	3 aft.	Apply to the keeper; closed September and October.
Museums of the Louvre	9 ,,	5 ,,	See Louvre.

DAYS AND HOURS FOR VISITING PUBLIC BUILDINGS, &c.—*Continued.*

LIST OF THE MOST REMARKABLE BUILDINGS, PALACES, &c.	Open to the Public.		REMARKS.
	From	To	
Museum of the Luxembourg, Rue de Vaugirard, 19..............................	10 mrn	4 aft.	Daily, Mondays excepted.
*Museum Orfila, at the School of Medicine	after	4 ,,	Apply to the keeper. Ladies are not admitted
*National Archives, Rue de Paradis du Temple, 20............................	12 non	3 ,,	(By Ticket on Thursdays; to the public on Sundays.
Notre Dame	...	...	Fee expected, if attendance be required.
Notre Dame de Lorette....	...	...	
Obelisk of Luxor	—	...	In Place de la Concorde.
Palace of Elysée	...	...	
Palace of the Legislative Body	...	...	Fee.
*Palace of the Tuileries	...	...	Re-building.
Palais des Archives	12 non	4 ,,	
Palais de l'Industrie	10 mrn	3 ,,	One franc
Palais de Justice	10 ,,	5 ,,	Open daily, except Sundays and Mondays.
Panorama, Champs Elysees	10 ,,	4 ,,	Two francs; Sunday, one franc.
Panthéon, now called Church of St. Geneviève	10 ,,	4 ,,	Dome and Vaults, ½ fr.
*Sainte Chapelle, Palais de Justice.............	12 non	4 ,,	(Daily; free by ticket (except Mondays and Fridays, by fee).
Salon, at Palais de l'Industrie	...	...	Daily, from 10th May
Sèvres, Museum	12 ,,	5 ,,	Daily by ticket; free on Sundays.
St. Cloud, Fountains	4 aft.	5 ,,	2nd Sunday.
St. Denis Church, by rail	11 mrn	3-30	Daily, except Sundays.
Tobacco Factory	10 to 12	2 to 4	Thursday, by card.
Tomb of Napoléon (Hôtel des Invalides)	12 non	3 aft.	Monday, Tuesday, Thursday, and Friday.
Trianon Gardens, at Versailles	...	...	Open all day.
Triumphal Arch of the Carrousel.............	...	...	
Triumphal Arch of the Étoile, Barrière de l'Étoile	until	dusk	Small fee to the keeper.
Trocadéro	...	...	
Vendôme Column	10 mrn	4 aft.	Daily; fee, 25 cents.
*Tuileries	...	...	Re-building.
Versailles	10 ,,	4 ,,	Daily, except Mondays.
Versailles, Museums and Carriages	12 ,,	4 ,,	
Water Color Institution, Rue Laffitte	10 ,,	6 ,,	
	8 aft.	11 ,,	One franc.
Zoological Gardens	12 non	4 ,,	At Jardin des Plantes

MINISTRIES (MINISTÈRES) OR GOVERNMENT OFFICES.

(Under the PRESIDENT, M. JULES GRÉVY, who resides at the Elysée Palace.)

Council of State, 101, Rue St. Grenelle St. Germain.

Ministry of the Interior (Home Office) and Public Worship, Place Beauveau, Faubourg St. Honoré. The Prefecture of Police (under the Minister) is at Caserne de la Cité, Palais de Justice; The Prefect of the Seine is at the Tuileries *(pro tem.)*

Ministry of Foreign Affairs, 130, Rue de l'Université. For Passports, 11 to 4.

Ministry of War, 14, Rue St. Dominique.

Ministry of Marine (Navy) and Colonies, 2, Rue Royale, St. Honoré.

Ministry of Finance, at the Louvre, Rue de Rivoli

Ministry of Justice, 11 and 13, Place Vendôme.

Ministry of Posts and Telegraphs, 101, Rue de Grenelle-St. Germain.

Ministry of Public Instruction and Fine Arts, 110, Rue de Grenelle-St. Germain.

Minister of Public Works, 246, Boulevard St. German.

Ministry of Agriculture and Commerce, 244, Boulevard St. Germain.

ADDRESSES OF EMBASSIES IN PARIS.

Austria, 7, Rue Las Cases; open 1 to 3.

Belgium, 153, Rue du Faubourg St. Honoré; 12 to 2.

Brazil, 13, Rue de Téhéran; 12 to 2.

China, 27, Avenue Kléber.

Denmark, 29, Rue de Courcelles; 1 to 3.

England, 39, Faubourg St. Honoré: 10 to 3.

Germany, 78, Rue de Lille; 12 to 1 30.

Greece, 15, Avenue de Messine.

Italy, Embassy, 53, Rue St. Dominique; Consul, 74, Rue de Lisbonne; 1 to 3.

Japan, 75, Avenue Marceau.

Netherlands, 2, Avenue Bosquet; 12 to 2.

Portugal, 30, Avenue Friedland; Consul, 10, Rue d' Hebe.

Russia, 79, Rue de Grenelle; 12 to 2.

Spain, 25, Quai d'Orsay; 1 to 4.

Sweden and Norway, 29, Avenue Montaigne; 12 to 2.

Switzerland, 3, Rue Blanche; 10 to 3.

Turkey, 17, Rue Laffitte; 12 to 3.

United States, 95, Rue de Challiot; 10 to 3.

FORTIFICATIONS.

Since the Revolution of 1789, the project of building fortifications round Paris has been several times entertained. After the disasters of 1815, Napoleon expressed at St. Helena bitter regret at the Parisians having been forced to open their gates to the allied armies, for want of sufficient protection, and he repeated the regret in the *Mémorial de Sainte-Hélène*.

At length, after long parliamentary debates, the fortifications were voted in 1841, and completed 1846. The building of them cost 140,000,000 fr. They form a gigantic undertaking, and consist :—

1. Of a continuous *enceinte* of about 23 miles in length, surmounted with 94 bastions and terraces, and a wall 33 feet thick, with a ditch and glacis outside;

2. Of seventeen detached Forts with several fosses. The whole system is united by strategic roads, and it includes all the new communes annexed since 1860, as Batignolles, La Villette, Bercy, &c.

The following is a list of the detached Forts: Charenton, Nogent, Rosny, Noisy, Romainville, Aubervilliers, de l'Est, Couronne du Nord, la Briche, Mont Valérien, Vanves, Issy, Montrouge, Bicêtre, Ivry, Stains, Rouvray; and the redoubts of Faisanderie and Gravelle.

The fort of Vincennes has also been strengthened.

The complete circle of fortifications round Paris requires upwards of 2,800 mortars, guns, &c., to defend it; most of which were given up to the Germans, 1871. The chief advocate for the erection of the fortifications was M. Thiers, when minister to Louis Philippe; who lived to see their efficiency strangely tested in the five months' siege of 1870-1. They served to delay the progress of the German forces, and though they could not save Paris from being finally occupied by the enemy, they gave the defenders of the country outside opportunities of making a rally, though unavailing. Vanves, Issy, and other forts were captured in the siege; and Mont Valérien (600 feet above the river), which made the greatest figure, was at length given up and dismantled. Forts Bicêtre and Ivry were occupied by the Commune, 1871. Most of them have been restored since the war. New forts are in progress upon an outer circle, distant 14 to 16 miles from Paris.

OMNIBUSES.

The omnibuses of the Compagnie Générale des Omnibus (the only one in Paris) are nearly 700 in number, follow 32 different lines (distinguished by letters of the alphabet), and run from 8 mrn. to after midnight. **Fares:** interior, 30 cents; imperial 15 cents.

Most of these lines correspond with each other. In paying your fare be careful to ask for your ticket of correspondence (if required).

OMNIBUS ITINERARY.

LETTER FOR LINES—PLACE OF START AND ARRIVAL—COLOURS OF OMNIBUS, AND OF LAMPS—AND ROUTE.

[For example, in the first mentioned—A is the omnibus *letter for the line*. Auteuil is the *place of start*; Palais Royal the *place of arrival*. Yellow is the *omnibus* colour; red the *colour of the lamp*.]

A. Auteuil to Madeleine; yellow, red. Along the Cours la Reine and the quays. Also a Tram.

B. Trocadéro to Gare de Strasbourg; yellow, red and green. Avenue des Champs Elysées; St. Philippe du Roule; Boulevard Malesherbes; Versailles terminus; Rue de Châteaudun; Rue Lafayette. Tram.

C. Porte Maillot to Hotel de Ville; yellow, red. Rue du Louvre; Place du Palais Royal; Avenue des Champs Elysées. Correspondence with tramway to La Villette.

D. Ternes to Boulevard Filles du Calvaire; yellow, red. St. Philippe du Roule; Place de la Madeleine; Rue St. Honoré. Correspondence with G. H. Tram.

E. Bastille to Madeleine; yellow, red. Along the Boulevards. Correspondence with D. Tram.

F. Bastille to Place Wagram; dark red, brown. Boulevard Malesherbes; Place du Havre; Rue Catinat; Rue Rambuteau. Tram.

G. Batignolles to Jardin des Plantes; light green, brown. Place du Palais Royal; Rue du Louvre; Place du Châtelet. Tram.

H. Clichy to Odéon; yellow, red. Rue de Châteaudun; Boulevard des Italiens; Place du Palais Royal; Place St. Sulpice. Tram.

I. Place Pigalle to Halle aux Vins; green, red. Place de la Bourse; Rue Croix des Petits-Champs; Place du Pont St. Michel. Correspondence with A B. Tram.

J. Montmartre, Boulevard Rochechouart to Palais Royal; yellow, red. Place du Châtelet; Pont St. Michel; Boulevard St. Michel. Tram.

K. Montsouris to Great Northern Terminus; yellow, green, and red.

L. Villette to St. Germain des Prés; yellow, red.

M. Belleville (Lac St. Fargeau) to Arts et Metiers; dark brown, red and green.

N. Belleville to Louvre; green, red. Boulevard du Temple; Porte St. Martin; Porte St. Denis.

O. Ménilmontant to Montparnasse; green, red and green. Boulevard des Filles du Calvaire Place du Châtelet; Place Gozlin; Western Railway Station (Left Bank). Tram.

P. Charonne (in Père la Chaise) to Place d'Italie; yellow, red. Place de la Bastille.

Q. Plaisance to Hotel de Ville; dark green, red. Rue du Louvre; Place du Châtelet. Correspondence with A D, A F, A G, C, G, &c.

R. Avenue de Wagram to Bastille; green, violet and red.

S. Porte de Charenton to Château d'Eau; yellow, red, and white. Rue du Louvre Châtelet; Place de la Bastille. Tram.

T. Gare d'Orleans to Place Montholon yellow, red. Porte St. Denis; Rue Rambuteau Pont d'Austerlitz; Jardin des Plantes and Orleans Railway Station. Tram.

U. Porte d'Ivry to Halles Centralles; yellow, green, and red.

V. Barrière du Maine to Gare du Nord; light brown, green, red. Rue de Sèvres; Rue du Louvre; Rue Croix des Petits-Champs. correspondence with N, I, and F. Tram.

X. Vaugirard to Gare St. Lazare; yellow, green, and red. Place du Palais Royal; Rue de Grenelle St. Germain; Rue de Sèvres.

Y. Grenelle to Porte St. Martin; light brown, red, and white. Rue du Théâtre; Rue St. Dominique; Place du Palais Royal.

Z. Grenelle to the Bastille; light brown, green. Rue de Grenelle; Place St. Sulpice; Boulevard St. Germain. Tram.

AB. Passy to the Bourse; green, green. Boulevard de la Madeleine; St. Philippe du Roule. Tram.

AC. Petite Villette to Champs Elysées; green, red, and green. Boulevard de la Madeleine; Rue de Châteaudun; Rue Lafayette. Tram.

AD. Château d'Eau to Ecole Militaire; green, green. Rue St. Dominique; Rue St. Denis. Tram.

AE. Forges d'Ivry to Pont St. Michel; green, green. Château d'Eau; Place du Trône. Correspondence with E. Tram.

AF. Place du Panthéon to Courcelles; green, red. Place de la Madeleine; Cours la Reine; Rue St. Dominique. Correspondence with AB, E, and A. Tram.

AG. Vaugirard to Louvre; dark brown, red and white.

AH. Auteuil to Place St. Sulpice to the Bastille; green, orange.

An Omnibus key (clef) may be bought for 1 fr.

It is not an unpleasant way to view Paris, to take two or three omnibus drives (outside price, 15c.; with correspondence, 30c.), through the great thoroughfares. One good drive is from the Madeleine to the Bastille, and thus back by the Rue de Rivoli and Rue St. Honoré, to St. Philippe du Roule. The last route is followed from the Place de la Bastille, by the Charenton Omnibus.

Another pleasant trip may be made from the Place de la Bourse to Passy, through the principal Boulevards. A third, from the Parc de Monceaux to the Odéon, Rive Gauche. Some of the omnibuses have an awning, and staircase to mount behind.

Tramway Cars now run in different parts of Paris, distinguished by numbers, 1, 2, 3, etc. Many run in correspondence with the Omnibuses; some are worked by steam. Charge, 15c. to 1fr. The routes are—

Those of the *General Omnibus Company*, run from the Louvre, L'Etoile, Villette, Halles Centralles, Montrouge, La Chapelle, Bastille, etc., to places in the suburbs.

Those of the *North* (Nord) Lines, run from L'Etoile, St. Augustine, Place Clichy, and La Chapelle, to the neighbouring suburbs.

Those of the *South* (Sud) Lines, from L'Etoile, St. Germain des Prés, Montparnasse, Bastille, etc., to the neighbouring suburbs.

TELEGRAPH OFFICES.

(Charge to United Kingdom 2½d. per word.)

At the General Post Office, 55, Rue Jean-Jacques Rousseau; 2, Avenue de la République; the Luxembourg; Rue La Fayette, 35; Place Vendôme, 15 (till 6 p.m.); Place de la Bourse, 12 (all night); Boulevard Malesherbes, 4; Auteuil, Grand Rue, 10; Passy, Place de la Mairie, 4; Avenue des Champs Elysées, 33 or 67 (till 12 p.m.); Rue de Rivoli, 17; Boulevard des Capucines, 12 (Ecole Militaire Pavillon de l'Artillerie); Boulevard du Temple, 41 (till midnight); Boulevard du Prince Eugéne, 34; Place St. Michel, 6; Rue Pagevin (Hôtel des Postes); Rue aux Ours,

32; Place Roubaix (till midnight); Rue de Lyon, 55 (day and night); Les Ternes, Avenue de la Grande Armeè, 80; Rue de Strasbourg, 8; Belleville, Rue de Paris, 58; Ministère de l'Intérieur, 103, Rue de Grenelle St. Germain (allnight); 112, Rue St. Lazaire; Grand Hotel; 16, Boulevard St. Denis; Gare du Nord, and all the other Railway Stations.

PROTESTANT CHURCHES AND CHAPELS.

CHURCH OF ENGLAND.—*Chapel of the British Embassy*, 5, Rue d'Aguesseau, Faubourg St. Honoré (at 11, 3½, and 8). *Marbœuf Chapel*, 10, Avenue Marbœuf (at 11 and 3½); *English Chapel*, 38, Rue St. Hippolyte, Passy; built by Mr. Albert Way, 1844, and now under restoration. *Christ Church*, near the English Orphanage, Boulevard Bineau, Neuilly. For hours of service, clergy, &c., see *Galignani's Messenger*.

WESLEYAN.—4, Rue Roquépine, Boulevard Malesherbes (Sundays, 11½ and 7½; Wednesdays, 7½).

CONGREGATIONAL.—23, Rue Royale St. Honoré (Sundays 11½ and 7½; Tuesdays 7½).

SCOTCH CHURCH. — The Oratoire, near Palais Royal, at 11 and 3.

BAPTIST.—48, Rue de Lille.

AMERICAN CHAPEL.—21, Rue de Berry.

AMERICAN EPISCOPAL CHURCH.—17, Rue Bayard.

GALLICAN CATHOLIC CHURCH.—Service conducted by M. Hyacinthe Loyson (Pére Hyacinthe).

REFORMED CHURCH OF PARIS.—*(Consistoire de Paris)*.—The Reformed Church of Paris comprises five parishes and two annexes, Vincennes and Courbevoie. The four principal places of worship (Temples Protestants) are the Church of the Oratory (Oratoire), 147, Rue St. Honoré; Eglise Saint Esprit, 5, Rue Roquépine; Pentémont, 106, Rue Grenelle St. Germain; Ste. Marie, 216, Rue St. Antoine.

D

In these churches service commences at noon There are also services as follows:—At 3 at the Oratoire; at 3, in German, at St. Marie; at half-past 12 in the Church of Batignolles; at 12 in that of Belleville, 17, Square Napoléon; at half-past 10 at Passy, 11, Passage des Eaux Minérales; at 1 in the Church de Plaisance, 97, Rue de l'Ouest; at 5, in German, in the same place; at 1, in the Church at Vincennes, 96, Rue de Montreuil; at 10, in the Asile des Vieillards; at 3, at the House of the Deaconesses, 95, Rue de Revilly; every Wednesday, at 8 aft., at the House of the Deaconesses; and every Thursday, at the same hour, at the Pentémont and Ste. Marie (see above).

An occasional change in the hours of service may take place according to the time of the year, or from personal causes. See *Bradshaw's Continental Railway Guide*. The principal services are also usually recorded in *Galignani's Messenger*. of Saturday.

St. Joseph's Roman Catholic Church, for English speaking Catholics, Avenue de la Reine Hortense. *Synagogue*, 15, Rue N. D. de Nazareth, at 7 a.m. and sunset.

Clubs.—Among these are the *French Jockey Club*, Boulevard des Capucines; *Washington*, 4, Place de l'Opéra; *Agricole (or Farmers' Club)*, Quai d'Orsay.

For useful information affecting English-speaking Residents at Paris, see *Galignani's Guide*.

Water Supply of Paris.

Water, either for the streets and sewers, or for drinking purposes, is brought in by five canals, and four or five aqueducts. which supply 18 to 20 reservoirs; numerous fountains, of which 35 are monumental and 90 plain; and above 2,000 waterplugs (bornes fontaines) for washing the streets. Several Drinking Fountains have been opened at the cost of Sir Richard Wallace. The Artesian Wells are those of Grenello,

Passy, Ménilmontant, and La Chapelle. The *Aqueducts* are those of Arceuil, built 1624, on the south of the city: de Ceinture, on the north; Belleville, on the nor h; and de Romanville.

On the 11th September, 1865, at 1-40 p.m. the waters of the Dhuys reached Paris by the immense aqueduct which has been constructed to convey them to the vast reservoirs of Ménilmontant.

The aqueduct of the Dhuys begins in the parish of Pargny in the department of the Aisne; and passes through the departments of the Aisne, of the Seine et Marne, of the Seine et Oise, and of the Seine. Its length is about 135 kilomètres (83 miles), of which 16 are syphons or conduits, crossing valleys, &c., and 10 are tunnels. The principal tunnels are those of Montménard, Montretout, Monceaux, and Quincy, which have a length of from 700 to 2,000 mètres. The principal syphons are those of the Petit-Morin, of the Grand-Morin, of the Marne, and of Villemouble, which have a length of from 1,000 to 4,500 mètres, and a rise of 56 and 75 mètres. The works were begun in June, 1863. The water was let into the aqueducts to try the syphons August 2nd, 1865. The total expense of the works was 16 millions of francs, including indemnities for land and premises.

Before this addition, Paris received 147 million litres of water in 24 hours; proceeding from the Canal de l'Ourcq, from the water works of Chaillot and Austerlitz, from the Bridge of Arcueil, from the Artesian Well de Grenelle, and the sources du Nord above mentioned.

The Dhuys has added at least 40 litres daily to this supply, and the spring at Saint Maur yields as much more. Thus Paris receives at present a daily supply of 252 millions litres of water.

An additional supply can be obtained directly it is required. It will be derived from waters in the valley of the Somme and the Sonde, in a district of Champagne. This supply would amount to 60 million litres daily, and if the increase of the population of Paris rendered it necessary, an additional supply could be obtained from the sources of the Vanne, between Troyes and Sens. The latter would yield a supply of 70 million litres in 24 hours, and would be received in a reservoir at Montrouge. Part of the *Sewage* is sent by Conduit to *Gennevilliers*, near the Clichy outfall; where 2000 acres are given to Market Gardeners for reclamation. Another Conduit for the excess is in progress towards St. Germains. The Paris Sewers may be seen by ticket, from the Préfect of the Seine.

WATER CLOSETS—called "Cabinets d' Aisance"—are a very useful institution in Paris. They are lit up at night like the front of a theatre; and are used by men and women indiscriminately; which is rather apt to shock the raw English traveller. They are private speculations. Usual charge, 15c. To the list given at page 384 of *Bradshaw's Continental Guide*, the following may be added :—Boulevard Sebastopol, No. 119 (Passage du Ponceau); Boulevard des Italiens (No. 17, "Goffard"); Passage next Corps de Garde in Boulevard Bonne Nouvelle, No. 23; and in same Boulevard, No. 48, next the Gymnase; Passage Jouffroy, opposite the Variétés, No. 45; Rue de la Ville Neuve, No. 66; Boulevard Bonne Nouvelle;

Notre Dame Bonne Nouvelle, No. 11; Passages des Panoramas, next Variétés (Galérie Montmartre, No. 27); Passage des Princes, 14 bis; Rue de Bondy, close to La Renaissance Theatre; Passages de l'Opéra (Galérie des Baromètre, No. 9), opposite Hotel de Castille; Passage du Saumon (Galérie des Bains, No. 5, first galérie to right); Rue Montorgueil, near Rue Poissonnière; Passage Vendôme, near Château d'Eau; Passage Choiseul, No. 28 (Bouffes P.) Nos. 2, 10, and 21, Rue de Beaujolais; Avenue Victoria (Châtelet), next Hotel Victoria; three in Palais Royal, viz., one in Galérie Beaujolais, one in Galérie Chartres (No. 7), one in Péristyle Joinville (Nos. 77-78); Passage Radziwill (Nos. 23 and 35, at back of Palais Royal); Boulevard Porte St. Martin, No. 2; Rue Montaigne, No. 23; Carré des Champs Elysées, to the right in going towards l'Arc de Triomphe; near Garden of Tuileries, in Passage Delorme, No. 16, between Rue Rivoli and Rue St. Honoré; Cour Bony, No. 9; Passage Brady, No. 83; Rue Sufflot, near the Panthéon; one in Garden of Luxembourg, in a little building between the great alley and Boulevard St. Michel; with several others on the left bank of river.

Gasworks, all under one company, chartered till 1906; the works are in the environs.

Paris Statistics.

The following facts relating to the area of Paris, during eighteen centuries, will probably be interesting to the visitor.

Paris occupied	Hectares (each 2½ acres).
Under Julins Cæsar	15
„ Julian	39
„ Phillip Augustus	253

Paris occupied—	Hectares (each 2½ acres).
„ Charles VI.	439
„ Henry II.	484
Henry IV.	568
„ Louis XIV.	1,104
Louis XV.	1,537
„ Louis XVI.	3,370
„ Louis XVIII.	3,404
Napoleon III.	7,450

The Bois de Boulogne which forms part of the recent annexations to Paris, contains 800 hectares (2,000 acres).

The number of boulevards and public *places* has more than doubled since the annexation of the ancient district, situated between the former customs limit and the covered way (Rue Militaire) inside the fortifications.

Independently of the first exterior boulevards, which now form an excellent walk, of the Park of the Buttes-Chaumont, now just completed, and of the park projected on Mont Souris, the old banlieue of Paris has already received the addition of numerous districts covering an area of above 60,000 mètres, or distributed thus:—

	Mètres.
District of Vaugirard	4,134
„ Belleville	11,273
„ Grenelle	4,395
„ Beau-Grenelle	3,200
„ Montrouge	7,124
„ Place Malesherbes	9,794
„ Batignolles	19.246
„ Charonne	1,808
Total	60,974

Paris, for civil purposes, is divided into 20 Arrondissements and 80 Quartiers or Quarters, as follow:—

Arrondissements and Quarters.

1st. LOUVRE.

1. St. Germain l'Auxerrois.—2. Halles. —3. Palais Royal.—4. Place Vendôme.

2nd. BOURSE.

5. Gaillon.—6. Vivienne.—7. Mail.—8. Bonne Nouvelle.

3rd. TEMPLE.

9. Arts et Métiers.—10. Enfants Rouges.—11. Archives.—12. Ste. Avoie.

4th. HOTEL-DE-VILLE.

13. St. Merri.—14. St. Gervais.—15. Arsenal.—16. Notre Dame.

5th. PANTHEON.

17. St. Victor.—18. Jardin des Plantes.—19. Val de Grâce.—20. Sorbonne.

6th. LUXEMBOURG.

21. Monnaie.—22. Odéon.—23. Notre Dame des Champs.—24. St. Germain des Prés.

7th. PALAIS BOURBON.

25. St. Thomas d'Aquin.—26. Invalides.—27. Ecole Militaire.—28. Gros-Caillou.

8th. ELYSEE.

29. Champs Elysées.—30. Faubourg du Roule.—31. Madeleine.—32. Europe.

9th. OPERA.

33. St. Georges.—34. Chausée d'Antin.—35. Faubourg Montmartre.—36. Rochechouart.

10th. ENCLOS ST. LAURENT.

37. St. Vincent de Paul.—38. Porte St. Denis.—39. Porte St. Martin.—40. Hôpital St. Louis.

11th. POPINCOURT.

41. Folie-Méricourt.—42. St. Ambroise.—43. Roquette.—44. Ste. Marguerite.

12th. REUILLY.

45. Bel Air.—46. Picpus.—47. Bercy.—48. Quinze-Vingts.

13th. GOBELINS.

49. Salpétrière.—50. Gare.—51. Maison Blanche.—52. Croulebarbe.

14th. OBSERVATOIRE.

53. Montparnasse.—54. Santé.—55. Petit-Montrouge.—56. Plaisance.

15th. VAUGIRARD.

57. St. Lambert.—58. Necker.—59. Grenelle.—60. Javel.

16th. PASSY.

61. Autenil.—62. La Muette.—63. Porte Dauphine.—64. Des Bassins.

17th. BATIGNOLLES MONCEAUX.

65. Ternes.—66. Plaine Monceaux.—67. Batignolles.—68. Epinettes.

18th. BUTTE MONTMARTRE.

69. Grandes Carrières.—70. Clignancourt.—71. Goutte d'Or.—72. La Chapelle.

19th. BUTTES CHAUMONT.

73. La Villette.—74. Pont de Flandre.—75. Amérique.—76. Combat.

20th. MENILMONTANT.

77. Belleville.—78. St. Fargeau.—79. Pére-Lachaise.—80. Charonne.

There is a mayor to each Arrondissement; the chief mayor being the Préfect of the Seine (resident at the Tuileries, *pro tem*, till the Hotel de Ville is rebuilt). The Préfect of the Police is at the City Barrack, Palais de Justice. The police are called "Sergents de Ville."

Population.

The existing *population* of Paris is three times larger than that ascertained by the census of 1806. The following has been the rate of increase (by official documents):—

1806 580,600
1811 622,636
1817 713,000
1836 866,438
1846 1,053,801
1861 1,596,141

1871 1,696,141
1873 1,851,792
1876 1,936,738

In 1864 the Births amounted to 53,835; and in the same year there was

1 Birth to 31 inhabitants,
1 Death to 35 inhabitants.

The proportion in France was

1 Birth to 35 inhabitants,
1 Death to 41 inhabitants.

In 1876, Deaths were only 1 to 53, or 26 per 1000.

In 1878 the Births in Paris were 55,000; Deaths, 48,000; Marriages, 20,000.

The recent improvements in drainage at Paris have considerably diminished the rate of mortality.

TRADES.—In a late return the Paris trades are classed thus:—Establishments ministering to Food, 29,069, with 38,859 hands; Building, 5,378, and 71,242 hands; Furniture, 7,391, and 37,951 hands; Clothing, 23,805, and 78,377 hands; Textile Fabrics, 2,836, and 26,810 hands; Metals, 3,440, and 28,806 hands; Jewellery, &c., 3,199, and 18,731 hands; Chemistry, porcelain, 2,719, and 14,397 hands; Printing, engraving, &c., 2,759, and 19,507 hands; Other trades, 20,580, and 82,071 hands.

The poor are assisted by means of a *Mont de Piété*, or public pawnshop; such as those at 17, Rue des Blanc Manteaux, and 7, Rue du Paradis, au Marais; where loans, &c., can be obtained. *Savings Banks* are established in each arrondissement, the head one being at 9, Rue Coq Héron. A *Maison de Santé*, for the use of persons who can afford to pay, is here and there opened by the municipality; the head one being in Rue du Faubourg St. Denis.

ELECTORS.—Every Frenchman under the present constitution, aged 25 and upwards, is an elector, under certain conditions.

CITY REVENUE.—About 10 millions sterling; of which the house, furniture, and window duties yield about 2 millions; trade licenses (patentes) about £60,000; but a great portion (above 5 millions) is derived from the *Octroi* duties taken at the city gates or Barrières (corresponding to the old Bars in the city of London). This octroi includes duties on wine, spirits, beer, oil, charcoal, wood, hay and straw, meat, &c., and involves inspection of all carriages passing in. The City *Expenditure* includes £600,000 for the poor; £400,000 for education; £200,000 for lighting; £200,000 for water; £800,000 for police; and 1 million to the State and the Department of the Seine. Debt, 79½ millions; interest on Debt, 4 millions.

BRIDGES.—There are 25 *Bridges* on the Seine, all comparatively short ones; and about 11 miles of *Quays* on both sides, with wharfs for landing wine, wood, stone, coal, &c.

IMPROVEMENTS.—The changes at Paris since 1861 have completely transformed it. We may enumerate—1. The clearance of the Rookeries, near the Palais Royal, to make room for the new street from the new Opera to the Louvre, by the head of Rue Richelieu. 2. The Boulevard St. Germain in the Faubourg of that name. 3. Place du Roi de Rome, opposite Champs de Mars. 4. The fine new Avenue, north-east from the Arc de Triomphe. 5. The whole quarter of the New Opera, and the Chausséed'Antin. 6. The new clearances near the Rue Rambuteau, behind the Rue de Rivoli, &c.

Events of the last Hundred Years.

1774 Louis XVI.'s accession.
1789 Meeting of States-General.
—— Constituent Assembly.
—— Bastille taken, 14 July.
1791 Legislative Assembly.
1792 Republic and Convention.
  Execution of Louis XVI.
1793 Reign of Terror.
1795 Directory.
1799 Bonaparte First Consul.
1804 Napoleon I. Emperor.
1814 Allied Sovereigns at Paris.
  Louis XVIII. King.
1815 Hundred Days. Waterloo, 18 June.
  Return of Louis XVIII.
1825 Charles X.
1830 Three Days, 27, 38, 29 July. Flight
  of Charles X.
  Louis Philippe, King of the French.
1848 Second Republic, 24 February.
  Louis Napoleon, President.
1851 Coup d'Etat, 2 December.
1852 Napoleon II. Emperor.
1870 War declared against Prussia,
  18 July.
  Defeat at Sedan, 2 September. Surrender of the Emperor.
  Republic proclaimed, Government of
  National Defence, 4 September.

Paris invested by the Germans,
  18 September.
Gambetta leaves in a balloon, 7 Oct.
First Communist rising.
1871 King of Prussia proclaimed German
  Emperor at Versailles, 18 January
  Second Communist rising, 22 Jan.
  National Assembly at Bordeaux,
  12 February.
  M. Thiers, Chief of the Executive
  Power, 17 February.
  German army occupies Paris, 1, 2,
  March.
  Communist Rising at Paris, 18 Mar.
  The Government and M. Thiers retire
  to Versailles, 19th March.
  Second Siege of Paris, 2 April.
  Troops enter Paris, 21 May. The
  rising put down, 29 May.
  Third Republic, M. Thiers, Presi-
  dent, 31 July.
1873 Marshal MacMahon, President,
  24 May.
  His powers prolonged for seven years
  20 November.
1876 New Senate and Chamber elected.
1877 Death of M. Thiers.
  The Dufaure Ministry take office.
1879 M. Jules Grévy, President (for
  seven years) 30 January, on the
  resignation of Marshal Mac Mahon.
  The Waddington Ministry.
1880 De Freycinet Ministry.

DISTANCES OF PARIS

From some of the Chief Cities of the World.

	Leagues.		Leagues
Alexandria	756	Leipsic	189
Amsterdam	112	London	98
Antwerp	78	Madrid	300
Bâle	117	Mexico	2189
Berlin	225	Milan	153
Brussels	69	Moscow	620
Cadiz	395	Naples	410
Cape of Good Hope	2406	Palermo	406
Constantinople	556	Parma	225
Copenhagen	250	Pekin	2350
Dantzic	300	Philadelphia	1100
Dover	75	Pondicherry	2390
Dresden	213	Rome	325
Dublin	185	St. Petersburg	500
Edinburgh	190	Smyrna	630
Geneva	145	Stockholm	380
Ghent	70	Turin	167
Gibraltar	410	Warsaw	375
Hague (The)	90	Venice	248
Jerusalem	810	Vienna	275

4

RAILWAY SERVICE TO AND FROM PARIS.

FOR DETAILS, SEE "BRADSHAW'S CONTINENTAL GUIDE," PUBLISHED MONTHLY.
OMNIBUSES RUN FROM THE SUB-OFFICES (BUREAUX SUCCURSALES) OF
EACH LINE TO MEET THE TRAINS.

1. WESTERN LINES (l'Ouest).—From the terminus, Rue St. Lazare or Rue d'Amsterdam (for Normandy): To Rouen, Yvetot, Havre, Dieppe; to Mantes, Evreux, Lisieux, Caen, Bayeux, and Cherbourg.

From the **terminus, Boulevard Mont Parnasse (for Brittany):** To Rambouillet, Chartres, Le Mans, Laval, Rennes, Brest, Nantes. From St. Lazare or Mont Parnasse, for the **Ceinture Line,** and the **Banlieue Lines,** to Neuilly and Auteuil; to Asnières, St. Cloud, Sèvres, and Versailles ; to St. Germain; to St. Denis, Enghien, and Argenteuil. A new Branch connects *Champ de Mars* with the Western.

2. EASTERN LINES (l'Est).—From the terminus, Place de Strasbourg: To Meaux, Epernay, Chalons, Blesme, Bar-le-Duc, Commercy, Toul, Frouard, Nancy, Luneville, Sarrebourg, and Strasbourg; to Carlsruhe, Stuttgart, Augsburg, Munich, and Vienna ; to Nancy, Metz, Forbach, and Frankfort; to Chalons, Strasbourg, Frankfort, and Wiesbaden; to Epernay, Rheims, Mézières, Namur, and Brussels; to Marseilles and Switzerland by several routes; to Meaux; to Longueville and Provins. *Gare de Vincennes,* to Vincennes, &c., from Place de la Bastille.

3. NORTHERN LINES (Du Nord).—From the terminus, Place Roubaix: To Creil, Compiègne, Noyon, Bussigny, Charlerol, Namur, Cologne, and Frankfort; to Maubeuge, Mons, and Brussels; to Creil, Amiens, Abbeville, and Boulogne; to Creil, Amiens, Arras, and Calais; to Amiens, Douai, Lille, and Ghent; to Dammartin, Soissons, Reims, and Thionville. A junction is open between the Plain of St Denis Station and the St. Ouen Docks, on the Seine.

4. ORLEANS and DU MIDI (South) LINES.—From the terminus, Quai d'Austerlitz: To Choissy, Etampes, Orléans, Tours, Chatellerault, Poitiers, Angoulême, Bordeaux, and thence to the South of France and to Spain ; to Poitiers, Niort, and La Rochelle; to Tours, Saumur, Angers, Nantes, Savenay, and St. Nazaire; to Orléans, Tours, and Mans. *Gare de Sceaux,* for Arcueil, Fontenay, and Sceaux; and to Orsay.

5. LYONS and MEDITERRANEAN.—Terminus, Boulevard Mazas (opposite Mazas Prison) : To Mâcon, Lyons, Valence, Avignon, Marseilles, Toulon, Nice, Geneva, Mont Cenis, &c.; to Charenton, Brunoy, and Corbeil.

CHEMIN DE FER DE CEINTURE (Girdle Line.)—Connects all the lines round Paris in the **Banlieue** or suburbs, and makes junctions with the Main lines. It runs just inside the fortifications, is 23 miles long, with 28 stations, and makes the round *de Paris à Paris* in 2½ hours. Starting from Place du Havre, the principal station, it serves, among others, Batignolles (for the Western), Courcelles, Bois de Boulogne, Ouest-Ceinture (for Versailles, &c.), Orleans-Ceinture (for Orleans), La Glacière (for Sceaux), Bell Air, Ménilmontant, La Chapelle (for St. Denis), Avenue de St. Ouen, to Courcelles and St. Lazare again. See page 20, *Bradshaw's Continental Guide.* A section is open from Plain St. Denis to Pantin. For the Banlieue to Versailles, St. Germans, &c., see page 32 of *Continental Guide.* A **Metropolitan or Underground Line,** in progress, will comprise the following sections:—Batignolles-Girdle, Gentilly-Girdle, and Ornans-Girdle, to Palais Royal as a Central Station, with a Branch from Orleans Terminus, and the extension of Moulineaux Girdle to Orleans Terminus.

Passengers by railway are supposed to be at the station at least ten minutes before the trains start. There are always commodious waiting-rooms.

PARIS.

HISTORICAL.

HE soil of Paris has, in remote ages, been covered by the sea three times, each submersion having left evidence of a special creation. Much of the soil, consisting of cretaceous formations, giving rise to the noted plaster of Paris, is the production of early animal life. The traces of nummulites are very plentiful. Impressions of palms and cedars have been found, and paleotheric and anoplotheric animals (extinct species), recovered by the genius of Cuvier, were frequent. Above the thick bed of gypsum (sulphate of lime) you reach the marly and flint beds and rocks.

In the quaternary age a great cataclysm gave the basin of Paris its present form, scooping out the Valley of the Seine, and shaping Montmartre, Mont Valérien, and other high points. From traces that occur, it appears that at that time the forests on the site of Paris were peopled with mammoths, monster stags, bisons, beavers, and primitive man, as can be proved by the rude flint instruments found amongst the remains of those animals. In the time of Julius Cæsar, Paris, to which the name of *Lutetia*, a corruption of Lutuhesi (river dwelling), was given by the Romans, was only a collection of mud huts, inhabited by the *Parisii*, a rude and savage tribe, on a small island, with the Seine for its foss. That island is now the Ile de la Cité. The Latin rule removed, in some degree, the traces of this ancient barbarism. The Roman emperors frequently made the rising city a place of residence, and under Julian, especially, Paris assumed a greater degree of importance, and obtained considerable political privileges.

In 496, Clovis, who had been elected chief of the Franks at the age of fifteen, became king. The wife of Clovis (Ste. Clothilde) was a Christian, and, by her influence, a church, dedicated to Ste. Geneviève, the patron saint of Paris, was built. Under the reign of this prince, the city was first securely fortified. For nearly two centuries after, little addition was made, but in the reign of Hugh Capet, the mason and carpenter were again at work. The place had also acquired sufficient dimensions to be divided into four administrative quarters. Under Philip Augustus, A.D. 1180-1223, the streets were first paved; several churches erected; a considerable portion of Notre Dame finished; the tower of the Louvre remodelled and fortified, and a great part of the suburbs enclosed with walls. During the age of Louis XI., Robert Sorbonne founded his schools in the locality still called the Sorbonne. Under Charles V., the faubourgs being much extended and in danger, from the frequent incursions of the English, the fortifications were enlarged, and Paris was surrounded with new fosses.

Fresh improvements went on under the reign of Francis I. The old tower of the Louvre was pulled down, and the foundations of a palace laid upon its site. The Hôtel de Ville was commenced; better means of communication were opened up between different parts of the city, and its defences again enlarged and strengthened. Henry IV. was also a great benefactor to his capital. The Pont Neuf, the building of which had been delayed for want of funds, was completed at his private expense; the hospital of St. Louis founded; many streets, squares, and quays added to the beauty and importance of the place; the Tuileries and Louvre were continued; and everywhere embellishments were vigorously executed.

When Louis XIV. mounted the throne, he lent a great part of his restless energy to the improvement of Paris. In his reign, more than thirty churches, and a corresponding number of streets, were built; with the Hôtel des Invalides, Observatory, Colonnade of the Louvre, and Pont Royal. The Champs Elysées was improved; the Institut de France and the manufacture of the Gobelins tapestry were established. About 1670, the then outer walls were cleared away, and their sites converted into broad planted roads, thenceforward called *Boulevards* (for bulwarks). The Portes St. Denis and St. Martin were erected in commemoration of two victories. In the two following reigns magnificent hotels, or private mansions were built in the Faubourgs of St. Germain and St. Honoré; the foundations of the Panthéon, St. Sulpice, and the Madeleine were laid; the Place de la Concorde was beautified; the manufactory of porcelain was removed from Vincennes to Sèvres; the Ecole Militaire and Collége de France were instituted; the Jardin des Plantes was enlarged; and a wall, for levying the *octroi*, was built about 1770, inclosing the new suburbs.

Under the Directory, and the Consular and Imperial governments, new improvements were pressed forward with vigour, and the city began to assume an aspect of unwonted magnificence. The Place du Carrousel was enlarged; the northern gallery of the Louvre and the Rue de Rivoli were commenced; spacious markets were projected; and three handsome bridges thrown over the river. Since 1815, the hand of renovation and embellishment has not been slack. The Place de la Concorde has been remodelled; the Obelisk de Luxor, brought from Egypt, has been reared in the centre; with two magnificent Fountains on either side of it; the Arc de l'Etoile has been completed; the Church of the Madeleine opened for public worship; the Hôtel de Ville renewed; the exterior of Notre Dame cleansed; the Palais du Quai d'Orsay and the Palais des Beaux Arts finished; several new and open streets constructed through the densest and unhealthiest parts of the city; and handsome houses and bridges erected. In Louis Philippe's time, 1841-4, under the Government of Thiers, the present line of Fortifications or Enceinte was completed (cost five millions sterling); and in their neighbourhood, both inside and outside, newer boulevards have grown up. The reign of Napoleon III. was marked by the completion of the new Palace of the Louvre, the splendid new Rue de Rivoli, the Boulevards de Strasbourg, du Prince Eugène, de Sébastopol (about 2 miles long), and de Magenta, and the new Boulevards in the environs, with the Halles Centrales, the Pont d'Alma, the Bois de Boulogne, and other improvements, mostly due to Baron Haussmann; all of which contributed to transform Paris, and to make it the most splendid city of Europe; when it was overtaken by the fearful disasters consequent upon the Franco-German war of 1870-1.

The principal events in this dark period of Paris history are, the flight of the Empress after the surrender of the Emperor at Sedan; the appointment of the government of National Defence, under General Trochu, in September; the complete investment of the capital on 19th September by the Germans; the repeated attempts of the Parisians to break out, during a *Siege* of four months, till the starving condition of the population led to a capitulation on 28th Jan., 1871; and the surrender of the forts to the new German Emperor, whose head-quarters were at Versailles. An armistice being agreed on, the National Assembly was summoned by M. Thiers; the party of the Reds, however, rose against his government, 18th March, occupied the Hôtel de Ville, killed Generals Lecomte and Clement Thomas, and proclaimed the *Commune*, which lasted till 22-6 May; when Paris was recaptured by the French army under Marshal MacMahon, the National Assembly having in the meantime fixed itself at Versailles. The disastrous rule of the fanatical Commune was finally marked by the destruction of the Vendôme Column, the burning of the Tuileries, Palais Royal, Hôtel de Ville, and other public buildings, much injury done to the Louvre, Luxembourg, &c., and the murder of Archbishop Darboy, President Bonjean, and various persons, who had been seized as hostages, and were put to death in the Roquette Prison and in Rue Haxo. The injuries done to the buildings in this miserable week of the last reign of terror (May 20th to 28th) are noticed under their proper heads in the following description. Some which were entirely destroyed have been rebuilt on a new design; the restoration of others is in progress.

Among the streets and localities which suffered most, are Rue Royale, Rue St. Honoré, Rue de Rivoli, Rue de Bac, Rue de Lille, Place de la Concorde, Avenue de la Grande Armée, Porte St. Martin, Bois de Boulogne, Buttes Chaumont, and Père la Chaise Cemetery; and the following buildings, in addition to those above mentioned, viz., the Ministries of Finances and Foreign Affairs, Palace of the Legion of Honour, the Lyrique and Porte St. Martin Theatres, the Arsenal, Grenier de Reserve, Cour des Comptes, Conseil d'État, Préfecture, Palais de Justice, Gobelins Factory, École des Mines, Prince Eugène and Bonaparte Barracks. The Louvre and Notre Dame, though threatened by the Communists, were fortunately saved in time; but the library of the Louvre was injured. Most of the Forts in the environs were ruined in the German siege, but are in course of restoration. The Passy, Auteuil, Vincennes, and Lyons Stations were injured; and the villages of Châtillon, St. Denis, St. Cloud, Meudon, Sèvres, Champigny, Clamart, &c., suffered more or less in the war, or in the second siege, when the Commune held the capital.

The population of Paris, which, in the fifteenth century, contained only 100,000 souls, and under Louis XIV. 500,000, was in 1860, 1,525,942; in 1867, 1,825,300; in 1873, 1,851,792; in 1876, 1,936,738.

DESCRIPTIVE.

PARIS, the metropolis of France, is one of the largest and richest cities of Europe. It is situated in a valley on both banks of the Seine. The river crosses it from east to west, dividing it into two nearly equal parts; it then divides itself into two branches, which again unite after forming three considerable islands. The communication between the banks of the river and the islands is effected by a great number of bridges, many of which are remarkable for the beauty of their construction, and join the quays, which are intended rather for ornament than for business. The environs do not exhibit the same variety as those of London; instead of the gardens, parks, and country seats which surround our great metropolis Paris, on several sides, presents large tracts of uninclosed corn fields. The stream of life in the great streets, the crowd of wagons, carriages, and horsemen, is not so great as in the neighbourhood of our metropolis, though some of the busier streets approach the activity of our own. There is a great difference in this respect, according to the season of the year. In winter and spring (during the height of the season) the great thoroughfares, such as the Boulevards, from the Madeleine to the Rue Vivienne, are almost as crowded with vehicles as Regent Street in May. Most of the streets, however, are wide, airy, watered by numerous fountains, and full of magnificent hotels and shops. A history of Paris is, to a considerable degree, a history of France, so much has this city, during the last centuries, concentrated in itself all the vital action of France. The preponderance of Paris over all France, not only in a political sense, but in literature, arts, customs, &c., is immense, and has been most strikingly manifested during the revolutions of the last century. Paris—the common phrase runs—is France.

Paris is, without doubt, one of the most charming and luxurious capitals in the world. There is a perfect adaptability in its position, and construction, to all the ends and purposes of pleasure. The climate is, however, far from perfect, offering frequently a very cold, wet season in winter, and scorching glare in summer, which strips the trees early of their leaves. All that is possible is done to relieve this by an admirable system of irrigation, at great cost; yet the dust in summer, and mud in winter are, notwithstanding, a frequent nuisance. There is, however, a certain charm in the very aspect of Paris, in her boulevards, her gardens, her public promenades, which produces a fascination upon the senses, whilst there are few spots that have not some interest with which to attract the eye. May is the best time to enjoy Paris.

Standing on the Pont du Carrousel, a picture rich with beauty presents itself. Towards the east, and immediately before you, stands out, in bold relief, the Ile de la Cité, with its mass of irregular, tall, white houses; the solemn towers of Notre Dame; the gorgeous pinnacle of the Sainte Chapelle; the solid domes of the Palais de Justice; and the spired turrets of the Conciergerie. The river, descending by two channels, and here uniting, adds a peculiar grace to the scene. Immediately on our left extends the long line of lofty streets, abutting on the Quais, the houses of which gleam in the warm light of the sun and blue azure of the heavens. Sometimes a huge pile of building; sometimes a high Gothic tower; sometimes a colossal statue; sometimes a tiny spire rears itself in the midst. On the other side stands the Institute of France, with its domed centre, and circular wings; and between these two lines of buildings flows the swift current of the Seine, animated by the motion of boats, and the presence of floating-houses, decorated with flags. If we turn to the west, a no less charming picture presents itself. On the right, the elegant façade of the Louvre, and the thickly-leaved avenue of the Tuileries. On the left, the Quai de Voltaire and the Palais d'Orsay, behind which, the river loses itself by a graceful bend, interrupt the view; whilst beyond, the green heights of Chaillot and Passy, dotted with glaring houses close a scene of unwonted character.

There are few streets in London—in fact there are none—which will bear comparison with the Boulevards of Paris; the oldest parts of which, from Rue St. Antoine to Rue St. Martin and Rue St. Honoré, mark the bounds of the first Paris Wall (page 2). They form wide and magnificent promenades, in the middle of which is an unpaved road; on each side of the road is a row of trees, and between each row of trees and the row of houses are wide asphalte walks for pedestrians. The waving line which these streets assume, adds greatly to the beauty of the Boulevards; the eye cannot reach the end of the prospect, and the uncommon width is productive of no vacuity or dulness. Among the attractions are the covered *Passages*, full of gay shops (like the Burlington Arcade), as Passage Vivienne and Colbert, near the Bourse; de l'Opéra and Choiseul, near the Opera; des Panoramas and Jouffroy, in Boulevard Montmartre; Delorme, in Rue Rivoli; du Saumon, in Rue Montmartre; du Pont Neuf, on Quai Conti; and others. The *Bazaars* are those of Montmartre, Jouffroy, &c. The massy stone structures of Paris appear to greater advantage here than in the narrower streets. On the southern side of Paris the Boulevards extend a still greater length, and are planted with trees, but they are not considered equal to those on the other side of the city,

The Court of the Louvre

The banks of the Seine present but few attractions to the visitor, except in the quarter of the Tuileries, where, on one side are the Louvre and the Tuileries, with its gardens, and on the other, from the Palais du Corps Législatif to the Pont Neuf, a succession of fine buildings.

But it is not here that we pause to exhaust the beauties of Paris. We shall everywhere find something to attract us, something to admire; and must allow that Paris is unrivalled, if not as a city of beauty, at least as a city of pleasure.

In 1600, Paris possessed 339 streets; 1856, **1,474** public ways, including 1,168 streets and 44 roads. To-day Paris contains 65,000 houses, 3,000 streets, 80 squares, 80 churches, and 30 bridges. Streets often change their names here: among the latest are Rue St. Morny, now Rue Pierre Charron; and Rue d'Enfer, now Rue Denfert Rochambeau, after the defender of Belfort.

Since 1852, some 4,000 houses have been demolished to make way for improvements, and about 10,000 have been built, most of them in a peculiarly handsome and substantial style. On the 1st January, 1860, the bounds of the city were extended to the fortifications, in consequence of which, the old Barrières, or octroi gates, have been removed, and the Arrondissements increased from 12 to 20; the new ones being styled Gobelins, Observatoire, Vaugirard, Passy, Batignolles - Monceaux, Butte - Montmartre, Buttes - Chaumont, and Ménilmontant. This enlarged area is 19,280 acres, or 30 square miles, within a double circle of Boulevards; the newer and outer circle of which is not yet filled up. Its circumference is 21 to 22 miles.

FIRST DAY.

THE TUILERIES—PLACE DU CARROUSEL—LOUVRE—ST. GERMAIN L'AUXERROIS—PALAIS ROYAL—FONTAINE MOLIÈRE—THÉÂTRE FRANÇAIS—RUE DU REMPART

THE TUILERIES—(NOW IN COURSE OF RESTORATION.)

The Tuileries and the Louvre, which now form as it were, but one grand building, will be the primary object of attraction to the visitor, the former as being intimately connected with the modern history, the second with the fine arts, of France. This splendid palace is situated along the side of the river Seine; and fronted on the west by the gardens of the Tuileries, the Place de la Concorde, and the Champs Elysées. On the spot where it now stands, existed formerly, tile-fields, from whence the name is derived, the word *Tuilerie* signifying a tile-field, or more properly a tile-kiln. These fields were converted into gardens, and laid out in 1665, according to the taste of the age of Louis XIV., by Le Nôtre, but have since his time undergone considerable alteration. These gardens form a grand parallelogram, containing about 67 acres, and are flanked by the Rue de Rivoli on the north, and the Seine on the south. They consist of flower-beds and public walks in front of the palace, a grove of trees in the centre, and another walk and flower-beds on the western side of the grove. Two elevated avenues of lime trees run parallel with the Rue de Rivoli and the Seine. A sunk fence with a sloping green sward and white stone finishings separates a portion of the flower garden in front of the Tuileries, and this portion now, as well as the rest, is open to the public. An elegant new bridge, of white stone, crosses the southern avenue and leads to the terrace which is next to the Seine. A *Laocoon* and a *Diana* in bronze, amongst other statues, ornament this garden, and on each side of the road-way leading up to the grand entrance may be also seen bronze figures of the *Sicilian Knife Grinder* and *Venus sitting on a Tortoise*. Three circular basins, with jets, d'eau, and full of gold and silver fish, ornament the public gardens; and around the centre one are collected several fine groups of statuary, among which *Æneas rescuing Anchises and leading Ascanius*, the *Death of Lucretia*, and *Atlas changed into a Rock*, may easily be distinguished. On the north side, parallel with the Rue de Rivoli, runs the *Allée des Orangers*, so called from the *orange trees*, which in summer are brought out and arranged along it. At the further extremity is a fine Grecian statue of *Meleager*. The horse-chestnut trees, which form the principal trees in the grove, have long been celebrated for their size and beauty. Beneath them, a most agreeable shade may be obtained; and in the afternoon of a sunny day, crowds people come here to enjoy an hour's recreation. In the summer military bands in Paris play, affording a delightful concert at the price of a few sous.

After a fatiguing morning in the Louvre it is a very agreeable relief to enjoy the afternoon, listening to this excellent music in the shade of these fine gardens. The bands play (in summer) between 4 and 6 p.m. This grove is divided by a broad open avenue, leading from the Pavilion de l'Horloge, to the Place de la Concorde, and used on state occasions as a carriage way up to the Tuileries. From this avenue, a fine view of the Obelisk de Luxor, the Avenue de Neuilly, and the Triumphal Arch at the Barrière de l'Étoile may be obtained. The best time, however, for viewing this scene, is the evening, when the sun, being in the west, lights up the whole with a peculiar radiance. On either side of the broad avenue are open spots amongst the trees, converted into small gardens, and decorated with statues. The semi-circular banks of white marble nearest the Tuileries, containing the nude figures of a man and a woman, were designed by Robespierre, and intended for the seats of a court of old men, which, after the manner of the ancient Greeks, were to preside over the games to be held in honour of the god Germinal. There are also a *Centaur conquered by Cupid*, a *Hercules in his Youth*, and a fine *Boar* in marble, beneath the trees. At the eastern extremity, figures of ancient Roman and Greek celebrities are ranged alternately with some beautifully-executed marble vases. On the west side is the second garden. In the centre is a fine octagonal basin, with a jet d'eau, which, when the waters are in full play, throws up a stream to a height considerably above the level of the trees. *La Petite Provence* is a name given to the parterre on the northern side, from the genial character of its position, which faces the south, and is sheltered from the eastern and northern winds. Here invalids and nurses and old men flock in abundance. The building on the elevated avenue on the south side is the *orangerie*, where the orange trees are kept during the winter months. Allegorical statues of the Seasons, the principal rivers of France, and the Muses, adorn this garden. To the west is the gateway leading into the Place de la Concorde; on either side is a fine group in marble, representing *Victory*, *Mercury*, and *Fame*, on winged steeds. A shady terrace faces the *Place*, from which a good view may be had.

PALACE OF THE TUILERIES.

[Not open to the public. The Pavilion de l'Horloge, on the west side, facing the Garden, is a ruin, having been set fire to by the Communists 22-3 May, 1871. The north wing and Flora Pavilion have been restored; and the Marsan Pavilion has been rebuilt by Lefuel. They are occupied by the Prefect of the Seine and the Municipality. The Flora Pavilion contains a *Museum of Decorative Art;* open daily for 1 fr., 10 to 4. A short description will give an idea of its former condition.]

The palace was begun 1564, on the site of a tile work (tuilerie), as a residence for Catherine de Medicis, the plans being furnished by Delorme and Bullant. The central pavilion, now

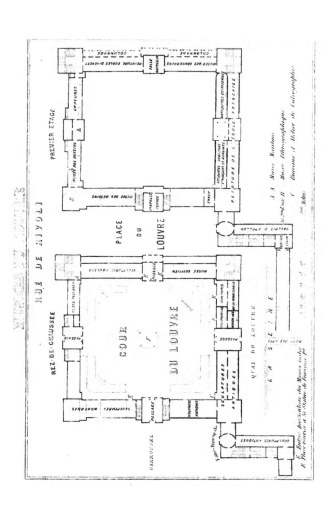

called the Pavilion de l'Horloge, is the oldest part; the adjoining wings and two low pavilions were next added; and at length the building was extended to its present length by Henry IV., and terminated by the two pavilions, the Pavillon Marsan and the Pavillon de Flore. Louis XIII first took up his residence here; Louis XIV. occasionally lived here during the building of the Château of Versailles; in the reign of Louis XVI. it was only occupied by persons connected with the court, but, after the restoration, it became habitually a royal residence. When Louis Phillippe and his family were expelled, it became a hospital for the wounded in the insurrection of June the same year; and in 1849, the annual exhibition of paintings was held there. It was the residence of Napoleon III., in whose reign the interior underwent considerable changes. The ante-room to the Salon on the right was called *Salon du Premier Consul*, from the admirable painting by Gros of the 1st Napoleon. In the *Salon des Maréchaux* were the portraits of the twelve first Marshals of the Empire. The *Salon de la Paix* contained a fine statue holding a cornucopia, and a ceiling, by Nic. Loyt, of the time of Louis XIV.

In the *Salle du Trône* there were neither pictures nor statues, only a bust of Napoleon I., and a ceiling, painted by Flamäel, "Religion protecting France." The *Salle du Conseil* had a chimney-piece of M. Fontaine. On its walls was a very fine portrait of "Le Grand Monarque," by Philippe de Champaigne. Another by Lebrun, and a Maintenon as Governess to the Royal children of France. The *Galerie de Diane* was hung with pictures of the time of Louis XIV. and XV., amongst which were one or two chefs d'œuvre.

The *Galerie de Diane* led to the Pavillon de Flore, which was destined to be the future residence of the Prince Imperial, who took possession of it on attaining his 14th year. These Salons and Galleries all look on to the Court of the Tuileries. The apartments of the Empress looked on to the garden. The bed-room was formerly the library of Napoleon I. Near to the bed-room there was an oratory and a chapel. Next to these were the library and study, with portraits of the Princess Mathilde, the Princess Clothilde, and the Emperor—the celebrated one signed Cabanel. All the furniture was of the time of Louis XIV. and Louis XVI. Next followed three Salons, completely modern—a blue salon, a green salon, and a rose salon, or le Salon des Fleurs. The apartments of the Emperor and of the Imperial Prince were on the rez de chaussée. The wing flanking the Rue de Rivoli was formerly the residence of the Duchess of Orléans and her suite.

Leaving the Tuileries we find ourselves on the **Place du Carrousel**. That part of the Place which is enclosed by a barrier of elegant iron railing, is properly called the Court of the Tuileries, and was separated from the public place by the first Napoleon. The *Place* derives its name from a tournament, which was held here by Louis XIV. in 1662. At the grand entrance into the court stands the *Arc de Triomphe du Carrousel*, 45 feet high, erected in 1806 by Napoleon I. Eight Corinthian columns of red Languedoc marble, with bronze bases and capitals, decorate the arch, and support the entablature, above which is a car and Four Horses in bronze, modelled after the original group on the piazza of St. Mark, at Venice (Napoleon brought the original horses here; and they were restored at the peace). Colossal figures of Victory, Peace, History, and France surmount the stone bastions of the two gateways on either side of the arch. On the south side runs the long gallery which connects the Louvre with the Tuileries, and contains the French national collection of pictures; on the north is a corresponding gallery commenced by Napoleon I., and partially finished by nim, but afterwards completed by Napoleon

III. It had been intended by Percier and
Fontaine, the architects of the first Napoleon,
to erect a fountain, issuing from an enormous
rock in the centre of this place, to hide an
irreparable architectural defect which exists
in the construction of this vast square. This
was not, however, put into execution, but two
lateral buildings have been erected, forming
part of the whole, and in the centre of the
square a parterre has been formed, planted with
trees, which serve to hide the defect. At the
extreme end of the Carrousel is the

Louvre.—[Threatened by the Commune
1871, but happily saved, except part of the
Library, which was burnt, and robbed of
many books. It has been restored. New
galleries have been added.] Visitors to the
Louvre fall into two categories:—1st. Those
who can only give it a few hours, and therefore
carry away a vague impression of its contents.
2nd. Cursory visitors, yet can come more than
once; let them go over it, first to get a general
idea and know the place, and afterwards return to study some special part of it.

The Galleries of the Louvre are open daily
(except Monday), from 9 to 5 in summer, 10
to 4 in winter. Here books and paintings
are combined in one immense collection;
the pictures being on the first floor. The
different rooms cover nearly 20 acres, and
take about three hours just to walk through.
Good catalogues of each collection may be
had; and those who require it will find
guides at 2fr. an hour, who speak English
and other languages. The general arrange-
ment is as follows:—

Ground Floor—Assyrian Antiquities, col-
lected by M. Botta 1843-5. Antiquities from
Asia Minor. Egyptian Museum. Algerian
Museum. Mediæval and Renaissance Sculp-
tures—chiefly of the French, German, and
Italian schools, in five rooms. Christian
Museum. Jewish Room. Then a series of
Salles or Rooms—named after the works of
the artists which they contain—as Colombe,

who died 1514; Jean de Douai or de Bo-
logne, who died 1608; Goujon, who died
1572; the Brothers Anguier, who died 1669
and 1686. Museum of Engravings, where
they may be bought. Then the Rooms dedicated to Modern Sculpture—named after
Coysevox, who died 1720; Puget, who died
1694; the Brothers Coustou, who died 1733
and 1746; Houdon, who died 1828; Chaudet,
who died 1810. The last includes works by
Canova, Pradier, and other artists.

Museum of Ancient Marbles—including the
Rooms of the Caryatides; Achilles, or the
Rotonde (Round Room); the Seasons, or the
Emperors; Augustus; the Autel, or Altar;
the Tiber; the Gladiator; Minerva Room;
Melpomene Room; Room of **Venus of Milo**
(or Melos, in the Archipelago), otherwise
Venus Victrix, a very fine work; Psyche
Room; Sarcophagus Room; Room of Hercules
and Telephus; Medea Room; and the Room
of Pan.

First Floor (Premier Etage)—containing the
Paintings mostly in the New Louvre division
of the building. Catalogues of the different
schools of painting are 2 and 3 fr. each. Black
numbers are used to distinguish French pictures; blue for Dutch and German; red for
Spanish and Italian. The different collections are as follow:—La Caze Collection,
bequeathed 1869. Henry II.'s Room. Room
of the Sept Cheminées (Seven Chimneys),
dedicated to modern French artists. The
Bijoux Room, for mediæval ornaments.
Vestibule, or Salle Ronde (Round). Apollo
Gallery, a fine room, 210ft. long. Salon
Carré, or Square Room, full of the best
pictures of every school. The Sept (Seven)
Mètres Gallery—so called from its width—
for Italian pictures. Grande Galerie, about
a quarter of a mile long, containing Italian,
Spanish, German, Dutch, and Flemish pictures. Then the Rooms of the French
Schools, including Ancient French, French
before Louis XIV., and French since Louis

XIV.—the last two divided by the Denon Room.

In the Old Louvre division, on the first floor, are the Museum of Antiquities—Egyptian, Greek, Etruscan, and Roman. Ancient Bronzes. Museum of Drawings (Dessins), by masters of every school. Works of the Renaissance; and the Campana Museum of vases, bronzes, &c.

Second Floor—containing Supplementary Rooms, of Dutch and Flemish artists. The Naval Museum (de Marine) of Models. Ethnographical Museum of Chinese, Japanese, Mexican, Peruvian, and other objects.

The Grand Tour of the Louvre may be best performed in the following manner:— 1st. From the Cours pass to the five Salles of Modern Sculpture. 2nd. To the four Salles of the Sculpture of the Renaissance. 3rd. To the Assyrian and Phœnician Museum. Then back the same way to the passage, and on the opposite side to the *Parterre Salle* of the Egyptian Museum. Thence to the *Salle des Sept Cheminées*, to the nine Salles of the collection Campana, back again to the entrance through the vestibule to the East wing; five Salles of the *Musée des Souvenirs;* then the Musée Naval, the Faïences or Pottery, Musée des Bronzes Antiques, Salle des Bijoux, Galerie d'Apollon, Salon Carré, the Grande Galerie, the Lateral Salle of Italian Painters, the Gallery of Modern Painters; then all the way back, down the steps, to the Salle des Sculptures Antiques, which finishes the round.

On the site of the present palace stood formerly a castle, far outside the precincts of the ancient Paris. This château is said to have been the hunting seat of king Dagobert, and called *Louveterie*, or *wolf-hunting establishment.* It was remodelled, fortified, and converted by Philip Augustus in 1200 into a state prison, and by Charles V. into his treasury and library. Francis I., however, de-molished the entire building, determined to raise a more handsome one in its stead. Accordingly Pierre Lescot was ordered to supply the design, and the new palace was commenced in 1541. During the reign of Francis and that of his son, the wing now called the *Gallery of Apollo* was finished under Henry IV. considerable additions also were made; but Louis XIV. wishing to complete it, at once appealed to all the architects of Europe to send in plans. That of the Chevalier Bernini pleased the monarch, and he was sent for from Italy; but the capricious interference of the King disgusted the architect, who returned to his native country, after a twelvemonths' sojourn, leaving the physician Perrault, whose designs were afterwards adopted, to carry on the work. The attention of the king, however, was more directed towards the Château de Versailles, and the works of the Louvre were suffered to relax, so that the building was not completed, until Napoleon I. lent his energetic hand to it, when it was accomplished by Messrs. Percier and Fontaine, two hundred and fifty years after the first foundations were laid.

The Louvre was used as a place of residence by Charles IX., the persecutor of the Huguenots: the window is shewn from whence he viewed, according to an ancient tradition, the massacre on the eve of St. Bartholomew, 1562. It appears that in reality he was at the neighbouring Château de Bourbon during the massacre. It was also the residence of Henry III., Henry IV., Louis XIII., and Henrietta, widow of Charles I. of England. Since the time of Louis XV., who spent his minority here, it has been given up to the exhibition of works of art, though occasionally used for state ceremonies.

On the 28th and 29th July, 1830, the Louvre was attacked by the people, and obstinately defended by the Swiss guard. Those who fell on the occasion were buried beneath the green sward at the foot of the colonnade next to the Seine. They were, however, subsequently disinterred, and their remains deposited in the vaults beneath the Column of July, on the Place de la Bastile, which was erected in commemoration of that event.

On the two sides of the chief entrance to the Musées are engraved, "1541, François I commence le Louvre.—1564, Catherine de Medicis commence les Tuileries. 1852—1857. Napoleon III réunit les Tuileries au Louvre."

The attention of the visitor should be especially directed to the superb colonnade, by Perrault, consisting of twenty-eight double Corinthian pillars, which adorn the eastern front of the Louvre. This façade, by the beautiful symmetry of its parts, the fine execution of its ornaments, the just economy of their distribution, and by the imposing grandeur of its extent, is justly admired as a chef-d'œuvre in the architecture of the age of Louis XIV.

The southern front, by the same architect, is also very fine. Like the eastern front it has a highly ornamental pediment, and is beautifully decorated with forty Corinthian pilasters. The northern front consists of a central pavilion, with two lateral ones, slightly but tastefully ornamented. The western front is intended to harmonize with the buildings erected in the Place Napoleon. Within the court, the top and bottom stories of this façade have been adopted as patterns for the corresponding ones of the other sides of the quadrangle.

The lower storey is composed of a series of circular arcades, divided by Corinthian pilastres, with a lofty window beneath each arch. The windows of the second storey are tastefully adorned with carved and triangular pediments, a pillar of the Composite order dividing each window from the one adjoining. The windows of the upper storey are splendidly ornamented with groups in sculpture, trophies, &c.

The principal gateway to the Louvre occupies the centre of this façade, and bears the name of the *Pavillon de l'Horloge*, or *de Sully*. This pavilion is surmounted by a quadrangular dome, supported by gigantic Caryatides by Sarazin. The various projections of this side are richly ornamented with sculpture. All the gateways are surmounted by pediments, which have in their tympans sculptures by Coustou Ramey, and Lesueur.

Two ranges of Doric pillars, fluted, with a carriage road in the middle, form the southern entrance; pillars of different styles of the Ionic order, distinguish those of the northern and western; Doric, those of the eastern vestibule. The Court of the Louvre is also equally striking, as being one of the finest in Europe. It is lighted by 24 beautiful bronze lamps; its centre laid out in bitumen, bordered with beds of grass and shrubs, and surrounded with a low railing of cast iron.

A series of gardens enclosed by elegant iron railings, ornamented with laurel wreaths encircling the imperial "N." surround the whole of the palace, terminating at the new wing opposite the Rue de Rivoli.

The southern wing contains the former Imperial stables, and the Salle des Etats, 138 feet long and 69 wide, where the chief bodies of the state were received by him. It communicates with the picture galleries. The inauguration of the new Louvre took place here in 1857.

A series of galleries runs to the eastward from the *Salle Egyptienne* entirely round the building. In some of the rooms may be seen missals elaborately bound, belonging to various queens, and of a very early date; the chair of king Dagobert; a splendid *armoire à bijoux*, once Marie Antoinette's, of beautifully coloured wood, inlaid with pearl and jewels; the swords and sceptres of various monarchs; the crown of Charlemagne, and his sceptre, sword, and hand of justice; the armour of Henry II, and III. and Louis XIV.; the coronation robes of Napoleon and Charles X.; the tent-bed of the former, and some of the clothes he wore at St. Helena; a room, formerly the chapel of the Order of the Holy Ghost, and a variety of other very interesting curiosities. One room has a fine collection of armour, principally worn by the Kings of France; a magnificent casket, presented by Cardinal Richelieu to Anne d'Autriche; and at the end opposite, the font used at the baptism of Philip Augustus, St. Louis, and the Comte de Paris. The font is of silver, beautifully chased. It had previously occupied a position in the chapel of Vincennes.

All the objects of special historical interest, from Childeric to Napoleon, are in Salle 4. Among others, the Gospels of Charlemagne, written by Godescalc (781); the Psaltery of Charles the Bald, on parchment, by Linthard (869); the Baptismal Font of St. Louis; several relics of St. Louis, Armour of Henry II. and Charles IX., and Prayer Book of Mary Queen of Scots, Armour of Henry IV. and Louis XIII., Spurs of Louis XIX., and Shoe of Marie Antoinette.

In the 4th Salle of the Renaissance are some fine porcelain and pottery work of Bernard Palissy. The *Musée de la Marine*, which occupies the third storey, is also of interest; it contains models of vessels of all descriptions, of forts and guns; plans of the different naval arsenals of France, and every-thing connected with or relating to the im-provement of the marine department.

The ground-floor on three sides of the Louvre is taken up with the *Musée des Anti-quités Américaines*, and the *Musées de la Sculpture du Moyen Age et de la Renaissance.*

As the visitor will perhaps be perplexed by the multitude of pictures before him, and have but a short time to select those most worthy of his regard, it may be as well to assist him by pointing out a few of the best of the most celebrated masters.

SALON CARRÉ (Square Room).

(N.B. The numbers of the paintings are liable to change. Cheap Catalogues may be had.)

RAPHAEL.—La belle Jardinière (No. 375), estimated at 1,600*l.*

La Vierge au Voile, much copied (377).

The Holy Family (377) very often copied.

St. Michael treading the Dragon under his feet (382).

MURILLO.—Two paintings of The Immaculate Conception (546.) One was bought at the sale of Marshal Soult's collection in 1852 for 22,000*l.* by the Emperor, and given by him to the Louvre.

LEONARDO DA VINCI.—Portrait of Mona Lisa or Gioconda (484) estimated at 3,600*l.*

PAUL VERONESE.—The Marriage Feast at Cana (104) estimated at 40,000*l.*

Magdalene wiping the feet of Jesus with the hair of her head (103), estimated at 6,000*l.*

CORREGGIO.—Sleep of Antiope (28), estimated at 20,000*l.*

Mystic Marriage of St. Catherine (27), estimated at 14,000*l.*

FRANCIA.—A head (318).

VANDYKE.—Charles I. (142), a duplicate of this one is in the royal gallery at Hamp-ton Court. Said to be the finest of all the existing heads of Charles I.

TITIAN.—Portrait of his mistress (471), esti-mated at 1,800*l.*

Christ carried to the Tomb (465), 8,000*l.*

RIBERA, OR SPAGNOLETTO.—Adoration of the Infant Jesus (553), estimated at 1,600*l.*

GERARD DOW.—Administering a Cordial to a Dropsical Woman. His masterpiece, estimated at 1,200*l.*

GRANDE GALERIE (Long Room).

MURILLO.—Jesus and his Mother together with John (548).

Beggar Boy (551).

Nos. 550, 546, and 549 are beautiful small Murillos.

GUIDO.—The Magdalene (329), estimated at 400l.

Ecce Homo (328), well known.

RUBENS.—Series of Allegories.

TITIAN.—Portrait (462).

RUYSDAEL.—Sea View (471).

CUYP.—Meadow Scene with Cows (104).

PAUL POTTER.—Do.   do.   (400).

REMBRANDT.—Tobit and the Angel.

TENIERS.—Interior of an Inn (518).

CANALETTO.—Views of Venice.

CARACCI.—The Salutation of the Angel (126), The Nativity (134) estimated at 4,000l.

SALVATOR ROSA.—Battle Scene (360), estimated at 2,000l.

DOMENICHINO.—Saint Cecilia (494), much copied.

DA CORTONA.—Jacob and Laban (73).

In other rooms are a splendid collection of paintings by Rubens; a portrait by Raphael (Balthazar Castiglione) estimated at 2,000l.; a Plague Scene by Poussin; twelve exquisite paintings by Claude Lorraine; several fine landscapes by Van der Meulen. Fish, flesh, and fowl by Snyders, &c.

In the lateral Italian Room the following paintings claim attention: No. 459, Titian's Vierge au Lapin. 482, Leonardo da Vinci's Vierge aux Rochers, estimated at 16,000l. 379, Raphael's Saint Margaret and Palm, very often copied.

The Louvre is especially rich in Italian productions of the highest order, since these rooms contain fifteen paintings by Raphael; twenty-two by Titian; twenty-three by

Guido; nine by Leonardo da Vinci; three by Correggio; eleven by Canaletto; twenty-six by Annibale Caracci; and several by other Italian masters. Those amongst the French painters, to whose works attention may be drawn, are, Lebrun, David, Mignard, Jouvenet, Casanova, Greuze, Guerin, Leopold and Hubert Roberts, Vernet, &c.

The *Salle des Sept Cheminées*, rich, particularly in French paintings. The best of these are, the Sabines and Leonidas, by David; the Battle of Eylau, by Gros; a noble figure of Napoleon I; Cupid and Psyche, by Gerard; the Assumption of the Virgin, by Prud'hau is graceful, but almost profane in its treatment.

The *Galerie des Sept Mètres* has four paintings of Leonardo da Vinci; a Holy Family of Titian, and another of Giorgione, are magnificent.

In the *Grande Galerie*, the following additional paintings deserve attention:—

Hall I.—Italian Masters. No. 214, Fra Angelico's Coronation of the Virgin, one of the finest paintings of that master; G. A. Von Schlegel wrote a special treatise on this picture. The other paintings are chiefly Titian (458-464); Paolo Veronese (107); Guilio Romano (293), &c.

Hall II.—Italian and Spanish Masters. No. 32, Caravaggio, Death of the Virgin.

Hall III.—German and Flemish.

Hall IV.—Also known as the Rubens Salle, has many fine paintings of that master. 428 and from 434 to 450, Glorification of Henry IV. and Mary of Medicis.

The *Side Salle* of the Italian School or Sept Mètres out of the Salon Carré. No. 384 is a Raphael; 470 and 459, Titian; 99 and 100, Paul Veronese; 482 and 485, Leonardo da Vinci, &c.

Our limits preclude a minute notice of the treasures of the Louvre.

On leaving the Louvre and traversing the quadrangle, whose symmetrical proportions the visitor has already been admiring, a walk of three minutes will bring him to the gorgeously decorated *Church of St. Germain l'Auxerrois* (Place St. Germain l'Auxerrois) opposite the eastern façade of the building. A church was erected on this spot so early as the reign of Childeric, but was destroyed by the Normans in 886. A hundred and twelve years after it was rebuilt by king Robert, and dedicated to St. Germain l'Auxerrois. The present church, or part of it, was commenced in the fourteenth century. Owing to its proximity to the Louvre, it enjoyed the royal munificence, and became very rich.

No injury was done to it during the revolution of 1789, but when in 1831 an attempt was made to celebrate the anniversary of the death of the Duke de Berri in it, the populace rose against it, and everything within was destroyed; it was restored, 1837, and is again to be restored or re-built. Its white stone Gothic pillars and arches form a fine contrast to its richly painted windows, those in the transepts being some of the best in Paris. The centres of the arches are slightly but elegantly decorated. A fine fresco painting, by Guichard, adorns the side of one transept. The Lady Chapel is richly decorated. The porch to the west contains a double row of Gothic arches, five in front and three behind. To the Protestant this building has a peculiar interest, as it was the bell of this church that tolled the memorable signal for the commencement of the *Massacre of St. Bartholomew*, on the 24th August, 1572, which was responded to on the other side of the water by the tocsin of the *Conciergerie*. The memorable bell of St. Germains, however, is now removed, and a new set of chimes, of forty bells, is placed in the Gothic belfry between the church and the new Mairie. In the street close by, stood the mansion of Admiral Coligny, who was murdered on that dreadful night, in the cloisters of St. Germain l'Auxerrois.

Returning to the Rue de Rivoli, and directing our steps westward, we arrive n the Place. which faces the Palais Royal. The church on the right, the back of which we pass, is the *Oratoire*, a French Protestant place of worship.

The **Palais Royal**, whose fine façade we have before us, was built by Cardinal Richelieu, and from him called the Palais Cardinal. Later, however, he made a present of it to his royal master, Louis XIII., on condition that he should use it during his life time, and that after his death the crown should never part with it under any circumstance. Louis XIV., disregarding this stipulation, gave it, in 1692, to the Duke of Orléans and his heirs; and it was here that the orgies of the infamous Regent, and afterwards of Phillip Egalité, were celebrated. It is also deeply associated with the political intrigues of every reign, from the period of its founder, down to the accession of Louis Philippe. Here those assembled who were working for the destruction or the preservation of the crown; and those who are familiar with the memoirs of Cardinal Retz, will remember how many of the most dramatic scenes of the party of the *Fronde* took place here. In the early part of the first revolution the gardens belonging to the palace became the rendezvous of the most violent politicians of the day. In a circus that now no longer exists, the Jacobins and Thermidorians held their first sittings. Here the tricolor cockade was first assumed, and many of the most extreme measures of the Red Republicans taken. Camille Desmoulins here inflamed the populace by his wild eloquence; and in the Café oy the Dantonists, and in the Café de Chartres, the Girondists, met. After the death of "Egalité," the property became confiscated to the state, and was devoted partly to balls and restaurants, partly to a military commission; here, too, the Tribunate was established. During the empire it became the residence of Lucien Buonaparte, but in 1814 it was restored to the Orléans family. The Duke continued to reside in it till 1831, when he was called to the throne. In 1848 the Palace again fell a prey to the popular fury, and was thoroughly ransacked. It was however, subsequently reinstated as a residence of Prince Jerome, and the southern part became the residence of Prince Napoleon. The Palace adjoins the Cour d'Honneur, which was burnt by the Communists May, 1871, and restored 1873. The rest of the Palais and the shops were saved.

The principal entrance is from the Place du Palais Royal, and consists of a triple arched gateway leading into a large court. On either side are two wings which advance to the street; the front of the body facing the court is decorated with Ionic columns supporting a semi-circular pediment containing a clock supported by two figures. The façade towards the gardens is still more extended than that facing the Place, and is adorned by eight columns supporting figures. On the right and left are wings which join the building to the *Galerie d'Orléans.* The interior of this gallery is three hundred feet in length, covered with a glass roof, and with shops on each side.

Beyond this stretch other Galleries, forming, with the Galerie d'Orléans, a paralellogram, enclosing the much-frequented Garden of the Palais Royal. The regularity of their structure, and the tastefulness of the style, are very imposing. Here is ranged a collection of shops, glittering with articles of jewellery and bijouterie, which of themselves might well attract a stranger to Paris, though it is a universal practice here to charge strangers at least 50 per cent. more than Parisians. Every here and there we meet with a Café or a Restaurant, such as those of Véry, Véfour, les Trois Frères Provençaux,

Foy, de la Rotonde, &c.; and in the midst of the gardens is a small pavilion, at which the journals of the day are sold.

The *Garden* occupies an extent of 230 yards long by 100 broad, and consists of a long parterre down the centre, with a triple row of small elms, limes, &c., which afford a partial, but insufficient shade in warm weather. A fountain plays in the centre. Several marble and bronze figures are arranged in the parterres, and near that of *Eurydice Stung by a Serpent,* at the southern end of the gardens, is a cannon planned to be fired by the sun at midday. A military band plays here every evening in summer from 6 to 7, after which, till 10 or 11, the place is crowded with men, women, and children lounging about to enjoy the comparative coolness of the air. It is at this time, when the galleries are brilliantly lighted up, that the gardens are seen to most advantage; while the movements of the merry children, amusing themselves with every variety of game and dance, give the charm of animation to the whole scene.

Upwards of £1,520 is annually paid to the government for permission to supply the frequenters of these gardens with refreshments.

The *Théâtre du Palais Royal,* celebrated for its farces, accommodates 900 persons the performances commence at 8; prices ranging from 2 to 6 francs. The performances have so many equivoques and doubtful scenes that it is not usual for ladies to go to this theatre.

Passing out of the Palais Royal by one of the passages to the west, we enter the *Rue Richelieu,* No. 34 of which is the house where *Molière* died. A tablet, erected on the second storey, informs the passenger of this fact. Opposite to this is the

Fontaine Molière—A Fountain erected in honour of the father of French Comedy in 1844. It was designed by the late distinguished architect, M. Visconti, and is composed of a white marble pedestal resting on a base, surrounded by a stone cistern receiving jets of water issuing from the mouths of three lions. Two allegorical figures by Pradier are placed each side of the pedestal, and the whole is surmounted by a bronze statue of the poet sitting and reading one of his manuscripts. The whole cost of the erection amounted to £6,720. An inscription engraved on the pedestal bears the dates of the birth and death of Molière.

A handsome Arcade called *Passage Choiseul* near the Palais Royal, leads to the *Fontaine Louis le Grand.*

Passing down Rue Richelien towards the Rue St. Honoré, we pass by the

Théâtre Français, or de la République, as it was formerly called. This Theatre, built in 1787, is a dependence of the Palais Royal, with which several passages on the ground floor connect it. In 1799 it was conceded to the comedians of France, who took possession of it under the title of the Theatre of the Republic, and afterwards under that of *Comédie Française.* From the gallery, which surrounds it, we penetrate into a vestibule, adorned with a marble statue of Voltaire, who is represented sitting in an arm-chair, and in other parts of the house are a portrait of Molière, statues of Talma, Madlle. Rachel, &c. Four staircases lead from the vestibule into the interior of the theatre, which is elegant and commodious, and capable of holding 1,500 persons. Comedy and Tragedy find here their proper sphere; Fleury, Talma, Mold, Larochelle, Monrose Devienne, Mars, Armand, Dumas, Rachel, and Bernhardt, are amongst the most celebrated who have illustrated the French Drama on its boards.

The theatre is open all the year, at 7 or half-past 7 o'clock. The prices of admission range from 1 to 9 francs. This is almost the only theatre in Paris where unexceptional pieces are for the most part played.

Opposite the theatre stood a cluster of houses, recently demolished, which formed the street called the *Rue du Rempart,* which indicates that the ramparts of the city at one time extended so far. The spot has a historical interest to an Englishman, for it was here that Joan of Arc headed an attack when the Duke of Bedford was master of the town, and where she received a serious blow on the head from a stone hurled from a sling. She refused, however, to retire, and continued to fight on with unabated courage.

SECOND DAY.

CHAPELLE EXPIATOIRE—MADELEINE—PLACE DE LA CONCORDE—CHAMPS ELYSÉES—CIRQUE
DE L'IMPÉRATRICE — JARDIN MABILLE, JARDIN D'HIVER, AND CHÂTEAU DES FLEURS—
ARC DE L'ÉTOILE — PONT DES INVALIDES — PONT D'IENA —TROCEDERO—INVALIDES—
CHAMPS DE MARS — MINISTÈRE DES AFFAIRES ETRANGÈRES—CORPS LEGISLATIF—PONT
DE LA CONCORDE — PALAIS DE LA LEGION D'HONNEUR — PALAIS DE L'INDUSTRIE—
PALAIS DU QUAI D'ORSAY—BARRACKS—PONT ROYAL—QUAI DE VOLTAIRE.

WE will commence our sight-seeing this morning by a visit to the *Chapelle Expiatoire* (Expiatory Chapel), in the Rue d'Anjou St. Honoré, which may be approached either from the same street, the Rue de la Madeleine, which has been lengthened, or the Rue de l'Arcade.

This Chapel was built in memory of the unfortunate Louis XVI. and his wife, Marie Antoinette, whose remains were privately deposited here after her execution in 1793, by some zealous royalist. The spot was then an orchard. At the restoration, their remains were disinterred and laid with regal pomp amongst those of their ancestors, in the Abbey of St. Denis, June 21, 1815; and the present monument was erected over their former resting-place, that masses might be offered up for their repose. The building is of the Doric order, very elegant and imposing from its simplicity. It was originally surrounded by cypresses, but many of these have been removed. On the pillars that support the railings are sculptured appropriate emblems . of mourning. Over the portal is a tablet, recording the reason of its construction ; within is a statue of the King, and another of his Queen ; on the pedestal of the first is exhibited his will, on that of the second, extracts of his last letter to Madame Elizabeth. The remains of the Swiss Guards, who died so bravely defending their unfortunate sovereigns, are also deposited beneath in the same chapel. The chapel may be seen during mass at 9 mrn. daily ; at other times a fee is necessary. It was threatened by the Commune.

Leaving the Chapelle Expiatoire by the right, and descending the Rue de la Madeleine, we arrive at the

Madeleine.—This beautiful temple is one of the most attractive sights in Paris, and occupies a very fine open position, so that from any point it can be seen to great advantage. Where it now stands, stood formerly the church of the Ville-l'Evêque, but the latter edifice was pulled down in 1764, and the present one commenced by order of Louis XV., after designs by Constant d'Ivry. The works, however, were pushed forward very slowly, and during the revolution entirely suspended. In 1808 Napoleon resolved to finish it, intending to convert it into a Temple of Glory, dedicated to those who had fallen in the Prussian campaign. After his defeat in 1815, the building was again restored to its original purpose, but was not finally completed till the reign of Louis Philippe. It is erected on an elevated platform 328 feet in length, and 138 feet in breadth, and approached by a noble flight of twenty-eight steps ; it forms a paralellogram, and is constructed after the model of a Grecian temple. Forty-eight fluted columns of the Corinthian order surround it, 49 feet high, and 16½ feet in circum-

The Place

The Colonnade of the Louvre

The Triumph Arch   The Madeleine Church

ference; the distance between each column is two diameters, and corresponding with these distances are niches in the walls, containing statues of saints. The principal façade looks upon the Rue Royale and the Place de la Concorde, and is composed of a portico extending the whole breadth of the building, and supported by eight columns. The tympanum above is adorned with a bas-relief representing the Last Judgment. The effect of this beautiful façade is very striking; magnificent bronze doors, 33 feet high by 16½ broad, give admission to the principal entrance; the panels of the doors are adorned with illustrations of the Decalogue in alto relievo; the roof is of iron, and no wood has been allowed in the construction of the building. It is lighted internally from above by three domed windows.

The interior of the church is decorated with unusual splendour, gilt and marble being nowhere spared to give full effect to the idea of pomp and magnificence. It consists of a vast body without aisles, but with occasional recesses, which have been converted into chapels. As has been observed, it is lighted from above, and the effect of this upon the decorations is very striking; each chapel contains a statue of the saint to whom it is dedicated. Paintings, illustrative of the life of the Magdalene, ornament the tympans of the side arches, whilst sculptures, also representing passages in her career, and executed by the first masters, are distributed here and there. On the ceiling, over the high altar, is a painting exhibiting the principal events that have influenced the Romish Church from its first institution; the last event represented is the coronation of Napoleon by Pius VII. The high altar is very fine, and approached by a flight of white marble steps with balustrades of the same. The railing in front is of polished steel and ornamental brass. The Church was consecrated in 1842 by the Archbishop of Paris. The total cost of this building was £523,160. The lamps in front of the High Altar are remarkably massive and splendid. Open to the public at 2 o'clock; entrance at the side. There is a *Flower Market* here, Tuesday and Friday.

Descending the flight of steps at the grand entrance, and pursuing our way down the Rue Royale, we arrive upon the

Place de la Concorde.—This *Place* has received various names, having been called successively *Place Louis XV., Place de la Revolution, Place de la Concorde*; it was commenced in 1763, and was finished in 1772. It has, however, undergone several alterations since then, but was finally completed in 1854.

The *Place* consists of a fine open space, the entrances to which, at the four corners, are decorated by eight pavilions, bearing allegorical figures representing the towns of Strassburg and Lille, Bourdeaux and Nantes, Marseilles and Brest, Rouen and Lyons. In the centre stands the **Obelisk de Luxor,** brought from Egypt in 1833, and placed on its present pedestal in 1836 by Lebas, the celebrated engineer. The mode of raising it to its present elevation, and the machinery employed are engraved on the sides of the base. This monolith is one of those which were placed in front of the temple of Thebes, so long ago as the reign of Sesostris, 1550 years before the Christian era. The height of this single block of granite is 72 feet; it weighs more than a hundred-and-twenty tons. Eight hundred men were employed for three months in taking it from its place at Luxor, and conveying it to the Nile. A beautiful model of its transit to the Nile may be seen in the Musée de la Marine, in the Louvre. It stands on the spot where the Guillotine was erected in the "reign of terror," after the death of Louis XVI.

On either side of the Obelisk are two elegant fountains, richly embellished with allegorical subjects—the one dedicated to sea, the other to river, navigation. The figures and mouldings which adorn them represent the Genii of Commerce, Science, and Industry. The lower basins, which ought to have been in marble or bronze, stretch fifty feet across, and receive the waters of two superior basins and four jets d'eau, which issue from horns held by marine deities. The Place is also embellished by rows of elegant lamp posts, once highly gilt; the large ones are forty in number, and bear two lamps each. This fine promenade is surrounded on the north by a line of building separated by the Rue Royale, consisting on the west of the Hôtel de Crillon, held by private persons; on the east by the Ministére de la Marine, after which commences the Rue de Rivoli. On the east are the Gardens of the Tuileries, on the west the Champs Elysées, and on the south the river, the Corps Legislatif, and the Faubourg St. Germain, containing several of those noble mansions which once belonged to the nobility of the ancient régime.

In 1770, whilst the people were assembled to view the fêtes, given in honour of the marriage of Louis XVI. with Marie Antoinette, a rush was made by the multitude, on an alarm caused by the explosion of some fireworks, by which 1,200 were crushed and trampled to death, and more than 2,000 seriously injured. A collision took place here also between the troops and the people, which proved the signal for the attack on the Bastile in 1789. In 1793, Louis XVI. and Marie Antoinette were beheaded here, at scaffolds erected near the site of the present fountains. In 1848, the proclamation of the Republic was celebrated here. Here, and in the Champs Elysées, the Germans bivouacked, in March, 1871; and marks still remain of the injuries done to some of the statues (see that of Lille, &c.) by the insurgents, 21-2 May. On this occasion, 10 or 12 houses in the adjoining Rue Royale, with the Hôtel de la Rue Royale, and Weber's English Tavern, were set fire to by the Communists.

The **Champs Elysées** is properly speaking only a continuation of the promenade, which commences with the Gardens of the Tuileries. Up to the sixteenth century, the space it now occupies, as far as the Barrière de l'Etoile, the Rue du Faubourg St. Honoré, and the river, was but very partially cultivated, and dotted with a few straggling cottages belonging to poor labourers. In 1616, however, Marie de Médicis' had a portion of it, stretching along the banks of the Seine, and still called *Cours de la Reine*, laid out as a private promenade. Afterwards Coligny had the whole planted with trees and turfed, when it soon became a place of delightful resort, and received the flattering name it now bears. The Avenue des Champs Elysées, which rises by a gradual slope to the Arc de Triomphe at the summit of the hill, is upwards of a mile and a quarter in length from the Place de la Concorde.

Like every other part of Paris, the Champs Elysées has of late years been considerably improved, and adorned with embellishments of every kind. Beneath the trees are placed some graceful fountains, and, further up, breaking the long perspective of the grand road-way, an extremely elegant one throws out its waters to a considerable height in the form of a bouquet, and forms the centre of an open spot called the Rond Point. On either side are Cafés and Restaurants, and other places of public divertissement—amongst them the Folies Marigny—which, from the manner in which they are constructed, add considerably to the beauty of the picture. To the right is the *Cirque d'Eté* (late *de l'Impératrice*), a fine theatre, where the troop of Franconi go through their manœuvres to the delight of crowded audiences. It is open from the 1st of April to the 1st of October; prices one and two francs; commences at 8. Directly opposite, on the south side of the avenue, is a new building to match, devoted to a **Panorama** (2 fr.) From the Cirque, proceeding up the Avenue **Gabriel**, we reach the *Palace of the Elysée*, now the official seat of President Grévy; the garden of which is laid out in the English style, with alleys and grass-plots. The Elysée was built in 1718, and became the residence of Madame de Pompadour, and afterwards of the Duchess de Bourbon, who for a while gave her name to it. Under the Directory it became national property, and was occupied by officers of state; under the empire, Murat resided there, and Napoleon himself for a time; in 1814 the Emperor of Russia, and in 1815 the Duke of Wellington, took up their quarters here. In 1848 it was given to the President of the Republic. It is intended for the residence of any illustrious personages who may honour Paris with their presence, and was occupied by Queen Victoria during her stay in Paris, in 1855.

Opposite the Elysée Palace is the vast **Palais de l'Industrie**, erected between 1852 and 1855, for the French International Exhibitions of Manufactures, which take place every five years. Annual exhibitions of pictures and agricultural implements are also held here. That for Pictures, usually called the "Salon," opens like our Academy, in May. It is a commodious building, with no architectural pretensions. The prices of admission are fixed by Government, and are very moderate. Round the building are names of men, of all nations, eminent in science and the arts. At the South entrance there is an Exhibition of Products of Algeria and the Colonies, open on Sunday and other days; admission free.

From the *Rond Point*, several avenues branch off. The two on the left are the Avenue d'Antin (which is to be prolonged through the quarter of the Faubourg St. Honoré to St. Philippe du Roule) and the Avenue de Montaigne. In the latter is the late elegant new villa of Prince Napoleon, now sold. To the right is the

Jardin Mabille where, three or four times a week during the course of the summer, open-air balls are given. It is open on Tuesdays, Thursdays, and Saturdays, for 5 francs; on other evenings for 3 francs. It is much frequented by women of the demi-monde. The garden is open every day from 10 to 6, for promenade; admission, half-a-franc. On the left of the Avenue d'Antin, is an open air concert during the summer. It was here that Musard gained his European renown. Admittance, 1 franc. Good music from 8 till 11 aft.

A little further up the Champs Elysees, on the left, stood the splendid mansion (demolished) occupied by the mother of the Empress of the French, who resided near the Elysée, and still further on, in the Rue de Marignan, the

Jardin d'Hiver, or Winter Garden, opened in 1845. It is simply a vast green-house, within which are collected a great quantity of rare flowers and evergreens. Concerts and balls for charitable purposes are often held here. The ordinary price of admission to see the gardens is one franc, but on special occasions, when a ball or a concert is given, the price is increased accordingly.

A little further up the Avenue, still on the left, is the

Château des Fleurs, another garden where dancing takes place, and no less elegantly planned than the Jardin Mabille. Jets of light of different colours sparkle amongst the shrubs and flowers, while alcoves and seats occur at every turn; Chinese lanterns also hang from the boughs of the larger trees, and give a picturesque and Oriental appearance to the place. When the lilacs are in full blossom the gardens are quite pretty. A Kiosk in the centre of the grounds contains the orchestra. Fireworks are frequently added to the attractions of this Château. A Café and Restaurant supply refreshments. The gardens are open for promenade every day, for half a franc, and for dancing on Sundays, Mondays, Wednesdays, and Fridays. Admission—for gentlemen, 3 francs; ladies, 1 franc. The company is rather mixed and doubtful; in fact, it is a great resort of the Monde Interlope, or Demi Monde of Lorettes.

Crowning the hill, is the

Arc de Triomphe de l'Etoile, a triumphal arch, intended to celebrate the victories which Napoleon had gained over the Austrians and Prussians, and to signalise the entry of Marie Louise, the second wife of Napoleon, into Paris. It was commenced in 1806; in 1814 the works had advanced as far as the spring of the arch, when they were arrested until 1823. In that year the government determined to continue them, in honour of the success of the Duke d'Angonlême in Spain; the arch, however, was not completed until 1836. The total height of the structure is 152 feet, its breadth 137 feet, its depth 68 feet; the foundations which support its enormous weight are laid 25 feet under ground; the total cost was nearly £420,000. Each of the four principal groups which adorn the four fronts of the building is nearly forty feet high, and the figures twenty feet. On the side facing Paris the group on the right represents the *Departure for the Defence of One's Country*; on the left, *Napoleon, after a Triumph, receiving a crown from the hands of Victory.* On the front, towards Neuilly, the group to the right represents a young man surrounded by his family holding a dead child in his arms, and on the point of rushing out for the defence of his home; that on the left represents *Peace.* Competent critics in art have pronounced many of the groups in bas relief in bad taste, presenting, for example, a distorted Bellona and exaggerations, such as that of the fabled loss of Russians at Austerlitz, by the breaking of the ice. Still the general effect is good, and the pile is grand, especially when the moon

shines brightly through the colossal arches on a summer night.

This is one of the monuments of Paris which we would advise the visitor to mount; the ascent is comparatively easy, although there are 280 steps to climb; and the birds' eye view from the summit well worth the trouble. Looking over Paris, the Champs Elysées, and the Palace and Gardens of the Tuileries, with the Place de la Concorde between them, stand in front; to the left is the Madeleine, the Church of the Assumption, with its fine dome, the Column Vendôme, the Church of St. Eustache, the Tower of St. Jacques de la Boucherie and the Hôtel de Ville, the arches of St. Denis and St. Martin, the Strasbourg Railway Station, Montmartre and Belleville; on the right is the Seine and the Champs de Mars, beyond which the École Militaire, the Hôtel des Invalides, the Observatory, Val de Grace, the Panthéon, St. Sulpice, Notre Dame, the towers of the Palais de Justice, and the Conciergerie, stand out high above a vast mass of buildings; whilst beyond the Church of St. Gervais, the École de Charlemagne, the Column of July, on the Place de la Bastille, the two Columns at the Barrière du Trone, and the Château de Vincennes may easily be distinguished on a clear day. Turning to the west, a long line of hills surrounds the view, to the left of which may be seen Meudon and Mont Valérien, and beneath the Bois de Boulogne, to the north the low towers that rise in dim obscurity in the distance belong to the Abbey of St. Denis. The fee payable at the entrance is half-a-franc. Shot marks made in the siege of 1870-1 are visible. The German troops marched under it in March, 1871.

A new and very handsome **Russian Church** has been erected, Rue de la Croix de Roule, close to the Parc de Monceaux, and behind the Avenue de la Reine Hortense, opening east from the Arc de Triomphe. This church, with its kiosk-shaped cupolas, covered with gilt copper, and its handsome external fresco, richly gilt, over the portico, is a perfect specimen of the Byzantino-Muscovite style of church architecture, and transports the spectator at a bound from Paris to Moscow.

Erected in 1859–61, it consists of a Greek cross, with a court-yard. The exterior presents in the centre, and at the four corners, gilt cupolas of pyramidal form, each surmounted by a small elliptical dome and a cross. In the interior are a quantity of sculptured wood, frescoes in the principal dome, and paintings on the iconostasis. Under the church is a crypt 34 metres long and 28 wide.

The architects of this church were M. Kouzmine, who furnished the plan, and M. Strohem.

It is adorned with paintings from designs taken from St. Sophia, at Constantinople.

The principal painters who adorned it were M. Wassilieff, M. Eugraphe, and Sorokin; the figure of our Saviour outside the church is the production of M. Beidemann.

The frescoes which adorn the interior of the church are highly gilt in the Byzantine style, and represent the principal characters of the Old and New Testament, depicting the principal mysteries of the Faith.

The centre figure in the principal cupola is our Saviour in glory, surrounded by cherubim. The iconostasis, besides our Saviour and the Holy Virgin, has many images of saints, including St. Vladimir, who established Christianity in Russia in 988. For admission, apply to the concierge. Service at 11 and 3.

Close to the Russian church is the charming little public garden, the *Parc de Monceaux*, or *Monceau*, one of the best kept in Paris; once the private property of Egalité, Duke d'Orléans, father of Louis Philippe, and the scene of orgies and gambling. Many of the plants are rare, and its system of irrigation, imitating a gentle rain, is quite original and admirable.

The Parc de Monceaux opens on one side on the Boulevard Malesherbes, leading to the Madeleine, and on the West, to the Avenue de la Reine Hortense, leading to the Arc de Triomphe.

At the upper end of the Rue du Faubourg St. Honoré, is the *Chapelle de Beaujon*, a small building (No. 193) consisting of a neat and even elegant *Chapel*, erected in 1770 by the architect Girardin, with funds given by Nicolas Beaujon, the receiver of finance, who also erected the Hospital called after him, in the same street. At the time of the Revolution the chapel was profaned, and its monuments were mutilated, but the bust of Nicolas Beaujon was recovered and restored to the chapel, which is called after him *St. Nicolas*, and where his body lies.

The Curé of Saint Philippe du Roule has ceded the *Chapel of St. Nicolas* to the English Roman Catholic Fathers of the Passionist Order, for the use of English, Irish, and Americans of the Roman Catholic persuasion at Paris.

Sundays, Mass at seven, eight, and nine o'clock; a sermon at the nine o'clock Mass.

Vespers, sermon, and benediction at three o'clock. Week-days, Mass as on Sundays at seven, eight, and nine o'clock. Father Bernard, Provincial Consultor and Superior.

Address, Rue de Berry, 39.

A quarter of a mile from the Arc de Triomphe was the *Hippodrome*, which was opened in 1845 for equestrian evolutions, and was burnt May 1871. It was an irregular building, with a circus inside, capable of holding 7,000 or 8,000 spectators. Many balloon ascents were made from the Hippodrome.

When the weather is fine the Champs Elysées present a most animated appearance; about two or three o'clock in the afternoon the promenaders begin to appear; and from that hour to six or seven, a continual crowd of persons is thronging the principal pathways and alleys, between the Tuileries and the

Barrière de l'Etoile. In the road a perpetual stream of carriages, freighted beauty and fashion rolls on towards the Bois de Boulogne, outside the fortifications of the city.

In the evening, when the avenues are lighted up, and when the pavilions of the Cafés-chantants, decorated with flowers and silken festoons, are brilliant with jets of fire, the scene becomes still more attractive.

Returning to the Rond Point, and taking the Avenue d'Antin, we shall arrive upon the

Pont des Invalides.—This handsome bridge, consisting of four arches, serves as a communication between the Champs Elysées and the Invalides. It was erected by Napoleon III. in 1854-5, is 350 feet long and 24 broad, and admits of carriages as well as foot-passengers. The next bridge on the right is the new and elegant *Pont de l'Alma*, with colossal figures of soldiers between the arches. On Quai d'Orsay, you see the great *Manufacture des Tabacs*, or Government Tobacco Factory; nearly adjoining the Magasin Central, or Depôt of the Military Hospitals.

The next is the **Pont d'Iéna**, or de Jena, on elliptical arches, commenced in 1806, and completed in 1813, after designs by M. Dillon. It is 460 feet long, faces the Champs de Mar, and was named after the battle gained by Napoleon over Prussia, near Jena. In 1814, the Prussians, attempted to destroy the bridge; but Wellington prevented this outrage. It was called Pont des Invalides till 1830. It joins the Champ de Mars to the Trocadéro.

The **Champ de Mars** is an open space, half-a-mile by a quarter of a mile, noted for its reviews and for the great Exhibitions of 1867 and 1878 (p. 24). Remains of the latter are seen in the Pavilion of the City of Paris, and some gardens; as well as in the Trocadéro Palace, across the bridge, which stands on a plateau formerly called Place du Roi, but called by its present name after the capture of the Trocadéro at Cadiz, 1822. It forms a semi-circular colonnade in a gay Moorish style,

adorned with statues, and having pavilions at each end, with a circular Great Hall, to hold 6,000 persons, in the middle, 100 feet diameter, flanked by slender turrets 330 feet high, ascended by lifts. There is a fine view over Paris from the terrace. The top of the Hall is on a level with the top of Notre Dame. The Ministry of Public Instruction and Fine Arts seated here. In the Avenue du Roi de Rome (or Avenue de Trocadéro), in this quarter is the *Palias de Castile* (formerly Basilewsky), the residence of Queen Isabella, of Spain. Her country seat is *Chatean de Fontenay* (Seine-et-Marne). Towards the end of Avenue de Trocadéro, which leads to *La Muette Park* and Bois de Boulogne, is the *Flower Garden of the City*; open 1 to 4, by passport or ticket.

Crossing the Pont des Invalides, and proceeding to the left, we arrive at the *Esplanade des Invalides*, a fine open space, facing the river and the Champs Elysées, 1440 feet in length; devoted to the show of live stock in 1878. At the further end of it, and separated by a deep fosse, is the

Hôtel des Invalides, one of the chief public monuments of Paris. Until the reign of Henry IV. no provision was made for the soldier wounded and maimed in war: this humane monarch, however, instituted an asylum for them, which the numerous and severe wars waged by Louis XIV. soon proved to be too small in its accommodations. This prince accordingly determined to erect a magnificent edifice, which should be worthy of his reign, and of those whom he was pleased to call the participators of his glory. The present building was accordingly begun in 1671, after designs by Bruant, and the principal part of it finished in 1706: several additions have since been made. At the Revolution of 1793, it was called the *Temple of Humanity*; under Napoleon, the *Templ of Mars*; at the restoration, however, these inflated titles were annulled, and the institu-

Fontaine des Innocens

tion resumed its original name. The Hotel is entered by a railed court, which precedes a garden, divided into different alleys leading to the different courts. The sides of this court are enclosed by little gardens, left to the care of the invalids, who thus find occupation and amusement in attending to them. In front of the principal entrance, and on each side of the railing, is a battery of 18 cannons, which is fired on the occasion of any great event. These cannons are the spoils of victory, and were taken from the Venetians, Dutch, Austrians, Prussians, Russians, and Algerians. The façade of the Hotel gives the appearance of great solidity. Several pavilions, well proportioned, attract the eye. A grand Arch, sustained by columns and pedestals, forms the principal entrance; over this entrance is an equestrian statue of Louis XIV.; statues of Prudence and Justice are placed on the right and left, in bas-relief; whilst two fine figures of Mars and Minerva grace the sides of the gateway. The length of the front is 612 feet. There are in the interior fifteen courts, the principal of which, called the *Cour d'Honneur*, is 315 feet long by 192 feet broad.

At the bottom of this court is the porch of the church: this porch, which is of the Composite order, is crowned by a fine statue of the Emperor, executed by M. Seurre. The interior will be seen to consist of two churches, which are now thrown into one; and the high altar, which stands with such fine effect between them, serves for both churches. The first church is adorned with 54 flags, taken from different nations from the time of the Republic down to the present; amongst them the Russian Eagle which waved over the Malakoff Tower in the Crimea. In the time of Napoleon, 3,000 banners attested the brilliancy of his successes, but on the eve of the entrance of the allied armies, in 1814, the minister of war ordered them to be burnt, and the sword of Frederick the Great, preserved amongst its curiosities, to be broken. Beneath, in the vaults, repose the remains of several of the most celebrated warriors of France. To obtain a view of the Tomb of Napoleon, it is necessary to go round to the opposite entrance, in the Place Vauban; but, before doing so, it will be worth while to view the interior of the building. In the *Library*, the objects most interesting are two candlesticks which belonged to Marshal Turenne, and also the ball by which he was killed.

In the *Salle d'attente* and *Council Chamber* are portraits of the governors of the Hospital; also models of the different forts and fortresses of France, such as Cherbourg, Dunkerque, Strasbourg, &c. After this the visitor will be shown the dining-rooms, kitchens, and dormitories; a small gratuity is expected by the guide, and by the sub-officer who shews the library.

The internal arrangements of this institution are under the direction of a governor, usually a Marshal of France, assisted by a staff. The building is capable of receiving 5,000 persons, and, with its adjoining dependencies, covers sixteen acres of ground; twenty-six sisters of charity and two-hundred-and-sixty servants attend upon the inmates. Marshal Baraguay d'Hilliers was buried here 1878.

Having seen these places, pass out by the way you came in, and by taking the turning to the right, on crossing the fosse, and going round the building, you will find yourself in the Place Vauban, and opposite the principal front of the *Invalides*, the portico of which is exceedingly beautiful; it is composed of two rows of columns, one above the other, of the Doric and Ionic order, supporting a delta, above which rises the magnificent Dome, decorated by forty columns.

This Dome, with its campanile, is one of the finest chef d'œuvres of Mansard, who took nearly thirty years in constructing it. It has recently been plated with gold leaf which is not at all in keeping with the rest of the structure. The dome has been restored.

The interior of the dome-church, however, with its eight-arched chapels and painted cupola, is most beautiful. The tombs of Turenne and Vauban stand opposite to one another. To the left and right are the tombs of the Emperor's two brothers, Jerome Bonaparte (a magnificent sarcophagus designed by himself), and Joseph Bonaparte. In the centre is the grand *Mausoleum of Napoleon*, containing his remains, which were brought from St. Helena, in 1840, by Prince de Joinville; it stands immediately under the centre of the dome, where the ground is open, and galleries of white marble encircle the sarcophagus, which is of red Finland granite. In the crypt, which is beautifully decorated in mosaic, is a little recess illuminated by a lamp, and closed by an iron screen in which are the sword and hat worn by the Emperor at Austerlitz, the golden crown given by the town of Cherbourg, the decorations worn by Napoleon, and 70 flags taken from the enemy. Over the doorway leading into the crypt is the inscription taken from the will of Napoleon:—*Je désire que mes cendres reposent sur les bords de la Seine, au milieu de ce peuple Français que j'ai tant aimé.* (I desire that my ashes may repose on the banks of the Seine, in the midst of the French people whom I have loved so well.)

The altar, which is the work of the late M. Visconti, is surmounted by a canopy supported by four columns of black marble, consisting each of an entire block, and measuring 22 feet in height. The capitals are gilded, but the light, which is admitted through painted windows, is so arranged as to give them the appearance of being of mother of pearl. A beautiful Christ, in bronze, with gilded cross, adorns the altar. The colours taken from the Austrians at Magenta and Solferino, with many others, are placed in the old chapel adjoining, in which several marshals and governors are buried. Bertrand and Duroc lie near the Emperor.

The Hôtel can be seen every day except Sunday. The dome church and the tomb of Napoleon are open, Monday, Tuesday, Thursday, and Friday, from 12 to 3; on Saturdays, by passport. They are in a separate building at the back of the Hotel, with an entrance in Avenue Tourville, Boulevard des Invalides.

On leaving the Invalides, the visitor should return to the Place Vauban, turn to the right, and pass down by the Avenue de Tourville, by which he will arrive in a few minutes upon the **Champs de Mars**, already mentioned (page 22. In this arena took place the *Fête de la Fédération*, on the 14th July, 1790, when an altar, called the *Autel de la Patrie*, was erected in the centre, around which thousands of people crowded. Opposite the front of the Ecole Militaire stood a pavilion, richly decorated, for the King; and here Louis XVI. swore to observe the new constitution. It was here also that Napoleon held his famous *Champs de Mai*, in 1815, previous to setting out on his fatal campaign in Belgium; and in the same month, in the year 1852, Louis Napoleon distributed the eagles to the army. On this field all kinds of military exercises take place every day, and horse-racing nearly every Sunday in summer. The building at the south end, facing the Exhibition site, is the

École Militaire.—It is a plain building, without any architectural pretensions, and was established by Louis XV. for the gratuitous education of five hundred sons of poor noblemen, but more especially for the children of those who had perished in battle. The building was commenced in 1752, and completed in 1762. Ten Corinthian columns, which rise the whole height of the edifice, support an attic adorned with bas-reliefs. In 1788 the school was abolished, and the scholars were drafted off into other colleges, or took their commissions at once in the army. In 1789 it was converted into a cavalry barracks,— Napoleon made it his head-quarters for some time;—it is now a barracks for infantry, cavalry, and artillery corps, with the official residence of the General commanding the garrison of Paris. In the dome of the edifice an observatory was erected, which exists still. Strangers are not admitted into the interior.

Near this, in Place de Breteuil, is the *Artesian Well de Grenelle*, 1,800 feet deep, bored 1834–41, through the Paris gypsum.

Returning in front of the Invalides, the nearest way to which is by the *Avenue de la Motte Piquet*, and retracing our steps to the river, we must turn to the right, and thus continue our route along the Quais. The first object of interest will be the *Hôtel des Affaires Etrangères*, or Foreign Office; which, after having been completed at a cost of £200,000, was burnt May 1871, along with houses in Rue de Lille and Rue de Bac, &c., in this neighbourhood. The Caserne Bonaparte, the Cour des Comptes and Conseil d'Etat, and the Palais de la Legion d'Honneur in Rue de Lille, were half ruined at the same time. The Foreign Office consists of a main body, terminated at each extremity by a pavilion, and two wings project on the side facing the Rue de Lille, forming a grand court. The lower part is of the Doric, the upper the Ionic order.

As we proceed up the quay, we arrive at the *Pont de la Concorde*, a fine bridge, 470 feet in length and 60 in breadth, consisting of five elliptical stone arches. It was commenced in 1787 and finished in 1790, when it was called the *Pont de Louis XVI*. In 1792 it was called *Pont de la Révolution*, and in 1800 the name was again changed to the one it now bears. The materials of which it is built were taken from the *débris* of the Bastille. Perronet was the architect.

A little further on, and opposite the Pont de la Concorde is the **Palais du Corps Legislatif**, or *Palais Bourbon*, as it is commonly called. This palace was built by the Duchess Dowager of Bourbon, in 1722. Eight hundred thousand francs were afterwards expended on it by the Prince de Condé, and the works were still in progress when the first revolution broke out. The mansion was then pillaged, and for some years remained unoccupied; but, in 1795, it was chosen as a place of meeting for the council of the Five Hundred. It reverted after the revolution to the Prince de Condé, and that part of it used formerly by the council was retained for the Chamber of Deputies. On the death of the Prince it became the property of the Duc d'Aumale, when the private apartments were rented by the state for the President of the Assembly. The whole of it was shortly afterwards purchased by the nation. It was here that Louis Philippe was proclaimed, in 1830, King of the French; and it was to the Salle des Séances, in this palace, that, at the revolution of 1848, the Duchess of Orléans and her children flew for shelter. It was occupied by the Corps Législatif during the second empire, and is now the seat of the *Chamber of Deputies* and the official residence of the President of the Assembly.

The fine peristyle, consisting of twelve Corinthian columns which decorates the river front, was built in 1804. The base of the delta is 95 feet, and its height, 17 feet. A bas-relief representing France standing on a tribune and holding the constitution in her right hand, is by Carlos. On the side of France are Minerva and Themis, the representatives of Force and Justice; on the left an allegorical group, representing Navigation, the Army, Industry, Peace, and Eloquence; on the right, Commerce, Agriculture, the Arts, and the two rivers, the Seine and the Marne. A broad flight of steps leads up to this noble porch, at the foot of which are statues of Justice and Prudence. Statues of Sully, Colbert, L'Hôpital, and D'Aguessau rest upon pillars that strengthen and adorn the iron railing surrounding the building.

F

The principal entrance, however, is from the Rue de l'Université. The gateway placed in the centre of a Corinthian colonnade, terminated by two pavilions, has a very fine appearance. The court, which is of considerable size, and surrounded by a fine line of buildings, is adorned with a portico of fluted columns, which serves as the entrance into the *Salle des Séances.* This saloon is on a level with the platform of the peristyle, and arranged in the form of an amphitheatre. It is adorned by a colonnade of twenty-four Ionic pillars of white marble, each a single block. A great number of historical pictures, by the best masters, decorate its walls. When the Duchess of Orléans came here, as above-mentioned, in 1848, she endeavoured, but without success, to engage the Chamber to acknowledge her son, the Count de Paris, as king. In the *Salle de la Paix,* a Laocoon, a Virginius, a Minerva in bronze, and a ceiling, painted by Horace Vernet, are worthy of notice. In the *Salle de Casimir Périer* are statues of the Republic, by Barre; of Casimir Périer, by Duret; of Bailly and Mirabeau, by Jaley; and bas-reliefs, by Triquetti. In the *Salle des Conférences,* besides some paintings illustrating French History, will be observed figures of Prudence, Justice, Vigilance, and Power, as well as medallion portraits of Sully, Montesquieu, Colbert, and others. The *Library* of the Corps Législatif contains about 50,000 volumes, consisting of a collection of all the laws passed, and procès-verbal of the legislative assemblies held here, and also of works relating to diplomatic subjects. The Palace is, for the present, not open to the public.

Near the Corps Legislatif, in the Place Bellechasse, is the modern church of *Ste. Clothilde,* built by the effort of Queen Marie Amelia (begun 1846.) Finished by Ballu in 1847. The design was furnished by a German architect. It is the only modern French church in the Gothic style.

The frescoes of the five Chapels of the Choir are by Picot. Those of the transept by Lehman. The painted glass windows of the transept are by Amaury-Duval, and others. The basso-relievos, in stone, of the Via Crucis, are by Pradier and Duret. The edifice cost eight million francs.

Proceeding onward, down the Rue de Bourgogne, and taking the first street to the right, the *Rue de Lille,* the visitor will arrive in front of the

Palais de la Legion d'Honneur, built in 1786, and designed as a residence for the Prince de Salm-Salm, who was guillotined in 1792. It was burnt by the Communists, May, 1871; but is in course of restoration from funds collected by public subscription. After the death of the owner, in 1792, it was put up to a raffle, and fell to the lot of a barber. In 1804, Napoleon gave it to the Chancellor of the Legion of Honour, which institution had recently been established. This building is very rich in sculpture and ornament. The gate at the entrance represents a triumphal arch, decorated with Ionic columns, and bas-reliefs and statues. Two galleries of the same order, placed on the right and left, lead to the principal building, the façade of which is adorned with Corinthian columns, and a fine Ionic portico. A flight of steps leads up to this portico, and on the frieze above is the inscription of the Order, "Honneur et Patrie."

Opposite the Palais de la Legion d'Honneur is the **Palais d'Orsay,** in design, one of the finest and most imposing edifices of its kind in Paris; but half ruined by the Commune, 1871. It was commenced in the latter days of the empire by Napoleon, and completed under Louis Philippe. It was intended as an Exhibition of the works of Industry of France, but was, under the Republic, devoted to the sittings of the *Cours des Comptes* and the *Conseil d'État.* The building of this splendid palace cost upwards of a half a million sterling. The principal front is towards the Rue de Lille, containing a spacious court, enclosed by an elegant range of buildings; the façade towards the Quay is also very fine. On the walls of the staircase were frescoes by M. Chasserian, representing Study, Agriculture, Commerce, War, Peace, &c. In the Salle du Comité de l'Intérieur were some fine paintings, amongst them Moses and Justinian, by Marigny. The Salle des Séances Administratives is a very splendid hall, decorated with twenty-four Corinthian columns of white marble, with gilt capitals. Portraits of Turgot, Richelieu, Cambacérès, Colbert, and others, graced its walls. The interior cannot be visited. In front of this Palace is the new Pont de Solferino, an iron bridge, leading over the Seine to the Tuileries Gardens, about 500 feet long.

The building next to the Palais is a cavalry barracks. By the side of this is the Hôtel de Praslin, and beyond this the Quai Voltaire. In the house at the corner of the quay and the Rue de Beaune died this celebrated satirist. The bridge opposite is the

Pont Royal.—It has, however, changed names with the change of times, and has been known as the Pont National, and the Pont Impérial. It was built in 1684 by Frère Romain, a Dominican priest, after designs by Mansard. It is of stone, and consists of five semi-circular arches. Its length is 432 feet, and breadth 52. On one of the buttresses to the west is an index marking the height to which the waters of the Seine have risen during different inundations. The highest rise was in 1740, when they rose twenty-five feet. This bridge leads from the Tuileries to the Quais Voltaire and d'Orsay, and the Rue du Bac—in which about twenty houses were burnt by the Communists, May, 1871.

THIRD DAY.

PLACE VENDÔME—FONTAINE DES CAPUCINS—ST. ROCH—ST. JACQUES DE LA BOUCHERIE—PONT NEUF—PLACE DAUPHINE—PALAIS DE JUSTICE—FONTAINE DE ST. MICHEL—SAINTE CHAPELLE — CONCIERGERIE—THE NEW MORGUE—HÔTEL DIEU—NOTRE DAME—PONT DE LA REFORME—HÔTEL DE VILLE—CASERNE NAPOLEON — ST. GERVAIS — HENRY IV ASSASSINATED — HALLES CENTRALES — ST. EUSTACHE — HALLE AUX BLÉS — BANK OF FRANCE — PLACE DES VICTOIRES— THE BOULEVARDS.

THIS morning shall be directed to some of the older monuments of Paris; but first it will be as well to visit the Place and Column Vendôme, at the end of Rue de la Paix, a half English street.

This place or square, which forms an irregular octagon, was commenced in 1688, after designs by Mansard, on the spot where formerly a monastery stood. It was intended by Louis XIV., who originated the place, to contain the Mint, the Royal Library, and the Hotels of Special Ambassadors. The project was, however, abandoned, and the property disposed of to the corporation of Paris, who agreed to carry out so much of the king's intention as related to the formation of a place, which was accordingly done. At this time a colossal equestrian statue of Louis stood in the centre, but this was destroyed in 1792. In 1806, Napoleon ordered a triumphal **Column**, after the model of Trajan's triumphal pillar at Rome, to be erected in commemoration of the successes of the French armies. The shaft is formed of 276 plates of metal, derived from 1,200 pieces of cannon taken from the Austrians and Prussians, and weighing altogether more than 120 tons. The height of the column is about 140 feet, the pedestal is 22 feet high, and 16 feet wide. It was, after its completion, surmounted by a statue of Napoleon as emperor; in 1814 this statue was melted down to aid in forming the equestrian statue of Henry IV., now on the Pont Neuf; during the reign of Louis Philippe, a statue representing the Emperor in the familiar great coat and cocked hat, which was cast from Algerian cannon, was erected; and in the reign of Napoleon III. the statue was placed at the summit. This beautiful column was overturned by the Communists in May, 1871; but has been pieced together again and restored, out of the surplus funds collected for rebuilding the Palace of the Legion of Honour; and the Emperor's statue figures on the summit. The perpetrators have been condemned to pay the cost of the restoration, above £12,000.

The plates of which the column is formed, are arranged in a spiral manner, and adorned with bas-reliefs, representing the principal events which signalised the campaign of 1805, up to the battle of Austerlitz. The figures in the spiral are about 3 feet high. Its pedestal is ornamented with casts of helmets, cannons, and military instruments of every kind, in good keeping with the rest of the design. In the interior of the column a narrow staircase has been formed of 176 steps, by which the visitor may reach the gallery over the capital. View of Paris good, but not the best.

Descending the Rue Castiglione, and continuing by the Rue St. Honoré eastward, we see on the left the

Church of St Roch—One of the wealthiest and most privileged churches of Paris The first stone was laid in 1653, by Louis XIV. and his mother, Anne of Austria, but the building was not completed until nearly a century afterwards The plan was furnished by Jacques Mercier. The external architecture is somewhat plain; the internal, which is of the Doric order, suggests massiveness and strength. The nave, the roof of which is supported by twenty columns, is 160 feet long. Eighteen chapels surround the aisles. At the further end is the *Chapelle du Calvaire*, a very curious chapel. In a large niche, lighted from an invisible opening above, is represented the top of Mount Calvary, our Saviour on the cross, and the Magdalene at the foot weeping. To the right of this chapel we see large rocks and the mouth of a cavern, before which are groups of figures representing the burial of Jesus. The Chapel of the Virgin behind the choir is considered a chef-d'œuvre. It is circular, ornamented with Corinthian pilasters, and crowned by a cupola painted in fresco. The subject is the Assumption. There are several pictures of value in this church; amongst them—the Raising the Daughter of Jairus, by Delorme; the Raising of Lazarus, by Vien; Jesus Blessing Children, by the same; Saint Sebastian, by Bellard. The shrine behind the choir is made of the cedar of Lebanon.

Here, in 1720, the famous *Law* professed his conversion to the Roman Catholic faith, to be made controller-general of the finances, when he made a present to the church of 100,000*l.* From the portal of this church Napoleon's cannon was directed against the insurgents who rose against the National Convention. The unfortunate Louis Philippe and his family used regularly to attend mass in this church. Many illustrious persons lie buried here; amongst others Pierre Corneille. On the steps of this church many popular tumults have taken place. Here an eager multitude thronged to witness the unfortunate Louis XVI., and afterwards the beautiful Marie Antoinette, led on to execution. In 1830, a valiant stand was made here by the people against the soldiers of Charles X.

At Easter, and on other great festivals, the music at this church is very good, though it has not the vogue now of some of the other churches of Paris.

Passing down the Rue St. Honoré, crossing the Place du Palais Royal into the Rue de Rivoli some little distance, we arrive opposite one of the purest specimens of Gothic architecture in Paris,

The Tower of St. Jacques de la Boucherie.
The *Church* to which it was attached, and the date of which is lost in antiquity, was destroyed during the revolution of 1789; and the tower, built 1508 to 1522, which alone remains to attest its magnificence, sold to a private individual to erect a foundry in. In 1836 it was purchased by the city of Paris, with a view to its preservation and renewal. The height is 160 feet. It has lately been renewed, and now stands in the centre of a large square planted with shrubs and flowers (open daily, 11 to 4). In this Tower, Pascal made his experiments on the weight of the atmosphere; and the statue of the philosopher, by Cavalier, is appropriately placed within it. There is a fine view of Paris from the top. *St. Merri's* Gothic Church of the 16th century is near it, in Rue St. Martin.

Close to this is the *Place du Châtelet*, and turning a little to the right the Pont Neuf. The *Place du Châtelet* is so called from a châtelet or fortress which formerly stood there, from the earliest times of the French monarchy to the year 1812, when it was completely pulled down. The fortress contained both a court of justice and a prison. In the centre stands a fountain, consisting of a circular basin 21 feet in diameter, and a column 54 feet high. This column, representing a palm-tree, the leaves of which form the capital, was erected in 1807, and was intended to commemorate the victories of the republic and Napoleon. Fame holding a wreath in each hand, standing on a globe, and borne up by the four winds, sur-

mounts the column. Four figures—Prudence, Vigilance, Law, and Force, adorn the base. This fountain was removed to its present site on the construction of the Boulevard de Sebastopol. To the right, looking towards the Pont au Change, is the *Théâtre du Châtelet*, near the site of the *Théâtre Lyrique*. It is a fine commodious structure, lighted from the ceiling outside, which has a charming effect, and prevents that excessive heat which is so common. The Théâtre du Châtelet commences at half-past seven; the prices varying from 75 centimes to 6 francs. The Lyrique, which held 1,700 persons, was burnt by the Communists, 24th May, 1871. It was much noted for the excellent performance of Faust, with Madame Carvalho as Marguerite, for whom the opera was expressly written by Gounod. At the Théâtre du Châtelet the performances are sometimes rather free.

Passing on to the *Pont Neuf* we have a fine view of the Cité, the quays, the river, and the *Pont des Arts*. This latter bridge is very light, though constructed of nine iron arches. It is 518 feet long and 31 feet broad, and derives its name from the Palais des Beaux Arts, to which it leads from the Louvre. It was built in 1804, and cost 56,000*l*. To the right, on the Quai de l'École, is the *Place de l'École*, containing a fountain, surrounded by a basin surmounted by a stone vase and flanked by lions, which cast the water into the cistern.

Immediately below the bridge, to the west, are the elegant *Baths* of the Samaritan, where every kind of warm and shower bath may be had, from early in the morning to 10 or 11 at night. Opposite are the baths of Henry IV. where swimming is taught. In the summer season this establishment, as well as others lower down on the Seine, is crowded by bathers. It may be as well to observe that the Baths of Henry IV., and the Baths along the Quai de Voltaire, commonly known in Paris as the Bains Deligny, and perfectly thronged in the afternoon on scorching July days, are the best swimming baths. There are, however, numerous warm baths in every part of Paris, moderate in price.

The **Pont Neuf** is perhaps the most frequented of all the bridges of Paris. Walk on it "and you are sure to meet a white horse, a soldier, and a priest," became of old a proverb, to indicate the crowd of people of every sort and every condition which crossed it. This bridge connects the two banks of the Seine with the Ile de la Cité, and opens up a communication between the most populous and busy quarters of Paris. It was commenced in 1578, but, owing to the civil troubles that afflicted France at this period, it was not completed till 1604. Henry IV. was so anxious for its construction that he defrayed the expenses out of his private purse. The entire length of the bridge is 1,008 feet, and its breadth 86 feet. Formerly shops were established along the sides of the parapets; but during the recent improvements, these houses have been taken down. The ground on which the centre of the bridge rests was formerly a separate island, called l'Ile aux Vaches. Here, in 1304, Jacques Molay, grand master of the Templars, was publicly burnt to death. The statue of Henry IV., which fills the open space between the two bridges, was placed there in 1818, and replaces the one erected there by his widow, Marie de Médicis, but which was destroyed in 1793. Opposite the statue is the entrance into the former *Place Dauphine*, which was planned by Henry IV. in 1608, and so called in commemoration of the birth of the Dauphin Louis XIII., son of that monarch.

Proceeding straight through the Place, and passing down the Quai des Orfèvres and the Rue de la Sainte Chapelle we see the new *Tribunal of Commerce*—a building in the Renaissance style, built by Bailly, 1866, covered by a dome, and enclosing a handsome public room. It is light and elegant in construction, and has a handsome double staircase. Flower Market on the Quai, Wednesday and Saturday.

Palais de Justice (or Law Courts, open daily), the front of which, however, faces the Place of the same name. Some of it had been just rebuilt when it was partially burnt by the Communists, including the Salle des Pas Perdus; which latter has been restored by Viollet le Duc, and contains a statue of Berryer. The Cour de Cassation was destroyed. The *Préfecture de Police*, on Quai des Orfèvres, adjoining the Palais, was also burnt, 24th May, by Ferré and his gang, and 150 prisoners were shot or burnt. It is now rebuilt, by Diet, in a plain style, for 200,000*l.*; and contains several courts, the Prefect's Hotel, passport office, &c. Place Dauphine and the Desaix Pillar have been cleared away.

The Palais, by the antiquity of parts of it, and by its associations, is one of the most curious monuments of the capital. It was here that from the time of Hugh Capet or his son Robert, who is said by some to have built it in 1000, down to the reign of Charles V., who left it in 1354, that all the French kings dwelt. The first edifice was small, but it was successively enlarged by St. Louis, Philippe le Bel, Louis XI., Charles VIII., and Louis XIII. The towers with conical roofs, which face the quays, are referred back to the time of Philippe Auguste; and the square tower, known by the name of the *Tour de l'Horloge*, which forms the angle with the Quay and the Marché aux Fleurs, belongs also to the same early period. This tower contains the famous clock, made in 1370 by a German, and presented to Charles V. It was restored 1852, and was the first clock of the kind that the Parisians had seen. In the lantern over this tower formerly hung the *Tocsin*, or clock alarm-bell, which was rung on the occasion of the death of the king, or the birth of the dauphin. It was this bell too that, on the fatal 24th of August, 1572, responded to the death-signal from the bell of St. Germain l'Auxerrois, for the St. Bartholomew massacre. It was destroyed, however, in 1789.

Before 1618, in the great hall of the palace, the king was accustomed to receive ambassadors, to give banquets, and celebrate the marriage of the princes or princesses of royal blood. Around it were arranged, in chronological order, statues of the Kings of France, from Pharamond down to the last deceased. At one end stood an immense marble table, it is said, of one block, at which kings and persons of the highest degree were privileged to eat. It afterwards became the stage upon which the first theatrical representations, such as the Mysteries, took place. The hall, however, was burnt down early in the seventeenth century, and the *Salle des Pas Perdus* constructed in its place. The entrance into the old building was by no means graceful, but within the last few years great improvements have been made, and the beautiful façade that at present exists has been constructed. The principal front is towards the Boulevard du Palais. A spacious court, the *Cour de Mai*, enclosed by a magnificent railing and two side buildings, leads up to the main building. This is again approached by a noble flight of steps, the largest in Paris, and adorned by Ionic columns.

The *Salle des Pas Perdus* (not yet restored), to which these steps lead, is a fine hall, 230 feet in length and 86 in breadth. It is divided into two naves by a row of columns and arcades which support the vaulted roof, and ornamented by a monumental statue of Malesherbes, the advocate of Louis XVI.; it was constructed by M. Desbrosses in the Renaissance style of architecture In the old chamber Henry II. of England was received and fêted when he came to do homage to the King of France for his Norman possessions.

Passages diverging from this grand saloon lead to the different courts of law, and over the entrance of each is inscribed the name of the court. The Court of Cassation is erected on the place of the ancient Salle Saint Louis, which Louis XII had repaired and decorated on the occasion of his marriage with Mary Tudor, the beautiful sister of Henry VIII. It is now enriched with bas-reliefs representing Louis XIV. between Justice and Truth. The chambers of the Court of Appeal, as well as those of the *Première Instance*, and Police are here.

To the curious and the antiquarian in taste, a visit to the *Dépôt des Archives Judiciaires* will be very interesting. It is situated in three long galleries, immediately above the grand salle and next to the roof, and is ascended by a tortuous and difficult staircase. Amongst its undisturbed treasures may be found the form of proceedings on the trial of Ravaillac, the assassin of Henry IV., and others whose crimes have rendered them notorious. In an old box in the same chambers are contained the clothes which Damien, the regicide, wore when led to punishment, and the rope-ladder so ingeniously made by Latude, when he attempted to escape from the Bastille.

On leaving these interesting antiquities and descending into the Cour de Mai, the visitor must next seek out the **Sainte Chapelle**, which is on the south side of the Palais. This is one of the most curious monuments of the 13th century, and interesting, not only from its historical associations, but as being one of the most beautiful and pure specimens of Gothic architecture which exists. It was built in 1242 by Saint Louis, as a depository for the *crown of thorns worn by our Saviour during the crucifixion, a piece of the true cross, the spear-head which pierced our Saviour's side,* and other such relics, which this superstitious monarch had purchased from the emperor Baldwin for two millions of francs. What is principally admired in this building is the extreme lightness of its construction, the magnificence of its stained glass windows, and the elegance of the groups of columns which spring up to support the vault and form the mouldings. The chapel was surmounted by a spire, elegant as the rest of the building, but destroyed by fire in 1620. The architects which Louis XIV. had around him attempted to restore it, but their genius and skill failed in the attempt; it was, however, replaced in 1853, by one in beautiful harmony with the edifice, and light and airy as can well be imagined. The height of the present one is 70 feet above the roof. It is superbly gilt. The height of the building from the ground is 110 feet. The interior consists of a single nave and choir. Four beautifully designed windows, illustrating the principal events in the life of St. Louis and his two crusades, adorn each side, while seven narrow pointed ones surround the choir. The whole is gorgeously decorated. At the extremity of the choir is a low chapel, remarkable for its beauty. The roof is supported by seven arches, resting on a cluster of seven small columns. Every part, external and internal, of this chapel, ought to be examined for the delicacy, as well as splendour, of the details of its architecture. A stone marks the spot of the famous reading desk, which was the subject of the best poem of Boileau, the satirical poet, who was buried here in 1711. The reading desk has been removed to the Abbey of St. Denis, and the organ to the church of St. Germain l'Auxerrois. The floor is paved in mosaic. Admission daily, free.

Forming a part of the Palais de Justice, but at the back of it, is the

Conciergerie, a prison, some of whose cells and dungeons descend many feet below the level of the Seine. It is approached by one of the streets leading out of the Quai des Orfevres. It was formerly the prison of the Parliament, and at a later period replaced that of the Châtelet. The cell in which Marie Antoinette was confined has been converted into a chapel, and several pictures hang around it to illustrate the history of her misfortunes. It was in the same chamber, too, that the Girondists held their last banquet before being led out to execution. In the dungeons of this gloomy edifice, Madame Elizabeth and the terrible Robespierre were also confined; and here several republicans, in the year 1794, condemned for their ultra and dangerous opinions, underwent the execution of their sentence, including Danton, St. Just, &c. The entrance facing the quay is flanked, as we have mentioned already, by two round towers with conical roofs. The one to the west is called the *Tour de César,* that to the east the *Tour Bombée.* A third tower, called Tour d'Argent, was burnt by the communists, and the public are not now admitted. The whole of this façade is in keeping with its character, and the eye has only to rest upon it for a moment, for the heart to be penetrated by a gloomy and ominous feeling.

The *Fontaine St. Michel,* in the Place of that name, deserves more than a passing glance. The figures of St. Michael and the Dragon are peculiarly effective, and the whole fountain is classic and grand in its design and execution. It was erected in 1860, by the city of Paris.

Passing on and entering the open space, the *Place du Parvis Notre Dame,* we have before us that ancient cathedral, and on our left,

The Hôtel Dieu.—This immense Hospital, which occupies a space of more than five acres, near the Quai Napoléon, takes its name from a refuge for the sick dating back to the seventh century, when a similar institution was said to have been established on the spot. Philip Augustus was the first king whose generosity prompted him to endow this hospital. Saint Louis after him granted to the institution the tax upon provisions brought to the markets; and subsequently various kings, nobles, and wealthy men, have enriched it by gifts and legacies,

Rue de Rivoli

Barrière du Faubourg St. Germain

Val de Grace

Notre Dame

Chapel of the Virgin

until it has become the richest hospital in Paris. Under the first republic it received the fantastic name of *Hospice d'Humanité*. The old building, with the exception of its size, and its object, is unimposing. The entrance is adorned by a portico supported by Doric columns, very simple and neat. Busts and portraits of the most celebrated physicians who have been connected with the institution adorn the vestibule. The interior is divided into numerous large and airy chambers, containing nearly 1,000 beds. The regulations of this establishment are upon the most liberal scale. The new Hôtel Dieu consists of two blocks, fronting Notre Dame, 410 feet by 520 feet; containing 6 pavilions, 20 wards, and 530 beds; with a Chapel at the end.

The hospital may be visited by applying with a passport, or stamped card, to the Bureau Central d'Admission dans les Hôpitaux, No. 2, Place du Parvis Notre Dame, opposite the Hôtel Dieu.

NOTRE DAME.

Open daily (the Choir closed from 10 to 1). Fee to tower, 20 cents. The Communists intended to burn it, 1871. A temple dedicated to Jupiter, is said to have occupied the spot on which this celebrated metropolitan cathedral is built. When this temple ceased to exist is not known, but, in 522, Childebert, son of Clovis, raised a Christian house of worship here. All but the foundations of this structure was destroyed by the Normans, who invaded France, and took Paris in the ninth century. This building remained in a state of ruin till 1160, when Maurice de Sully, who had risen from a very obscure origin to be Archbishop of Paris, signalised his accession to the archiepiscopal chair by undertaking the reconstruction of the church. The first stone was laid by Pope Alexander the Third, who had taken refuge at the court of Louis le Jeune. Although that

part containing the high altar was consecrated twenty-two years after—in 1182—the works went on very slowly, and it was not until 1223, in the reign of Philip Augustus, that the western façade was completed. Even yet it was but partially completed, for the north transept was not built until the year 1312, when Philippe le Bel bestowed a portion of the confiscated property of the Templars upon it, to sanctify his unjust method of suppressing the order; and the *Porte Rouge*, which was so called because it was erected by the Duke of Burgundy in expiation of his crime, the assassination of the Duke of Orléans, was not finished until 1420, so that this magnificent monument of ancient times took nearly three hundred years in building. For the last few years it has been under repair, and the restorations have been made in the spirit of the original plans. The ceremony of dedication, which was very grand, took place on the 31st of May, 1864.

The church is built in the form of a Latin cross. Within, it is divided by two rows of pillars and pointed arches, 120 in number, surmounted by galleries decorated by light columns into three naves. The vaulting of the roof, which has nothing particular about it, except its imposing height, rises 102 feet from the pavement. The doors at the side are highly ornamented with scrolls of iron-work, of great elegance. The gilt iron-railing that separates the choir from the nave is also a chef-d'œuvre of its kind. The choir, which is paved with marble, is surrounded by a magnificent wainscoating, containing the twenty-six stalls of the ecclesiastical dignitaries belonging to the church, upon which are engraved scenes in the lives of our Saviour and the Virgin. The high altar, approached by steps of Languedoc marble, with its rich canopy and fine bas-relief, is particularly worthy of remark. Behind is a fine group of sculpture by Coustou, representing the Descent from the

Cross. Around the choir are also arranged some good paintings by Philippe de Champagne, Vanloo, Antoine Coypel, Jouvenet, &c. Four magnificent rose-windows, 36 feet in diameter, highly sculptured, and filled with beautifully stained glass, illustrating Scripture history, decorate the windows at the north and south transepts, and east and west ends. The monuments commemorating cardinals and archbishops will also be much admired. The church is surrounded by twenty-four chapels, one of which is dedicated to St. Thomas of Canterbury.

A bas-relief of the Last Judgment, near the southern door, is noteworthy. The visitor will not fail to notice a beautiful monument to the memory of Archbishop Affre, who was killed during the revolution of 1848, in the streets of Paris. The memorial, which is in white marble, represents the archbishop falling, holding an olive branch. His last words: "*Puisse mon sang être le dernier versé*" (May my blood be the last that is shed); and "*Le bon pasteur donne sa vie pour les brebis;*" with the representation of the scene in which he lost his life; and the simple record of his birth and death, form a very suggestive memento of a stirring historic episode.

Amongst the curiosities to be seen in the church are the golden cup of the Emperor Emanuel Comnenus (12th century); the cross held by St. Vincent of Paul to the dying Louis XIII.; the ball that struck Archbishop Affre in 1848; and several relics attributed to apostolic times, some having been brought from the East by St. Louis. They may be seen for ½ franc. There are also splendid vestments, coronation robes, &c., to be seen for another ½ franc.

The exterior of the church of Notre Dame is more striking than the interior, which has, however, been much improved latterly. The western façade is pierced by three doorways, composed of retiring pointed arches, sumptuously sculptured. The Resurrection, and bas-reliefs illustrating the seven cardinal virtues and their opposite vices, decorate the principal porch. The porch to the right is ornamented with a statue of St. Marcel, treading a dragon under his feet, and other subjects, taken from the life of our Saviour and St. Joseph; the porch to the left, by the death and coronation, as queen of heaven, of the Virgin Mary. The visitor may also see a memorial of the popular fury of the French revolution. On the right porch, may still be traced, though faintly, the words, "Liberté, Egalité, Fraternité." Above the arches runs a gallery extending the whole length of the façade, and called formerly the *Galerie des Rois*, because it contained statues of the kings of France. These were destroyed during the revolution of 1793, but are now being restored.

This front is terminated by two large square towers, 280 feet high, mounted by a staircase of 380 steps placed in the north tower. In the south tower is the famous *Bourdon*, a great bell weighing 32,000 lbs., which is only rung on great occasions. It was founded in 1685, and baptised with great ceremony, having Louis XIV. and his wife for sponsors, hence its other name, Emmanuel Louise Thérèse. The clapper weighs nearly a thousand pounds. The portal of the south transept of the church is adorned with sculptures illustrating the life of St. Stephen, and that of the north transept by sculptures illustrating the story of the Nativity, and the expulsion of evil spirits from those possessed of them. The church may conveniently be seen immediately after service any day. A fee is expected for any assistance in viewing the objects of interest. In Lent and Advent, some of the best preaching in France may be heard in what are called the Conferences of Notre Dame, being lectures on passing topics of interest, especially to literary and scientific men, who crowd to them in such

umbers, that it is necessary to go two hours efore the time to get a good place for hearing. [[M]]any of the most eminent men in France [[m]]ay often be seen at these conferences.

At the back of the Cathedral is the **New [[M]]orgue**, or Dead House. It is a long, low uilding, not so repulsive as the old one, but aving no architectural pretensions, as befits [[it]]s character. There are a dozen slabs, on [[w]]hich are placed the bodies of those who have [[b]]een found in the river, or who have otherwise [[c]]ome by violent deaths, by their own hands, [[o]]r those of others, and who are not known [[T]]he bodies can, of course, be exposed but for [[a]] short time, but the clothes of the deceased [[r]]emain suspended for a year. It is a sad and [[p]]ainful sight, and may not be without its [[u]]ses amid the glitter and gaiety of the French [[c]]apital. It is, however, more prudent to [[a]]void it, especially if the visitor have sensitive [[n]]erves.

Passing to the east of Notre Dame, we have [[b]]efore us the *Pont St. Louis*, reconstructed by [[N]]apoleon in 1861-2; the *Pont d'Arcole* and *Pont de la Réforme*, or the *Pont Louis Philippe*, [[r]]econstructed by Napoleon in 1861-2, which [[s]]tretches from the Ile de la Cité to the Ile [[S]]t. Louis ; and again from this island to [[t]]he Quai de la Grève. This bridge consists [[o]]f two suspensions, supported by cables formed [[o]]f 250 threads of iron wire. The span of [[e]]ach bridge is 250 feet. It was called the *Pont de Louis Philippe*, because it was opened [[i]]n 1834 under the auspices of that monarch, [[a]]nd Pont de la Réforme after the revolution of [[1]]848. It is opposite to this bridge that formerly [[s]]tood the house in which the unfortunate [[A]]belard and Heloise resided. From the centre [[a]] fine view of the river and of the Hôtel de Ville may be had.

Crossing the Pont d'Arcole we arrive upon [[t]]he Quai de la Grève, and a little further on [[a]]t the Paris

Hôtel de Ville, or Mansion House, ruined by the Communists, who made it their headquarters 19th March, 1871, and burnt it 22nd May, when 600 persons perished in the flames, with the Library, Statues, &c. It is rebuilding in the style of the former Hotel ; and will be completed about 1882. Meantime the seat of the Préfect of the Seine, who usually resides here, is fixed at the Luxembourg.

It originated in a house called the Maison de la Grève, which had been the residence of Charles V. when dauphin, and which was purchased by the corporation of Paris in 1357, for 2,880*l.*, for the purpose of holding their municipal meetings. In 1533 this mansion, with some others that environed it, was pulled down, and a more spacious one commenced. After a long interruption it was continued from designs by Dominic Certone, and finished in 1605, during the reign of Henry IV. During the revolution of 1793, it suffered greatly from the furious conduct of the populace, but, in 1801, it was rescued from neglect, and made by Napoleon the residence of the Prefect of the Seine. From that time, however, the whole edifice was entirely remodelled, and enlarged to nearly four times its original extent. Here Queen Victoria and the King of Sardinia were entertained by the municipal authorities, at their respective visits, in 1855. Over the principal doorway towards the west was an equestrian statue of Henry IV., over which again was an illuminated clock. It contained an elegant double marble staircase, variegated marble pavement, and pillars at the grand entrance. Besides the two pavilions at the extremities, there were two smaller ones over each entrance, and in the centre a lofty turret, from which sprung a gilded vane. The façade fronting the Seine was adorned with twelve allegorical figures representing Commerce, Justice, &c. The whole of the building was in the Renaissance style of architecture.

The apartments of the Prefect of the Seine

occupied the ground floor of the right wing; above these were the reception rooms, and over these again were the archives of the préfecture. In the left wing was the magnificent room known by the name of the *Salle de St. Jean*, where the public festivals of the city took place; besides other fine chambers, in which the sittings of the council general, as well as the meetings of learned and scientific societies, were held. The other rooms of the palace were devoted to offices and residences for the subordinate members of the administration. The staircase leading up to the principal rooms was of great beauty; the sculptures were the work of the celebrated Jean Goujon. In the *Salle du Trône* was a small equestrian statue of Henry IV., of exquisite workmanship, and in the court, which was also decorated with the productions of Jean Goujon, was a statue of Louis XIV.

It is hardly to be expected that a place of such municipal importance as the Hôtel de Ville should be wanting in historical associations. And in this we are not deceived. The various tumults, civil and religious, that have taken place on the troubled soil of France, have all had some connection with this building. It was here that, in 1358, the bloody insurrection of the Maillotins, so dreadfully suppressed by Charles VI., broke out; it was here that societies of the Fronde met; it was here that Robespierre held his blood-thirsty council; that Louis XVI. appeared wearing the *bonnet rouge* to gratify the people; it was here that Louis Philippe was presented to the French nation by Lafayette in 1830; and here, in 1848, M. Lamartine nobly declared to the excited people that, as long as he lived, the *red flag* should never be the *flag of France*. It was the seat of the Government of Defence from 4th Sept., 1870, till the Communists got possession, 1871. In front of the Hôtel de Ville is the Avenue Victoria, leading to the Tower of St. Jacques and the Place du Châtelet.

The Municipal or *Public Library*, which, before the fire, amounted to 100,000 volumes, is now fixed at **Hôtel de Carnavalet**, Rue de Sévigné; a mediæval house, which belonged to Madame de Sévigné, and is now restored. Here is an interesting historical Municipal Museum of old carvings, ornaments, utensils, &c.; with a Library, belonging to the city.

To the right of the large Caserne Napoléon, matched by Caserne Lobau, and near the new *mairie* of the arrondissement, is the

Church of St. Gervais.—This church was founded in the sixth century, but rebuilt in 1240, and restored and enlarged in 1581. The structure unites three orders of Grecian architecture—the Doric, Ionic, and Corinthian, all in excellent harmony the one with the other; and the approach of the western entrance has long been admired by connoisseurs. The portico, by Jacques Debrosses, is of the early part of the seventeenth century. In the interior the style is Gothic, and remarkable for the height of its vaulted roof. The stained glass of the choir, and several of the chapels, are very beautiful. The Chapel of the Virgin in the interior is considered a chef-d'œuvre, and contains a fine statue of Christ, by Cortot. In the Chapel of the Holy Ghost, in the south transept, is a good painting of the Tongues of Fire, and St. Ambrose shutting the Church Door on Theodosius the Great. In another chapel is an Ecce Homo, by Rouget. There are also other fine paintings in the style of the Italian masters, much admired. A monument to Chancellor Letellier has been erected in this church. At the extremity, figures of Religion and Fortitude, life-size, support the dying minister. A plaster Descent from the Cross here is also worth noticing. The street behind this church is the Rue St. Antoine, and leads to the site of the Bastille. It was in this quarter that, during revolutions and popular *émeutes*, the principal fighting occurred.

It is now necessary that we should retrace

our steps. Returning therefore to the Rue de Rivoli, at the north of the Hôtel de Ville, we must take the Rue du Temple on the right, and pursue it until we arrive at the Rue de la Ferronnerie, a street to the left. Continuing this street we enter the eastern end of the *Rue St. Honoré*, at No. 3 of which street stood Ravaillac, when he stabbed Henry IV. A bust of the king is placed in a niche between the third and fourth stories, with a Latin inscription upon it. The *Café de la Régence*, at No. 161, is the head quarters of Chess players.

The street opposite leads into the **Halles Centrales** of Paris, where the general marketing for the city takes place. A series of six blocks of buildings have been erected here, like our new Smithfield Market, on a site of nearly 20 acres, which form one of the finest markets in France. At an early hour of the morning, carts, conveying provisions of all kinds, come in from all parts, and when the wholesale business of buying is over, about 10 or 11, the retail dealers take their places to carry on their business. On the right, on entering, is a fine Fountain.

On the opposite side of the market is the **Church of St. Eustache**, one of the finest and loftiest in Paris, begun in 1532 and consecrated in 1637. In 1804 it was visited by Pius VII., when the ceremony of a second consecration was gone through. The interior has recently been cleaned and ornamented. It consists of a nave, two aisles, and shallow transept. It is remarkable for the height of its roof, the delicacy of its pillars, and the beautiful effect of its *tout ensemble*; as well as for a want of architectural harmony, for we see the Grecian orders blended together with the Gothic and the Renaissance styles. The roof is supported by ten parallel pillars, which rise a hundred feet from the ground, and which again support half-way up a gallery, running entirely round the church. There are some good paintings by Vanloo. Above the gallery are twelve handsome stained windows. The interior of the choir is also much admired for the beauty of its decorations. The high altar is of pure Parian marble, exquisitely sculptured, and cost upwards of 3,000*l*. The reading-desk is the same which stood in Notre Dame, down to 1793.

The church is surrounded by chapels, highly ornamented. In that dedicated to the Virgin is a marble statue of the Virgin, executed by Pigal; the sides of the chapel are adorned by some good bas-reliefs. In the same chapel is the tomb of Colbert, by Coysevox. The organ over the doorway has recently been built, and is considered one of the finest in Paris. The clock was set fire to in the siege of 1870-1. In Rue Aux Ours, is the restored *Burgundy Tower*, built by John Sans Peur, after the murder of the Duke of Burgundy, and now making part of the City of Paris Schools.

Either of the streets leading out from the west of the market will lead us to the *Halle aux Blés* and *Fontaine Médicis*.

The **Halle au Blé**, or Corn Market, is a large circular building, 126 feet in diameter, and covered by a vast dome. It is built on the spot where anciently stood the Hôtel de Soissons, a palace of Catherine de Medicis. This immense structure, which is divided into a gallery of 28 arches, is capable of holding 30,000 sacks of corn.

The only relic of the residence of Catherine de Medicis now existing is a Doric pillar, 95 feet high, situated on the south side of the hall. It was erected in 1572 as an observatory for that princess. At two-thirds of the height there is an ingenious sun-dial, constructed by a canon of the Church of St. Geneviève. This dial may be reached by a staircase in the inside, open to the public. At the base of the column is the *Fontaine Medicis*.

Passing down by the Rue Coquillière, and turning to the right on entering the Rue Croix des Petits Champs, we shall have opposite to us the

Banque de France.—This building was formerly the Hotel of the Counts of Toulouse. In 1720, it was rebuilt, after designs by Mansard, for the Duke de Vrillière, who gave his name to an adjoining street. It was, however, given, in 1811, to the administration of the Bank of France, which had been founded in 1803 by Napoleon. Near it is the *Caisse d' Amortissement* or National Debt Office. In Rue Neuve de la Banque, is the *Hôtel du Timbre*, or Stamp Office. Passing down the street, we arrive at the

Place des Victoires.—Some of the houses surrounding this circus, are from the designs of Mansard, and have their fronts regularly adorned by Ionic pilasters. In the centre, stood formerly, a statue of Louis XIV., crowned by Victory, surrounded by allegorical figures, in bronze. This monument was destroyed in 1792, and replaced by a pyramid, on which was inscribed the recent achievements of the French arms. In 1806, a colossal bronze statue of General Desaix, was erected in its place, but this was melted down on the Restoration, to form, with the statue of Napoleon, which surmounted the Column Vendôme, the statue of Henry IV. on the Pont Neuf. The present equestrian statue of the Grand Monarch, Louis XIV., habited as a Roman emperor, was erected in 1822, by Bosio. The two bas-reliefs on the pedestal are by his nephew.

A little behind the Place des Victoires, is the church of *Notre Dame des Victoires*, or *des Petits Pères*. This church was built by Louis XIII., in 1629, to express his gratitude to Providence for the series of victories he had gained, and which terminated in the taking of Rochelle. It is built in the form of a Roman cross. In the interior, which is very fine, are some admired pictures by Vanloo, embracing the history of St. Augustine. The altar is in better taste than we sometimes see in continental churches. A side altar, with a marble statue of the Virgin Mary (the Lady Chapel), is rich in votive offerings, and always crowded with devotees, being perhaps the most popular shrine in Paris. Many of the ornamental details of this chapel are very rich and costly. A rich velvet canopy covers it, and over the altar itself is the inscription "Toto corde credimus." The pulpit is singularly mean. In 1789, this church was converted into the Exchange, but has long since been restored to its former use.

The street to the west, the *Rue Neuve des Petits Champs*, will lead the visitor on to the *Rue de la Paix*, or the *Boulevard de la Madeleine*, when he will arrive at the locality he started from in the morning. All this quarter has been transformed by new streets.

The Boulevards. — Paris is perhaps unique in the plan of its construction. Most cities have their gardens, their parks, their public walks, their parades, their piazzas, or their arcades, in common with the metropolis of France; but those magnificent thoroughfares, lined with a fringe of trees, which stretch for miles within the busiest quarters of the city, and constitute the resort of nearly every class of citizen, are altogether peculiar to Paris. It is to these thoroughfares, the Boulevards, that we must go if we would study one of the most prominent features of French society, and acquire a knowledge of the open air habits of the Parisian. He who has made any stay within this city, and neglected to explore these fine avenues, lined with trees from Place de la Madeleine to Place de la Bastille, will have lost a splendid opportunity of seeing the French in their real element.

The Boulevards which are most frequented are those which lead from the Madeleine to the Bastille, viz., Boulevards de la Madeleine, des Capucines, des Italiens, de Montmartre (out of which runs *Rue Drouot*), Poissonnière, Bonne Nouvelle, St. Denis, St. Martin, du Temple, des Filles du

Calvaire, Beaumarchais (or St. Antoine), and, in another direction, the Boulevards de Sebastopol and de Strasbourg, on the former of which is a statue of the late Duke of Malakoff. In Boulevard des Italiens are two *Arcades* or **Passages**, viz.:—Passage de le Opéra and Passage des Princes. In *Boulevard Montemarte* are two handsome Arcades—*Passages des Panoramas* and *Passage Jouffroy;* the latter of which leads across Rue Grange de la Batalière to *Passage Verdeau*. In Rue Montmarte is *Passage du Saumon*. The best time for seeing these thoroughfares is in the evening, when the bourgeois and pleasure-seekers come out to gaze at the brilliant shops, or to sip their coffee at the numerous cafés.

On the left bank of the Seine, as it is called, the irregular circle of boulevards is continued: from the Pont d'Austerlitz run the Boulevards de l'Hôpital, des Gobelins, d'Italie, St. Jacques, d'Enfer, du Mont Parnasse, des Invalides, the last one leading into the Place Vauban and to the Hôtel des Invalides. Paris has improved, of late years, in its boulevards as in other things. The new Boulevard de Magenta runs from Montmartre, crossing the Rue Lafayette, and is to be prolonged to the Boulevard du Prince Eugène or Voltaire. This boulevard connects the Place de Château d'Eau (where fighting took place May, 1871), with the *Place du Trône*. The Fountain faces Caserne du Prince Eugène.

Other boulevards are in progress. The Boulevard de Strasbourg runs from the Strasbourg railway station into the Boulevard St. Denis. Here it is joined by the beautiful Boulevard de Sebastopol which runs in a south-westerly direction to the Seine, and to Boulevard du Palais and Boulevard St. Michel. The Boulevard Malesherbes connects the Madeleine, by way of the Place Delaborde, with the Parc de Monceaux ; and is intersected (near St. Augustin Church) by the Boulevard Haussmann, so named after the great improver

of Paris, under the Empire. There are also several other boulevards, among which may be mentioned two lines running from north-east of the city, that of Vincennes, and another from Vaugirard to the Pont de Grenelle. The new Avenue of Vincennes was inaugurated on the 30th May, 1864. It is five miles long, and connects the Place de la Bastille with Vincennes. Whatever boulevards are visited, the visitor, at all events, should see those to which we have specially alluded, as well as those of Magenta and Sebastopol.

The most remarkable feature along the boulevards are the numerous splendid *Cafés* such as the Grand Café, corner of Rue Scribe, Café de la Paix, and the Café Anglais ; and especially the Grand New Opera, the Grand Hotel, the Jockey Club (in Boulevard des Capucines), and a profusion of handsome shops. The Boulevards des Italiens and des Capucines are the centres of attraction and movement. The Maison Dorée is the most splendid and expensive café on the Boulevard des Italiens.

Along these boulevards, too, lie the principal theatres of Paris. The *Opéra Comique* is in the Rue Marivaux, Boulevard des Italiens ; the old Opera House, burnt 1873, was on the opposite side in the Rue Lepelletier. Here the attempt on the life of the Emperor and Empress was made on the 14th January, 1858, by Orsini and his gang of conspirators, by means of explosive shells, which killed 8 persons, and wounded 140 others. Orphée, one of the Emperor's carriage horses, received 14 wounds, which he survived. In the Boulevard des Italiens is the *Société Nationale des Beaux Arts*, consisting of some 200 paintings by celebrated modern artists. Admission : 1 fr. during the week ; 25 c. on Sundays. In the neighbourhood are the *Théâtre des Variétés* on the Boulevard Montmartre; *Th. de St. Martin* (burnt, May, 1871); and

Th. de l'Ambigu Comique, on the Boulevard St. Martin. Also, a cluster of theatres on the Boulevard du Temple, such as the *Th. Gymnase Dramatique; Th. de la Gaîte; Th. des Folies Dramatiques; Th. des Délassemens Comiques* (burnt 24th May, 1871, since rebuilt) ; and the *Théâtre Beaumarchais*, in Boulevard Beaumarchais. The *St. Martin Théâtre* above-mentioned, where A. Dumas' plays were acted, was set on fire by the Communists, 25th May, 1871, after they had killed about thirty persons at Deffieux's, a restaurateur, close by. It has been rebuilt ; and is not far from a handsome pile called *Théâtre de la Renaissance*, opened 1873. The magnificent **New Opera House**, in Boulevard des Capucines, begun 1861, by Garnier, was opened 1st January, 1875, in presence of the President of the Republic, and Lord Mayor Stone, who was invited over for the occasion. One part is 210 feet high; it is adorned within and without

with rich carving, gilding, statuary, ceiling and wall paintings, and has cost about 1¼ million sterling. It contains a lobby 180 feet long, fine saloons, crush room (foyer), a grand staircase, an enormous chandelier for lighting, and will hold 2,300 persons. The stage is 196 feet high and 178 feet wide, with a looking-glass at the back 32 feet by 22 feet, one of the largest ever cast. The former residence of Jacques Laffitte, at the corner of the Rues Laffitte and de Provence, was transformed into an Exhibition.

In Rue Cadet, No. 16, is the *Grand Orient*, or head lodge of the Freemasons; the only secret society in France permitted by the law. In Rue Neuve des Mathurins, is the *Hammam* or Turkish Bath, open all day.

In the Boulevard des Capucines is the *Paris Jockey Club*, consisting of between 600 and 700 members.

FOURTH DAY.

VERSAILLES.

We propose that this day should be devoted to the Château and Park of Versailles.

It depends upon the visitor, as to how much time he would like to give to this magnificent place; but the earlier he can arrange his departure the better, as a good day's work is before him. He may leave for Versailles either by the railway, in the *Place du Havre*, called the *Chemin-de-fer Rive Droite*; or by the railway on the *Boulevard Mont Parnasse*, called the *Chemin-de-fer Rive Gauche*; or by the *Chemin-de-fer Americain*, a tram-road by the river side, on which monster omnibuses are drawn by horses. Office—South side of the Place de la Concorde. Fare, 1 franc. But if he have taken up his abode in the quarter we have recommended, he will find it most convenient to take the former, as the station is within five minutes' walk of the Madeleine. The trains leave every hour from 7 30 a.m.

to 10 30 p.m. The prices are as follows: **1st** class, 1*f*. 50c.; 2nd class, 1*f*. 25c.

Independently of the purpose which the visitor has in view in making this little excursion, he must be reminded that the trip is one of no ordinary pleasure, and that, were there no Versailles at the end of it, the scenery, and the little pictures of half-urban, half-rural beauty, presented to him as he passes onward, would well repay a visit. The circuit which the railway makes enables him to have a fine distant view of the city, the windings of the Seine, and the aspect of the country in the immediate neighbourhood of Paris. As he will frequently find himself on a level high above the river, he will have a panorama stretched before him, full of points of beauty and objects of interest. To enable him, therefore, to understand this panorama better, we will mark out a few of the spots that stand in most prominent relief on its surface.

On leaving the station, the train passes through a short tunnel, and then a longer one, bored under a hill, forming a continuation of the rising ground, which, as with a natural barrier, encircles Paris, and of which Montmartre and Belleville are abrupt eminences. On emerging, he will see the *Docks Napoléon* on the right. These docks are close to the *Douane* (Custom House) the *Entrepôt des Sels* (Salt Warehouse) and the *Entrepôt de la Compagne des Douanes*, whither all the exciseable merchandise of Paris is first collected. A little further on, a line branches off to the west, to Passy and Auteuil, for the Bois de Boulogne. After this, the train passes the fortifications, and is fairly out of town. At first, the view is low, flat, and uninteresting, a large plain, extending on every side, which stretches away to the foot of a long line of hills towards the north. In this direction lie the town and abbey of St. Denis. Long strips of imperfectly cultivated land, producing every variety of vegetable and herb that the climate will admit of, gives a good idea to the foreigner, of the general style of husbandry throughout France. To the left, are the western banlieues of Paris, with the Arc de l'Etoile for their crowning point. Small villas, exhibiting the cockney-rustic taste of the citizens, line the sides of the railway. We now cross the Seine, and stop at Asnières, the favourite resort of the Parisian lovers of aquatics. This station is situated near the outskirts of the city. Its proximity to the river, on which pleasure boats, on a fine day, are always moving; the clusters of trees that embosom the residences, and extend down to the water's edge; the flower-gardens that peep out from the shade; all contribute to attract hither the fête-loving Parisians.

As the train continues rolling on, the scenery changes insensibly. The hills to the north-west begin to assume more shape and boldness. Villages may be discerned dotting their sides; amongst them, Eaubonne, Ermont, and Montmorency: to the left, the dimensions of Paris gradually enlarge themselves. The Arc de Triomphe which presents its side to us on leaving the station, now fronts us, and seems to have been acting as the centre to the circumference we have been describing. *Montmartre*, with its picturesque windmills and conspicuous houses, stands out in bold relief, as well as the minor eminences on which the city is built. A mass of buildings, indistinct in the hazy distance, fills up the back ground towards the Eastern horizon. The Bois de Boulogne lies at our feet, and becomes a spacious and beautiful foreground; whilst on the right, the villages of Boulogne and St Cloud, lining each bank of the river, seem to blend together into one large town, shaded by the wooded heights of Bellevue and Meudon beyond. Above us rises the hill on which stands *Fort Valerien*, 600 feet high, which figured in the war of 1870-1.

Passing beyond the station of St. Cloud, a still more pleasing picture discloses itself. We there come upon Ville d' Avray, the station for *Sèvres*, delightfully situated in the bosom of valleys. On every side the slopes are covered with vegetation. Where there are not vineyards there are woods, lawns, and flower-gardens; and the very look of the villas, all snugly enclosed in some pretty bosquet, cannot fail to be very agreeable, after the crowded streets of the city, so different to the balmy atmosphere of the country. With little change in the scenery after this, we enter the terminus at Versailles.

The first object that will strike the visitor on proceeding through the town will most probably be the regularity of the streets, and the uniformity of the houses. Eighty years ago, Versailles was the second place of importance in France. A hundred thousand inhabitants, all in one way or another connected with the most sumptuous court in Europe, contributed to its splendour and its luxury. Dukes, marquises, counts, foreigners as well as natives; all that was considered noble, whether from abroad or at home, was gathered within her walls, and this astonishing elevation was the work of scarcely a century. A small village, surrounded by woods and marshes, existed formerly where Versailles stands. The monarchs of France came here for the diversion of hunting, and left it as soon as the day's sport was finished. Louis XIII., however, fixed his affections a little more strongly upon it, and erected a hunting-box here, whither he might sometimes retire. This hunting-box was the germ of the present magnificent château.

In 1660, Louis XIV., tired of the incommodious palace of St. Germain, conceived, in one of his capricious moods, the project of converting this wild district into a beautiful park, and this pretty hunting-box into a splendid palace, which should contain himself and his numerous court. No expense was spared to carry into effect the king's design; Lenôtre laid out the park and the gardens; Mansard furnished the plans for the palace. Upwards of 80,000 soldiers were diverted from their martial occupations, and ordered to assist the workmen in making vast excavations, and raising the immense terraces; and it is estimated that not less than forty millions sterling were exhausted upon the laying out of these vast domains, and the erection of this superb château. While in consequence of the extraordinary vigour with which the works were pushed on, that in 1685, hardly twenty-five years after its commencement, the whole was in readiness to receive its royal master. But such was the oppressive nature of the taxes, resulting from these expenses, that the erection of this palace

and creation of this park are said to have had their share in accelerating the great Revolution. Here the royal family and the court resided until the revolution of 1789. Every part of the interior, as well as the exterior, was ornamented with the works of the most eminent masters of the time; but, during the turbulent period that followed the downfall of monarchy in France, the whole was ransacked, and few of its beautiful treasures were preserved. Louis Philippe conceived the design of converting it into a vast museum, where might be collected whatever illustrated the greatness and splendour of France. It was the head-quarters of the German army from 19th September, 1870, to 6th March, 1871, from which the King of Prussia was proclaimed Emperor of Germany on 18th January; and is now the temporary seat of the National Assembly.

On passing up from the station to the palace, the visitor will not fail to observe the *Statue of General Hoche*. Though not a native of the town, General Hoche was educated in it from earliest childhood, and here first displayed those talents that bespoke his future greatness. Turning to the right, we come in front of the palace. The railing which encircles the great court, is a very fine specimen of the kind. On either side of the court are statues of eminent statesmen and warriors of France. To the left, on entering, are: Duguesclin, Sully, Sugér, Lannes, Mortier, Suffren, Duquesne, Condé; on the right, Bayard, Colbert, Richelieu, Jourdan, Massena, Tourville, Duguay-Trouin, Turenne; whilst in the middle is placed a fine bronze equestrian statue of Louis XIV. The front of brick, which terminates the court, is the ancient hunting-seat erected by Louis XIII., and which the respect of his son left untouched. The palace is composed of three great divisions—*the main or central* body *the south wing;* and *the north wing.*

On either side of the eastern front of the left wing may be read the inscription : "*A toutes les gloires de la France,*" which indicates the present object to which the château has been applied.

The *Central part* contains, on the ground floor, a hall adorned with busts or statues, four suites of apartments, once royal residences, and several vestibules. On the first floor are the salons, seven in number, that adjoin the entrance to the chapel. They were formerly the grand apartments of Louis XIV.

The *South Wing* consists, on the ground floor, of twelve rooms, adorned with paintings, illustrating the political and military career of Napoleon, from 1796 to 1810, and containing busts of the emperor and his family ; and another, the Hall of Marengo, illustrating French history from 1789 to 1814. The busts of generals killed in battle occupy places in the windows. There is also a gallery of sepulchral monuments. On the first floor is the hall containing pictures of battles gained by the French, from that of Tolbiac, in the reign of Clovis, down to the battle of Wagram. The principal paintings in the *Galerie des Batailles* are, Gerard's Battle of Austerlitz, and H. Vernet's Battle of Wagram, with the Battle of Friedland. There is also a gallery of sculpture commencing with productions of the sixteenth century, and embracing those of the eighteenth.

The *North Wing* contains, on the ground-floor, a series of pictures representing the most remarkable events anterior to the reign of Louis XVI., and a gallery of busts, statues, and monuments. The first floor contains a continuation of these paintings, from the time of the first republic, down to the reign of Louis Philippe. The second storey contains portraits of eminent persons.

The *North Wing* is divided into 11 Salles, in which some of the principal paintings are the following :—Salle I.—No. 10, Ary Scheffer's Charlemagne presents the first Capitularies to the Assembly of the Francs. Salle II.—Brenet, Death of Duguesclin. Salle IV.—Ary Scheffer's Death of Gaston de Foix in the Battle of Ravenna. Salle VI.—Anne of Austria, by Delaroche. Salle VIII.-Chabord, Death of Turenne.

To obtain admission into the château, which is open every day, it used to be necessary for the visitor to show his passport to the porter, who occupies a bureau on the right hand side of the court, but it will not now be demanded.

On entering he will pass through the suite of rooms containing pictures illustrating the history of France, down to 1789, when he will arrive at the *Salle des Croisades*, containing five rooms, embellished by paintings of different battles, fought by the Crusaders in the Holy Land; or which influenced the Christian cause in the East. The ceilings are richly decorated with the arms and escutcheons of the principal French chevaliers who went to Palestine. These rooms also contain some beautifully carved doors of cedar wood, belonging formerly to the Knights of Rhodes, and given by the Sultan to Louis Philippe, in 1836.

The principal objects in the five *Salles des Croisades* are:—Taking of Jerusalem, by Signol; Battle of Las Navas de Tolosa, by Horace Vernet ; Battle of Ascalon, by Larivière, &c.

In the long *Sculpture Gallery* which follows, the visitor should observe among many other striking statues and busts, the beautiful statue of Joan of Arc, executed by the talented Princess Marie d'Orléans, and the fine statue of the Duke of Orléans in a sitting posture, by Pradier.

The pictures are labelled—in itself an immense advantage, but they often change places, which increases the difficulty of finding them.

The principal modern paintings are in Salles I., II., III., IV., V., VI., and VII., leading to the *Gallery of Statuary.* Among the principal paintings notice: Salle V., or of the Crimea, with scenes of the wars at Sebastopol and Solferino.

Ten Salles on the first floor leading to the Gardens, represent events of the first 30 years of this century; especially events in the life of Napoleon I. But the principal battle scenes are in the splendid *Galerie des Batailles*, 329 feet long and 40 feet wide.

The *Gallery of Louis Philippe* contains pictures illustrating his career from the time of his presentation to the people in 1830. The historical pictures of the war in Algiers, by Horace Vernet, are well worth a close inspection.

The Chapel, consisting of a nave and aisles, is very chaste and elegant. The pavement is of rich marble, divided into compartments, and elaborately wrought in mosaic. The ceiling is eighty-six feet high, and embellished by the pencil of Coypel, Lafosse, and Jouvenet. The high altar is very fine. In the Chapel of the Virgin, one of the seven which this building contains, Louis XVI. and Marie Antoinette were married.

The Theatre.—During representations the King and his suite occupied seats above the pit; the ambassadors, the central compartment of the first tier; and the rest of the guests, the different boxes arranged all around. The last representation that took place here was in 1844. On the 26th August, 1855, a grand ball was given in this room to Queen Victoria, Prince Albert, the Prince of Wales, &c. Her Majesty occupied the Petits Appartements of Marie Antoinette, during this visit to Versailles. Here the National Assembly held their meetings till the return to Paris 1880.

The *Grands Appartements*, amongst which the visitor will find

The *Salon d' Hercule*, which was formerly used as a chapel. Here Bossuet and Massillon preached to the court. *Salon d'Apollon*, or

Throne room, where Louis XIV., XV., and XVI. received ambassadors and other great functionaries. The *Grande Galerie de Louis XIV.*, the most splendid room in the château, and which, notwithstanding its immense size, 242 feet long by 35 feet broad, and 43 feet high, was daily crowded with courtiers. Here the King of Prussia was proclaimed German Emperor, 18th Jan., 1871. In the *Salon du Conseil*, or *Cabinet du Roi*, are the council table and arm chair of the Grand Monarque; with a curious clock that plays a chime when the hour strikes, and is set in motion by a curious machinery, by which sentinels are made to advance; a cock flaps his wings, Louis XIV. comes forward, and a figure of Victory or Fame descending from the skies crowns him with a golden chaplet. In this chamber many of the most important designs on which the state of Europe depended, were planned.

In the *Œil de Bœuf*, the courtiers were accustomed to await the King's rising, and many a scandalous intrigue was carried on. The *Salle des Pendules*, is so called from a curious clock in it. This clock shews the days of the month, the phases of the moon, the revolutions of the earth, and the motions of the planets, besides the hour, the minute, and the second of the day. A meridian traced on the floor by Louis XVI., and a marble table with a plan of the forest of St. Germain engraved upon it should be noticed here. After this, we enter the suite of apartments peculiarly associated with the memory of *Marie Antoinette*, amongst which we may mention the bed-chamber where the queen slept when the people burst into the palace on the 5th of October, 1789, and from which she escaped by a corridor leading to the Œil de Bœuf. The furniture of these apartments is very chaste, and is preserved just as that unfortunate queen left it. There is in a recess in one of the rooms a series of mirrors, so planted that the person who looks into either of them shall see everything but his head. The *Escalier de Marbre*, or marble staircase, should be remarked as being one of the finest in France.

The other rooms of the palace are too numerous to be mentioned individually, but we advise the visitor of the series of portrait galleries occupying the upper stories. Here may be seen portraits of the kings and queens of France from the earliest periods, also of the principal personages, military, civil, and ecclesiastical, of the kingdom. There are also portraits of foreign princes and high personages, amongst which will be seen those of George IV., the Queen, and Prince Albert, and we find among the notables of France the portraits of our countrymen Pitt, Fox, Locke, Newton, and Brougham. To view the private apartments of Louis XIV. and the theatre, it is necessary to have a special order which may be obtained on the spot.

Having thus satisfied ourselves with the beauties and curiosities of the interior of the château, we will take a ramble through the park, and admire the magnificent assemblage of works of art, contrasting immediately with those of nature, though it must be admitted that the gardens are tainted with the stiff artificial taste so dominant in France in the past, and still discernible in all their efforts to be natural. Immediately in front of the building is a vast terrace, adorned by four statues, representing Antinous, Silenus, Bacchus, and Apollo, by Keller. The gardens which surround it are decorated by fountains issuing from a variety of statuary. To the right, on leaving the château, is an avenue leading to the grand fountains called the *Basin of Neptune*. But descending the avenue, directly in front of the palace, called the *Tapis Vert*, we come upon a beautiful fountain, the *Basin of Latona*, from which we have a fine view of the *Fountain of Apollo* at the further end of the avenue, and the lake beyond. Turning down the alleys to the left, we shall come upon several beautiful fountains and parterres, amongst them is the *Bosquet du Roi*, the *Bosquet de la Salle du Bal*, where the court formerly danced on summer evenings, the *Quinconce du Midi* ornamented with eight termini, and the *Bosquet de la Colonnade*, an enclosed grove with a splendid rotunda composed of thirty-two marble pillars of the Ionic order, with jets d'eau thrown up between each of them. Descending the alleys still further, we arrive upon the *Basin of Apollo*, the largest fountain in the park, with the exception of the Basin of Neptune. Apollo is here represented issuing from the water in a chariot drawn by four horses, and surrounded by dolphins, tritons, and sea-monsters.

Pursuing the allé to the left, or now facing the palace, we shall find some of the finest fountains. Amongst them we would particularise the *Bains d' Apollon*, a beautiful artificial waterfall issuing from deep caverns, at the entrance of which are groups of nymphs. High rocks are here imitated with a very fine effect, and the delusion is so complete that we cannot but fancy we are looking upon a real and natural waterfall. When we have examined all these we must still reserve ourselves for the most splendid of all the fountains, the *Basin of Neptune*, behind the Parterre du Nord. Twenty-two vases are arranged around the margin. Against the side are three immense groups, representing Neptune and Amphitrite, Proteus and Ocean, whilst two colossal dragons, bearing cupids, repose upon pedestals at the angles. From these groups a flood of water is sent forth, which is further increased by magnificent jets arranged in different parts of this vast basin. The *Grandes Eaux*, or great fountains, play but seldom in the course of the year, and then on Sundays, at times announced beforehand. Should the visitor be fortunate enough to have it in his power to see them, he should follow the stream of people in their examination of the playing waters. They commence to play at 4 o'clock, and continue until 6 o'clock. When all the others are in full play, and the people have had time to inspect them, that is about 5 o'clock, then the magnificent waters of the Basin of Neptune are let forth. The volumes of water they exhaust are so great that they are not allowed to play more than half an hour or an hour.

Opposite the south wing of the château is the *Orangerie*, well worth seeing, where the orange trees and pomegranates are kept during the winter. One of the orange trees is called the *Grand Bourbon*, because it belonged to the constable Bourbon, whose property was confiscated, and with it this fruit tree. It is a contemporary of Francis I. The seeds from which it sprang were sown in 1421, by Leonora of Castille, wife of Charles III., King of Navarre, so that this tree has acquired a kind of historical notoriety.

From the Avenue d'Apollon, a road to the right, through the wood, leads direct to the *Grand Trianon*, a delightful little residence built by Louis XIV. in 1683, for Madame de Maintenon. It is nearly 400 feet long, contains only a ground floor, and is divided by a pavilion into two parts, united by a peristyle, supported by twenty-two Ionic pillars, eight of green marble, the remainder of red Languedoc marble. Mansard has the credit of being the architect, but he was also assisted in the design by Le Nôtre and Decotte.

We remark among the curiosities of the Grand Trianon, a bas-relief presented by the Queen Dowager of Naples, to the late Madame Adelaide, also portraits of Madame Maintenon, Marie Leczinski, wife of Louis XV., of Marie Thérése, Marie Antoinette, Louis XV. &c., and a circular bason of malachite resting on an ormolu tripod, presented to Napoleon by the Emperor Alexander. The long gallery contains valuable paintings by Roger, Bidault, Johannot, &c. The apartments have been successively used by Louis XIV., XV., and XVI., and Napoleon, and may now be seen left in the same condition as that in which they were arranged for the reception of Queen Victoria, who was expected to make a visit to Paris some time back. The gardens are laid out in the style of the grand gardens, and are decorated with fountains and statues. Here the court-martial of Marshal Bazaine took place in 1873, under the Duc d'Aumale; by which he was dismissed from the army.

To the right is the *Petit Trianon*, composed of a square pavilion, containing a ground floor and two stories. The interior is elegantly fitted up, and enriched with paintings by Dejeune. The Petit Trianon was occupied by the Duchess of Orléans. The gardens are laid out in the English style.

Visitors may view the Trianons three days a week, from 12 to 4, by passport.

FIFTH DAY.

WE will devote this day to visiting some of the Museums and Public Monuments of Paris which claim our notice, on the south side of the river. Taking them in the most convenient order, we commence with the **Musée d'Artillerie**, situated in the Place Saint Thomas d'Aquin, Rue du Bac. This museum is amongst the most curious and interesting in Paris, consisting of a fine collection of such arms, offensive and defensive, as have been used in war from the earliest periods. These are distributed in six grand saloons or galleries. In the *Galerie des Armures* which is divided into three departments by a fine colonnade, are arranged chronologically, according to the characteristic points of the age to which they belong, the defensive armour anciently employed in battle, such as entire suits of armour, coats of mail, cuirasses, casques, shields, &c. In a gallery parallel with this is placed a collection of swords and bayonets, ancient and modern. In the three other saloons of the museum is disposed in regular order the collection of protective fire-arms, which extends back as far as the arquebus, with its quaint and impracticable fire-lock, and comes down to the most finished improvement on the system of percussion locks. They are all inclosed under glass covers.

Opposite the stand of arms is a suite of tables upon which are placed models of machines and instruments, used in the artillery service, and models of machines, instruments, and tools, necessary for the construction of weapons of war, and to the different trades which form branches of it. On the walls, between the windows of the third and fourth galleries, are hung assortments of instruments, either for making or proving weapons of destruction.

The museum is open on Thursdays and Fridays, from 12 to 4.

In the *Boulevard St. Germain*, near to this and Rue du Bac, stands Bouchardot's handsome **Fountain** (formerly Fontaine de Grenelle St. Germain), erected 1739-45, in Rue de Grenelle, but moved to a better position in 1876. It makes a group 90 feet long by 36 feet high. At the corner of Rue Gregoire de Tours is the Publishers and Printers' Club House.

Returning to the Rue de l'Université, which crosses the Rue du Bac, near the Musée, and continuing along it to the right and the Rue Jacob, until he arrive at the Rue Bonaparte, the visitor must turn to the left, when he will come to the

Palais des Beaux Arts (École Nationale et Spéciale des Beaux Arts).—In 1791 the Convent des Petits Augustins was converted into a depository of the different works of art, taken from proscribed churches and châteaux. At the restoration, restitution was made to the proprietors of the different objects that had been collected here. However, in 1819, it was ordered that on this spot a suitable building should be erected, devoted to the teaching of the fine arts, to replace the old academies founded by Louis XIV.

The first stone was laid in 1820, and the edifice finished in 1832, after designs by Debret.

Two courts, separated by the *Arc Gaillon*, a relic of the Château d'Amboise, and enclosed by an iron railing, front the palace. In the first is the elegant portal, brought from the Château d'Anet, which was built for Diana of Poitiers in 1548. Round the walls of the inner court are sculptured the names of the most famous artists of all countries. The façade of the palace is 240 feet long and 60 feet high.

The ground floor is of the Tuscan order of architecture, the floor above this of the Ionic, whilst the attic which surmounts it is of the Renaissance style. A vestibule adorned with arches and marble columns leads to a double staircase, richly decorated, conducting to the first floor. Those of the pupils belonging to the school of the palace who obtain the first prize, are sent to Rome for three years, at the public expense, and an exhibition of the works they send home is annually held here. The galleries to the north are devoted to paintings (many copies), that to the south to architecture. On the second floor are kept all the pictures which have gained the highest prizes. In the *Salle des Modèles* are casts and models of the most celebrated Greek, Roman, Egyptian, and Indian monuments. The semicircle of the great amphitheatre is adorned with frescoes, by Paul Delaroche. It contains an Art Library; lectures are given. Open every day from 10 to 4, for 1 fr. During September it is open three days a week only.

On leaving the Palais the visitor may proceed to the *Palais de l'Institut*, or **Institute of France**, on Quai Conti. It is now the *locale* of five learned and scientific societies, the chief of which are the *Académie Française*, the *Académie des Sciences*, and the *Académie des Inscriptions et Belles Lettres*. The meetings of the *Académie Française* are every Thursday. For admission apply to the secretary. Going up the Rue Bonaparte, turning to the right, the visitor will come upon

Place St. Sulpice.—In this place which has recently been planted with trees, a flower market is held three times a week. A very elegant fountain, erected by order of the first Napoleon, after the designs of the late Visconti, stands in the centre. It presents the form of a pavilion, crowned by a dome. Around it are three basins placed one above the other, and flanked by lions. When playing, the water falls in a cascade into the basins. In the niches which adorn the pavilion, are figures of Fénélon, Bossuet, Flechier, and Massillon. On the south side is the great *Seminary* for Roman Catholic clerical students; to the right is a barrack, and opposite is the

Church of St. Sulpice. This church is founded on the remains of an ancient chapel, dedicated to St. Peter. The first stone of the present edifice was laid in 1646, by Anne of Austria, mother of Louis XIV., the first architect being Levau, but owing to several interruptions, and especially the want of money, it was not finished until 1745, by John Servandoni, a Florentine. The expense of the building was finally defrayed by a lottery. The façade of this church is very fine. Twelve Doric columns, forty-two feet high, supporting an entablature of thirteen feet in height, form the portico, over which is a gallery supported by a corresponding number of Ionic pillars. Two towers, one square, the other octangular, both surmounted with round turrets, terminate the front. These were erected at different periods. That to the south, begun so late as 1777, is still left in an unfinished state. The height of this tower measures 210 feet. During the first French revolution this church was called the Temple of Victory. The exterior and interior do not correspond in character, though both are striking. The dimensions of the church are: length of interior, 360 feet, width 185, height 180. There are large crypts, with statues by Pradier, under the church.

The building is in the form of a Latin

cross, at the further end of which is the choir. In the interior, which is grand and massive, the position of the high altar, which is between the nave and the choir, and surrounded by statues of the twelve apostles, produces a fine effect. At the entrance are two large shells, a present from the Venetian Republic to Francis I., resting upon rough rock, and containing holy water. Behind the choir is a chapel to the Virgin, lighted very artistically, so as to produce a mysterious effect. The statue of the Virgin, which is of white marble, is beautifully executed. Most of the chapels are embellished by good frescoes, and some of them by paintings. The pulpit, it should be observed, has no other support than the stairs. The visitor will remark the meridian line at the bottom of the lateral aisle on the north side. This meridian, which was fixed by Henri Sully, in 1743, marks the spring equinox, and winter solstice. The organ is by Cliquot, and very finely built, being supported by columns of the composite order. It has been lately repaired, and has 7,000 pipes and 118 stops.

On leaving the church, the visitor must take the street immediately to the left, the *Rue Férou*. This will bring him in two or three minutes to the

Palais du Luxembourg, where the Senate meet. The Museum and Gardens (but not the Palace) are open to the public. A palace was begun on this site so early as the end of the fifteenth century, by Robert de Sancy, but was not completed until 1583, when it was enlarged and finished by the Duke d'Epinay Luxembourg. Marie de Medicis, whilst regent of France, purchased it for 20,000*l.*; and requiring some adjacent land, had it demolished, and a more magnificent one built, after designs by Jacques Desbrosses. After passing through several ducal hands, it was sold in 1692, to Louis XIV. It became

the residence of the Count of Provence, who was driven from it in 1791. During the early part of the revolution, the palace was converted into a prison, in which Josephine Beauharnais, afterwards the empress Josephine, was confined with her husband. In 1795, the Directory used it as a place of assembly. Bonaparte made it the *Palais du Consulat et du Senat*. From 1814 to 1848, the peers of the kingdom legislated there; in the latter year some revolutionary sittings took place in it; and after the restoration of the empire, the Senate once more held their deliberations there, and the president of the senate occupied it as a place of residence. The Communists planned its destruction, 1871.

The plan of the building is that of a square; the court of the principal entrance, which measures 360 feet by 210, is enclosed on the side next the street by a façade which forms a terrace, in the middle of which is a pavilion, highly ornamented, and containing some fine sculpture. The beauty and richness of the architecture of this palace is much admired in all its details. At the extremities of the terrace, are two other pavilions, joined to the main body of the building by two connecting wings. The façade towards the garden differs little from that towards the street. The Pavillon de l'Horloge, in the middle, is embellished by allegorical figures.

In the various salons of the palace are some fine sculptures; amongst them, figures of Aristides, Cincinnatus, Leonidas, Solon, Pericles, Cicero, &c. In the *Salle de Messages*, a painting by Caminade, representing Charles IX. receiving the keys of Paris; St. Louis, by Flandrin, and the Duc de Guise, by Vinchon, should be observed; and in the *Salle des Conférences*, some beautiful Gobelin tapestry. The old *Salle des Séances* which was opened for the Peers of France in 1844, was unfortunately burnt in October, 1859, and the sittings of the senate now take place in a hall formed out of three others, called the *Salle du Trône*, and richly adorned. The *Library* of the palace contains upwards of 15,000 volumes, most of them of great value.

On the ground floor is the *Chapelle de Marie de Médicis*, a small quadrangular chamber of the Doric order, and highly decorated. Four pictures, representing the apostle Philip, St. Louis in Palestine, St. Louis pardoning traitors, and the Marriage of the Virgin, grace the walls opposite the windows; and behind the high altar, is a large fresco, the subject of which is taken from chapter IV. of the Revelations. Samuel White, an American artist, has supplied the *Adoration of the Shepherds*, which forms the altar-piece. The *Chambre à Coucher* of Marie de Médicis, is a splendid room, containing paintings by Rubens, Philip de Champagne, and Nicolas Poussin. The arm-chairs we see here were used at the ceremonial of the coronation of the first Napoleon.

After having seen these apartments, the private apartments of the palace, we will visit the *Musée des Tableaux*, or Picture Gallery. The entrance is on the eastern side of the building, and at the angle nearest the street. This gallery was commenced by Catherine de Médicis, and consisted principally of four and twenty pictures by Rubens; which were afterwards increased by various additions. It is now devoted to the works of living French artists, who have produced a painting considered sufficiently excellent to be purchased for the nation: but, owing to the rule, that on the decease of such artist, the pictures placed in the Luxembourg, shall be removed to the Louvre, a constant alteration is taking place in the arrangements. Amongst the present collection, those most worthy of inspection are:—

The Death of Queen Elizabeth, by PAUL DE LA ROCHE.

Landscape and Animals — BRASCASSAT.

Evening—CHARLES GLEYRE.

Cain after the Murder of Abel—PAULIN GUERIN.

The Malaria—AUGUST HEBERT.

Subject taken from the History of the Jews—HEIM

Shepherds, and view of the deserted port of Ambleteuse, near Boulogne—PHILLIPPE AUGUSTE JEANRON.

Desolation of the Oceanides, at the foot of the rock where Prometheus is bound—LEHMANN.

Lady Macbeth—CHARLES LOUIS MULLER.

Reading the list of names of the last victims of the Reign of Terror—MULLER.

Scene taken from the Coast of Normandy—CAMILLA ROQUEPLAN

Charlotte Corday, when she had just assassinated Marat—HENRI SCHEFFER.

Massacre of the Mamelukes, in the castle of Cairo, by order of Mehemet Ali—HORACE VERNET.

Judith and Holophernes—HORACE VERNET

Raphael at the Vatican—HORACE VERNET.

Landscape in Savoy—LOUIS ETIENNE WATELET.

Two exquisite Farm Paintings—ROSA BONHEUR.

The Museum of the Luxembourg is open every day, except Monday, from 10 to 4.

The **Jardin du Luxembourg** (open daily), a well-arranged garden, and the constant resort of the students of the Sorbonne, and the families of the middling classes of the neighbourhood. It was at first planted after the plans of Desbrosses, but during the period of the early revolution, it was much defaced, to make way for cafés, &c. During the empire, it was again restored to something of its original beauty, and has since been considerably embellished. To the west is a fine grove of trees, beneath which numbers of children sport on summer evenings. Immediately in front of the southern façade of the palace is a delightful flower-garden, stocked with the most beautiful flowers, and adorned with a fountain and basin, and several marble statues. A stone balustrade which is reached by a flight of steps, separates the flower-garden from the grove of trees, which encircles it almost entirely, leaving only space for the grand avenue facing the palace. Statues of the queens and heroines of France, from the time of Pharamond, down to the seventeenth century, are ranged round the outskirts of the trees, amongst which are those of *Joan of Arc* and *Marie Stuart*, on the eastern side. Having walked through the gardens, we will proceed down the grand avenue, and leaving the gardens by the iron gateway at the southern extremity, we shall pass out into the Avenue of the Observatory. On the left, about half-way down, is the Statue recently erected to the memory of **Marshall Ney**, exactly on the spot where he was shot as a traitor. The building at the end of the avenue is the

Observatoire Nationale.—This building was begun in 1667, in connection with the Academy of Sciences, then recently established, and finished in 1672, by Claude Perrault, for the sum of 2,000,000 livres. It was found, however, inconvenient for astronomical purposes, and a small building to the east of it was accordingly erected. It is a curious fact that neither wood nor iron enters into the construction of the building. The Observatoire contains a good collection of telescopes, magnetic instruments, globes, &c. In a room on the second story, is a meridian traced on the floor; and two instruments fixed here, give an account of the rain fall in Paris during the year. The *Bureau des Longitudes* holds its sittings here; and in one of the wings of the building is an amphitheatre, capable of holding eight hundred persons, where lectures are given to young students. Marble statues of Cassini, Laplace, and other illustrious astronomers, adorn the rooms of the interior. The late M. Arago had his residence here. Permission to visit the observatory is obtained with difficulty, but application may be made to the director. Once a month one day is given on which admission is more easy. On leaving the Observatoire, the visitor, having his back upon it, must take the first turning to the right, the *Rue Cassini*, and pursue it until he come to the *Rue St. Jacques*. In or near Rue d'Enfer are the *Foundling Hospital*, (Enfans Assistés,) founded 1638, by St. Vincent de Paul, and the *Horse Market*, (Marché aux Chevaux.) Turning to the left, and descending for a short distance, he will see before him the

Hôpital Militaire, and Church of Val-de-Grace, built by Anne of Austria, in 1650, after designs by Mansard. After being married twenty-two years to Louis XIII., and having no children, this queen made vows in several chapels, amongst others in that of Val-de-Grace, and promised to build a church if she had an heir. Shortly after this Louis XIV. was born to her, and, to perform her vow, she laid the first stone of the present edifice shortly after. In the court is a monument to Larrey, the celebrated surgeon, who served in the armies of Napoleon. The exterior and the interior of this *Church*, the plan of which is that of a Latin cross, is very fine. The dome is in the style of St. Peter's, Rome. The front is ornamented with a portico of Corinthian columns; the nave is intersected at the transept by four lofty arches. Above the arches are figures of the Virtues in high relief; the ceiling is also divided into compartments, highly decorated, and filled with figures of Saints. Behind the altars are chapels, separated by iron railings from the body of the building, where the nuns and superiors of the convent attend mass. The remains of Henrietta Maria, wife of Charles 1st, were placed in the vault beneath. Open, 10 to 11.

Descending the Rue St. Jacques until it crosses the *Rue Soufflot*, we have to the right of us

The Panthéon, now the *Church of Ste. Geneviève*, with its lofty porch and magnificent dome; though it can scarcely be called a building of a religious character. The Communists occupied the building, 1871; but no harm was done to it. Admission to the Vaults, 50c.; the Dome, 30c. On this site stood formerly a church, built by Clovis at the intercession of Ste. Geneviève and Clotilda, his wife; this church having fallen into decay, Louis XV. determined to erect a grand and magnificent one in its place. Soufflot furnished the plan, and on the 6th of September, 1764, the foundation stone of the new structure was laid by the king, in great pomp and solemnity, all his court attending. A lottery was also established to defray the expenses. The proportions of this building are truly noble. The tympanum of the portico, which is supported by twenty-two fluted Corinthian pillars, is 121 feet in breadth and 22 feet in height. Allegorical figures grace this tympanum, representing *Genius* and *Science* on either side of *France*. On the right of her are those amongst her sons who have illustrated their country by their pen, as Voltaire, Rousseau, Fénélon, Mirabeau, Lafayette, Carnot, &c.; on the left are grouped her military heroes, at the head of whom is placed Napoleon. *History* and *Liberty* are also represented at the feet of France, writing down the names of her great men, and weaving garlands for their brows. By a decree of the *Assemblée Constituante*, in 1791, the building was converted into a temple, where were to repose the ashes of the great men of the country. The inscription "*Aux grands hommes la Patrie reconnaissante,*" was written in characters of gold over the portico. To Mirabeau, who died the same year, the first honours of this sepulture were decreed. In 1822, it was again restored to the Church.

In the revolution of July, 1830, it once more became a secular institution; but, in 1852, the Emperor Napoleon III. by a decree caused it once again to revert to ecclesiastical uses. His monogram appears on several parts of the interior. The plan of the church is that of a Greek cross. The interior is devoid of much ornament, but the vastness of its size and sublimity of its triple dome, give it an imposing air, which would be destroyed were there introduced those details which so well embellish smaller edifices

The length of the building is 302 feet, its width 255 at the transept. The top of the cupola is 268 feet above the pavement, and reached by a flight of 475 steps. In the south transept is an altar to Ste. Geneviève, to whom the church is dedicated, and in the north another to the Virgin, both of them very elegant. Copies by M. Balze, of the frescoes of Michael Angelo and Raphael in the Vatican, adorn the walls; and on the spandrils of the arches which support the dome are four allegorical paintings, representing Death, Justice, France, and Napoleon. The cupola is painted by Baron Gros, and consists of four groups, each containing a monarch of France whose reign is supposed to form an epoch in her history. The four are Clovis, Charlemagne, St. Louis, and Louis XVIII. They each pay homage to Ste. Geneviève, who descends from the heavens in clouds to greet them. Louis XVI., Marie Antoinette, Louis XIV., and Madame Elizabeth, are conspicuous personages in this high drama. The painting covers 3,721 square yards; the artist received £4,000 for his work, besides being created a baron.

The Lantern that crowns the summit of the dome is very high, being not less than 450 feet above the level of the Seine. The ascent to it is as easy as with such an elevation it can be, and from the gallery on the outside a magnificent bird's eye view of Paris and the vicinity around may be obtained. The visitor by this time we presume is tolerably familiar with the aspect of most of the buildings and prominent objects of Paris, to determine many of the edifices for himself. However, as there are some places he has not seen, and therefore will not be able to recognise for himself, we will point them out. In front of the church are the Palais and Gardens of the Luxembourg, and beyond the Hôtel des Invalides, to the left, Val de Grace and the Observatoire. Inclining to the right, the visitor will observe the Sorbonne, the towers of St. Sulpice, the Tuileries, the church of the Assumption, recognised by its dome rising beyond the trees, and the Column Vendôme. To the east may be seen the Jardin des Plantes, the Wine Market, the Column of July, with its gilded figure of Victory, the twin-pillars at the Barrière du Trône, and away still further, emerging from the woods, the lofty and substantial towers of the Fortress of Vincennes. On the hills to the left, the long range of building visible there is the prison of the Bicêtre; to the north the eye ranges over a variety of buildings, and sees stretched out the greater part of Paris.

Crossing the river, the most prominent objects are the Hôtel de Ville, St. Gervais, and, further to the right, the *Lycée Charlemagne;* to the left the tower of St. Jacques de la Boucherie, behind which rise St. Eustache, the Bourse, the Portes St. Denis and St. Martin, and the Station of the Strasbourg railway, whilst the heights of Montmartre and Belleville bound this beautiful panorama. The river, which may be descried dividing the city into two unequal parts, may be traced towards the east, until its windings are lost far beyond St. Mandé and Charenton, and the distant vine-covered valley.

Immediately beneath the Panthéon will be perceived the Mairie of the 12th Arrondissement; the École de Droit; the *Bibliothèque de Ste. Geneviève; St. Etienne du Mont;* and the *Lycée Napoléon.* This last is an old building, with a church tower and cloisters. This college was formerly called the College of Henry IV.; in 1848 it received the name of Lycée Corneille, since 1851 it is known as the Lycée Napoléon. It was here that the sons of Louis Philippe were first educated.

In the *vaults of the Panthéon* are the tombs of Voltaire and Rousseau. The remains of Mirabeau were removed shortly after their interment by one of those capricious freaks which drive the people into a sudden determination, however unjust or absurd it may be. The remains of several distinguished marshals and generals of Napoleon's army repose here, also those of Soufflot, the architect of the edifice. The first interment of celebrity which we read of here, was that of Clovis, in the year A.D. 511.

During the insurrection of June, 1848, the Panthéon was the scene of a sanguinary conflict. The insurgents had taken possession of the building, and it was necessary to bring heavy pieces of artillery to bear upon them, to dislodge them; the marks of the firing might still be seen some time after on the walls of the church, and the bronze doors, but since the building has been converted into a church, the damage then done has been repaired. Traces of the conflict may, however, be seen in the holes pierced in the pictures that line the south and north walls, caused by bullets fired from muskets.

Opposite the north side of the Panthéon is the

Bibliothèque de St. Geneviève, which used to form part of the College of Henry IV., but which has recently been transferred to the present building. It contains 200,000 volumes and 30,000 MSS., besides busts and portraits of celebrated men. It is open every day, except Sundays and Fête-days, from 10 to 3; and from 6 to 10 for students. On the south side are inscribed names distinguished in science and literature of France and foreign countries. The *Collège St. Barbe* and the *École de Droit* are near it. To the right of the Library is the

Church of St. Etienne du Mont, the date of whose foundation goes so far back as the early part of the eleventh century, when the square tower and turret we now see were probably built. The portal was constructed in 1610. The interior of this church is very beautiful; a gallery consisting of a low elliptical arch, with two spiral staircases of exquisite detail leading up to it, traverses the body of the building in the middle. In the chapel of Ste. Geneviève, is the tomb of the saint, the patroness of Paris, enclosed by railings, upon which tapers are always burning. The painted glass which adorns the windows is very fine, and belongs to the 16th century. Several valuable pictures may be seen here; amongst them, the *Preaching of Stephen,* by Pujol; *Ste. Geneviève praying to Heaven to appease a Storm,* by Grenier; and *St. Peter curing the Sick,* by Jouvenet. The *Jews collecting manna,* and *St. Bernard praying,* are also good paintings. On the wall, near the chapel of St. Geneviève, is an epitaph written on Racine, by Boileau, and another on Pascal, who was buried in this church. The sacred building was, in 1857, desecrated by the assassination of Monseigneur Sibour, Archbishop of Paris, by a priest named Verger.

Behind this church, in Rue Descartes, is the *École Polytechnique.* (See page 83). In this neighbourhood is the **Ecole des Mines,** with a good Museum of Minerals (open Tu., Th., Sat., 11 to 8 30), at 62, Boulevard St. Michel; which leads to *Fontaine* and *Pont St. Michel.* Retracing our steps by the Rue Soufflot, as far as the *Rue de Cluny,* and descending it, we pass by, first, the *College of Henri IV.,* now the *Lycée Napoléon* (or *Fontaines*), which stands back a little way; and the *Sorbonne;* then the **Collége Louis le Grand,** or **Lycée Descartes,** as it has since been called. It was founded by the Jesuits in 1563, and re-constructed in 1682. It has, since the revolution, received several names; that of Lycée Descartes was given it in 1848. The building is of a very quaint style.

The Sorbonne.—This university derives its name from Robert Sorbon, chaplain to St. Louis, who founded the schools here about the middle of the 13th century. In 1629 the old building was restored by Cardinal Richelieu, who had graduated there, and still retained a feeling of filial veneration for the place. In the chapel attached to the Institution is the tomb of the Cardinal—a chef d'œuvre, by Bouchardon. The two figures, Science and Religion, are said to be portraits of the Duchesses of Guyon and Fronsac, nieces of the Cardinal. The Sorbonne became the great scholastic and theological authority of the middle ages and deserved the epithet, *Concile perpetuel des Gaules.* It favoured the League under Henry III. and IV., and became Gallican under Louis XIV. When Napoleon I. established his new University, it became the centre of the three faculties— Lettres, Science, and Theology, and of a new secular spirit. The building was begun by order of Richelieu, 1627. The church was finished 1653. The old bell of the Sorbonne used to ring the *contre feu* for the University. The three faculties of Lettres, Science, and Theology are taught here gratuitonsly, the professors being paid by the government. The public are admitted every day from 10 to 3.

There is a similar institution, the **Collége Nationale de France,** in Rue des Écoles, in this locality. It was founded, 1529, by Francis I., at the request of Budœus, Rabelais, and Du Bellay. Some of the greatest names of France have been associated with this college, which has reckoned Ampère, Champollion, Abel Remusat, Cuvier, and Biot among its professors. The College, which has thirty professors, who lecture daily, gratis (see prospectus at the College), occupies rather limited premises, enlarged at different times—1610, 1474, and 1831. The façade has been a little opened up (1854) by the opening of the Rue des Écoles.

Descending the street we arrive in front of **Hôtel Cluny** and **Palais des Thermes**, Boulevard St. Michel, one of the most interesting public places of Paris; containing a museum of antiquities; open daily, 11 to 4 (except Monday) by passport or card. The *Palais des Thermes*, of which some ruined walls and arches are still to be seen, in conjunction with the Hôtel Cluny, is supposed to have been built by the Emperor Julian, though others assert that Constantius Chlorus was the founder of it. Whatever may be the truth of these two assertions, there can be no doubt that the origin of the palace mounts up to a very early period. In the year 365, Valentinian and Valence resided in it; and at the same time it was occupied by Gratian, Maximus, and several others of the Cæsars. After them it became the residence of the early kings of France; it was, however, pillaged by the Normans during their devastating invasions, and finally sold by Philippe Augusto to his chamberlain. The palace was then divided into several distinct residences. In 1334 an Abbé of Cluny bought a part of it, to which he gave the name of the

Hôtel Cluny, whose history we will pursue a little further. The present building was erected in 1490. A hundred years later it was in the hands of a body of comedians, who acted their plays there, and gained such a reputation that it was jocularly said—The four best preachers in Paris, put together, failed to obtain so goodly an audience as the players. In 1625 it was bought by the Abbess of Port Royal, and continued in the hands of the sisterhood until the revolution, when the horrible Marat held his meetings there. After this epoch it passed into the hands of several proprietors, and lastly into those of M. Du Sommeraid, the distinguished savant, who spent large sums of money in forming a collection of the most rare objects of art, and curiosities of the middle age, and which he distributed in different apartments of his hotel. The museum became so valuable that the hotel and its contents were at length bought by the government.

In this palace Mary Tudor, sister of Henry VIII. of England, and widow of Louis XII., resided after the death of her husband; and the bedroom in which she slept is still known as the *Chamber of the White Queen*, it being the custom of the queens of France to wear white for their mourning. Here also James V. of Scotland celebrated his marriage with the daughter of Francis I.

The architecture of this building is admired for the grace, the finish, and the lightness of its sculptures. It partakes of the Gothic and Renaissance styles, and is in a state of perfect preservation. The visitor enters by a court, on the right of which is a bureau, where he has to deposit his stick or umbrella, if he has one. He then proceeds to the interior; the first room he passes through contains mosaics, reliefs, and plaster models, well worth examining. One relic is the original plaster *cast of Dante's face*, taken after death. The other rooms, retaining their ancient character, are adorned with magnificent fire-places, vast marble chimney pieces, beautifully stained glass windows, and all the decorations of the mediæval period. In the *Chambre de la Reine Blanche*, amongst a variety of other objects of art, such as ivory cabinets, curiously-painted vases. and all the paraphernalia of a lady's toilet in those days, are to be seen several fine bas-reliefs and paintings, of which we may enumerate the *Diana Venetrix*, by Primaticcio, and *Mary Magdalene at Marseilles*, painted by King René of Provence. The *Chapel* is considered a chef-d'œuvre for the airiness and delicacy of its decorations. A stone staircase leads down from the chapel into the garden, and from thence into the *Palais des Thermes*, of which only the cold baths remain; they are sixty feet in length, and thirty-five in width. The passages by which the water was conducted may easily be seen.

On the rez de chaussée, or ground floor, are three salles and compartments. On the first floor of the main building, four salles. In Salle III. is a cap of the Emperor Charles V.; also interesting watches of the 16th and 17th centuries. Salle IV., a relic of Molière. Many early Gaulish remains and Byzantine bas-reliefs. Room II.—The golden altar given to the Cathedral of Bâle, by Henry II.; and the noted Trésor de Guarrazar, found near Toledo, 1856, consisting of nine Crowns of the Visigothic Kings of Spain; one being the Crown of King Recesvinthus, A.D. 649. Russian trophies from Sebastopol.

The streets about this quarter of Paris are rather complicated, but if, on leaving the Hôtel de Cluny, the visitor descends by the Rue de l'Ecole de Medecine he will pass by the Écolè de Medecine, devoted to the education of the students of medicine. This edifice, which consists of four divisions enclosing a spacious court, was commenced in 1769, and finished in 1786. The peristyle is formed of four rows of pillars; another peristyle is surmounted by a triangular tympanum, upon which allegorical figures are sculptured. The interior is decorated with appropriate paintings and busts of the most celebrated physicians and surgeons of France, including a statue of Bichat. The amphitheatre will hold 1,200 persons. Twenty-three professors are attached to the Institution.

Pursuing the same street we shall arrive at the *Carrefour de l'Odéon*, or a place where several streets meet. Glancing up the centre one to our left, we see the front of the *Odéon Theatre*. A theatre was erected on this spot in 1779, but was burnt down in 1818. It is frequented by the students of the Latin Quarter, and for the quality of its performance only ranks second to the Théâtre Français; it is capable of containing 1,650 persons. The prices range from 60 cents to 8 francs. This theatre is closed during a part of the summer. Performances at 8.

Descending by the Rues Ancienne Comédie and Dauphine, we shall arrive on the *Quai Conti*. To the left, hardly fifty yards, is the handsome building of La Monnaie, or

Hôtel des Monnaies (the Mint), built in 1771. The principal entrance is by the richly-decorated gate in the centre of the façade. In the interior, which is beautifully adorned with pillars and galleries, is a cabinet of mineralogy, containing a vast number of specimens of minerals, collected with the greatest care by the late Lesage. The *Salon des Medailles* possesses a complete collection of medals struck from the time of Francis I.; the collection of medals and coins in this establishment is said to be one of the richest and most curious in Europe. There are other saloons devoted to their special object in the coinage of money. These cannot be visited without a special permission from the director. The cabinets of mineralogy and medals are open Tuesday and Friday, from ten to two.

Near this is the Passage *du Pont neuf*.

The very ancient church of **St. Germain des Prés**, at the end of Rue Bonaparte, in this neighbourhood, deserves examination, as well as the remains of the extensive Abbey, of which it was a part. The church was founded in 543, by Childeric I., at the advice of Bishop Germain, who was buried there. The Normans destroyed the old building, and the present edifice dates from the 11th and 12th centuries. The nave and foundation of the tower are of the former and the choir of the latter. The tombs of Casimir, one of the abbots, of Descartes, and Boileau; a statue of the Virgin, and several fine paintings are to be seen. The greatest curiosity of this church consists in the restoration of the old wall paintings, so usual in ancient churches of the Romanesque style, but which had been overlooked till the last twenty years, during which the architect, Baltard, has, with the painter, Hippolyte Flandrin, reproduced much of the half-effaced polychrome decorations of the interior.

St. Severin (Rue des Prétres, St. Severin, Rive Gauche), is an old building of Gothic style, dating from the 13th century, founded on the site of one of the 6th. It has stained glass of the 15th century. The chapels are adorned with modern frescoes.

SIXTH DAY.

BOIS DE BOULOGNE, ST. CLOUD, SEVRES, MEUDON.

We propose to pass this, the sixth day, in enjoying the fresh air of the country, and visiting the *Château of St. Cloud*, the *Porcelain Manufactory at Sèvres*, and the *beautiful terraces of Bellevue and Meudon.*

There are four ways to get to St. Cloud; one by the railway to Versailles, which makes a considerable detour around Paris; another by the railway to Auteuil; the third by omnibus from the Place de la Concorde, by the Cours la Reine, Pont de Jèna, Passy (where a new bridge connects with Javal), and Sèvres; the fourth by the tram, or Chemin-de-fer Americain, direct from the Place de la Concorde to the village of Boulogne. A walk of a few minutes across the bridge leads to the Château. We think that the railway *viâ* Auteuil will be the best, as it is by far the shortest, will diversify the trip, and enable the visitor to see the Wood and Lakes of Boulogne.

The trains start from the railway station, *Place-du-Havre*, about every half-hour. The office for the Bois de Boulogne is on the left. Having got a ticket, which costs six sous, second class, or eight sous first class, the visitor takes his place and proceeds the whole distance to Auteuil, passing Batignolles, Courcelles, &c. As part of the road is cut considerably under the level of the ground,

there is no opportunity afforded of seeing the country until we arrive at Passy, near the City Flower Garden. The next station is Auteuil.

From the train, the **Bois de Boulogne** is on the right, 1,980 acres in extent. This is the "Hyde Park" and "Kensington Gardens" of Paris. Having crossed the fortifications, the visitor will do well to penetrate into the wood by one of the avenues to th right, and he will then shortly arrive upon the lakes. These lakes afford abundant sources of recreation to the gay Parisians, who make the Bois de Boulogne one of their principal promenades. A steamer has been lately started for trips on the lake. N.B. The prices at the refreshment *Châlet des Iles* are high. The charge for admission is a franc during the day, and in the evening it varies according to the character of the fête. There are frequent concerts when many of the best military bands in Paris play in succession.

The Bois, or Wood, derives its name from a village to the west, which grew up round a pilgrim chapel which was a branch of the one at Boulogne-sur-Mer. Before the year 1790, the trees were of small growth, or decaying, from their great age. They were, during the revolution, cleared away in a great measure, and what was not then destroyed, was afterwards cut down in the year 1814, for the

H

defence of Paris against the approach of the allied forces. The English encamped here under Wellington in the following year. From that time the greater part of it has been planted, new walks have been made, and a variety of improvements have taken place. It suffered greatly in the siege of 1870-1; but restorations are in progress. Here a struggle took place with the insurgents, May, 1871.

The new Hippodrome, or Race Course of *Longchamp*, of 153 acres extent, near the village and river, is placed under the management of the French Jockey Club. An artificial *Cascade* or waterfall, 27 feet high, is a favourite resort. It is fed by the lake behind it, and is ornamented with rock work. In the western portion of the Bois is the *Jardin d'Acclimatation*, on a site of 50 acres. Here there are aviaries, silkworm nurseries, a good collection of rare animals, and an *Aquarium* and Waterfall. It is open every day; admission, 1 franc; Sunday ½ franc. The garden has been enriched with many exotic plants, and tropical as well as other animals, elephants, ostriches, &c., several of which have been sold to encourage their breed in France; we may specify among them the llama, alpaca, guanaco, kangaroo, wapiti stag, &c., some of which were killed for food in the siege. To the northwest of the Wood are the remains of the Abbey of Longchamp, celebrated towards the middle of the seventeenth century for its choir of nuns, and whither, on the Wednesday and Thursday in Passion Week, the élite of Paris flocked to hear the music and singing. From this circumstance has sprung up the *Fête de Longchamps*, when the wealthy display their fine equipages, and the fair, their fine habiliments, by driving out to the Wood and back. In fact, it is considered the time for commencing to wear the new fashions for the spring season. In the centre of the Bois is the *Pré Catalan*, a model dairy farm and a most charming resort, where shrubbery, flowers, and ever fresh grass delight the eye.

The **Cercle des Patineurs.**—One of the favourite resorts of the aristocracy in the Bois de Boulogne is the Cercle des Patineurs, or Grounds of the Skating Club; also used in summer for the *Tir aux Pigeons*, or pigeon shooting matches, and other similar amusements.

Shallow and suitable basins of artificial water have been prepared for the skaters, when the winter is severe enough to permit it. The first occasion on which it was used for this purpose was during the frost of January, 1867, when the frozen waters were largely frequented by fashionable skaters, and brilliantly illuminated with fireworks and electric lights, on the occasion of two fêtes that were given and attended by the Imperial Family and the Court. For the convenience of the members of the club some pretty châlets have been erected (tastefully decorated and furnished in cedar wood), providing cabinets for dressing and undressing, lounging, and refreshment rooms.

Entrance into the Skating Club is rendered rather difficult and expensive. In order to assist at one of the fêtes with illuminations it is necessary to obtain an order from a member, besides paying twenty francs.

Two or three ponds belong to the Club (one near Longchamp), but the principal one with the châlets and the site of the illuminations is in the direction of the district known by the name of Madrid.

Two handsome new churches have been completed in the N.W. quarter of Paris, Saint Augustin and La Trinité; the former half-way up the *Boulevard of Malesherbes*, near Boulevard Haussmann; the other in Rue St. Lazare, near Notre Dame de Lorette.

St. Augustin, built by M. Victor Baltard, is in the ogival style of the 15th century. Its paintings, which represent scriptural and ecclesiastical subjects, are by MM. Signol, Brissot, and others. The sculptures (evangelists, saints, &c.), are by MM. Jouffroy, Schroder, Cordier, Brunet, &c.

The portal consists of three arcades, contains statues of the 12 Apostles on the frieze, and a triangular salle above a rose window. In the centre of the building is a dome of 165ft. in height, and 83ft. in diameter, flanked with four turrets of cupola form, and surmounted with an elegant lantern. In the interior of the Church the length of the nave is 132ft. Underneath is a vast crypt.

La Trinité, a modern church, in a more perfect style, and of somewhat larger dimensions, facing Rue de la Chausseé d'Antin. It was completed in 1866, by M. Ballu, on the site of suburban gardens. The church has a length of 295 feet, and a breadth of 99 feet; and contains Français' large pictures of the Expulsion from Paradise and the Baptism of Christ. The façade, which is in the style of the Renaissance, consists of a vast porch, surmounted by an elegant clerestory, and a tower above 197 feet in height.

Nôtre Dame de Lorette (of Loreto), near Rue de La Fayette, is a handsome church, 204 feet long, built 1821; in a district not far from the Opera, inhabited by actresses and by women of the demi-monde; who are called "Lorettes," from the locality. The house of M. Thiers, in *Place St. George*, was built for him by the government after the destruction of his former house by the Communists. The Banque Parisienne, in Rue Chauchat, is a new building, by Souffron.

On retracing our steps to Auteuil, an omnibus will take us on to St. Cloud, across a corner of the Bois de Boulogne.

St. Cloud derives its name from Cleodald, grandson of Clovis, who escaped assassination when his two brothers were murdered by their uncles, Clotaire and Childebert, and hid himself in a hermitage in the wood that covered the hill. A village sprang up here, which has been the theatre of bloody conflicts. In 1358, it was pillaged and sacked by the English; again in 1411, by a party of Armagnacs; and during the wars of the League, it was frequently taken and burnt. It was here that Henry III. was assassinated, and in a house near the palace, Henry IV., his successor, resided after the event. During the minority of Louis XIV., the park had already become celebrated for the beauty of its gardens and its mansion; and the fine view, with the Seine winding along at its feet, was universally admired. The king, who was desirous of possessing himself of the estate, to make a residence for his brother, the Duke of Orléans, deputed Cardinal Mazarin to negociate the purchase of it. This he did, and by chicanery and force, wrested it from its proprietor, M. Fouquet, for the sum of 300,000*l.*, although it had cost the latter upwards of a million in erecting the château, and laying out the grounds. Three principal architects were then employed in harmonising the old, and erecting new buildings; whilst Lenôtre, taking advantage of the natural position of the grounds, designed the park, the admiration of all visitors.

It was the residence of the dukes of Orléans until the revolution, when it was made part of the national property. During the empire, Napoleon frequently resided here with Josephine, and from this palace Charles X. issued those celebrated ordonnances suggested by Prince Polignac, which led to his banishment in July, 1830. Louis Philippe subsequently inhabited the château, and rested there a few moments in February, 1848, during his flight from Paris. Here the Lord Mayor was entertained in 1854. Napoleon III. lived here in summer; and it was fitted up for the young Prince Imperial. It is now a ruin, having been set on fire, October, 1870, by French shells from Mont Velérien, to prevent its falling into the hands of the Germans. The barracks and part of the town were burnt at the same time, along with the station. Some of the Gobelins tapestry and several pictures by Vernet were saved; but all the other works of art were lost.

The principal building was after the designs of Mansard, and adorned with Corinthian pillars and bas-reliefs. The front faces the grand avenue of the park, whilst on the left are the cascades and jets d'eau, and on the right the private walks and flower-gardens.

The interior of the Château consisted of suites of apartments, approached by a very richly-ornamented vestibule. Among the rooms were the Salon de Mars, with paintings by Mignard in the ceiling. The Galerie d'Apollon, in which Pius VII. baptised the son of the King of Holland, afterwards Napoleon III., and in which the civil contract of marriage between Napoleon I. and Maria Louise was celebrated. Here also was a statue of Napoleon III.'s mother, Hortense. The Salon de Diana was painted like the others by Mignard, and used as a billiard room. This and the next rooms, the Salon de Jeu de Mercuriet, &c., were covered with Gobelins tapestry, some of which was rescued from the flames. The Salon de la Reception de la Reine had a clock with twelve dials on its face, marking the time in twelve different capitals of Europe. On the Grand Staircase was a painting of the Reception of Queen Victoria and the Prince Consort, by the Emperor and Empress, in 1855.

The Park lies on the road between St. Cloud and Sèvres, and is about ten miles in circumference.

The fountains and disposition of the waters in this park have for a long time been celebrated, and next to those at Versailles, merit an especial visit. The *Haute Cascade*, from which the water first issues, is adorned by a group of statues representing the Seine and Marne, and was designed by Lepantre. The second fall, called the *Basse Cascade*, receives the waters of the *Haute Cascade*, and

ejects them in a grand sheet into a canal, along which twelve jets d'eau are ranged. The effect of the waters issuing from urns and dolphins, and other emblematical figures, and falling after a graceful rise, into the different sculptured cisterns intended to receive them, is very magnificent. To the right of the *Cascade*, is the *Grand Jet*, also called *le jet géant*, which throws its waters one hundred and thirty feet above the level of the basin, and as it is situated on high ground, may be seen at a considerable distance sparkling in the sun, high above the green foliage of the trees. The rainbows, which the falling spray sometimes forms, are very beautiful. Other basins and fountains of extreme elegance are distributed about the grounds.

The part of the park now to be sought out is the high terrace in front of the river, from which a fine view of Paris and the surrounding country may be had. It is at the top of the grand avenue, facing the western front of the château, and was, till its destruction in 1870 by the Prussians, who occupied St. Cloud, distinguished by a kind of watch-tower, called the *Lantern of Demosthenes*, which was built on an open space here by order of Napoleon, and was designed after the original one by Lysicrates at Athens.

The waters play at St. Cloud during grand fête days and the first Sunday of every month from May till October.

Continuing our route by the avenue facing that we ascended from the palace, and taking a pathway to the left we shall, on arriving at the bottom of the hill, find ourselves at the town, and shortly after at the porcelain manufactory of

Sèvres.—The town of Sèvres is situated on the left bank of the Seine, on the high road between Paris and Versailles. In the rocks that environ it, are immense cellars of underground streets, divided into thirty compartments, where the wine is kept until it has attained a superior quality from age. These cellars are capable of containing upwards of fifteen thousand pipes of wine. But that for which Sèvres is chiefly celebrated, is its porcelain manufactory, which, though damaged in the war of 1870-1, is still at work. It was established originally at Vincennes, in the year 1738, under the superintendence of the Marquis de Fulvy, but was transferred to Sèvres in 1759, by order of Louis XV., and was made a government establishment. This manufactory contains a fine *Musée Céramique*, or museum of porcelains of every kind, foreign as well as French, modern as well as antique, and founded by Brongniart in 1800. The workshops where the vases, &c., are fabricated, are very difficult to be seen, but the rest of the establishment may be seen daily, on showing a passport, or by ticket. On Sundays or fête it is free. The new building was opened by Marshal MacMahon, when President, 1876.

At a short distance beyond Sèvres is the *Terrace of Bellerue* and the *Château of Meudon.* This Château stands at the end of a grand avenue, having before it a fine terrace, 1,730 feet in length, and 350 in breadth, constructed by Henri de Guise, in 1660. During the first revolution, the estate was seized by the government, and the grounds converted into a park for artillery practice. Shortly after this, a part of the château was burnt down, when Napoleon I. ordered the remaining portion to be repaired and enlarged, and the grounds to be laid out in gardens. At the restoration, it was made crown property, and subsequently used by the Duke of Bourdeaux until 1831, when it was given as a residence to the Duke of Orléans. It was occupied by Prince Napoleon Bonaparte, and was ruined in the bombardment of Paris, 1870-1.

The interior of the building was beautifully fitted up with rich silk and Gobelin tapestry, and contained many works of high eminence, by the first artists of the time. Amongst them may be mentioned the *Group of Cupid and*

Psyche, in marble, in the vestibule; and the paintings by Teniers, Schnetz, Vergnaud, which were all chef-d'œuvres. The Château may be visited any day, except Fridays, from 12 to 4.

From the terrace that lines the ground to the east, a most beautiful prospect may be had. Immediately beneath, in the valley, is the prettily situated village of *Meudon.* Unfortunately the place is infected with bad smells as in so many French towns. It is worth remarking that the satirist and wit, Rabelais, was formerly pastor in this village. On the opposite slope of the hill is *Fleury,* its cottages and summer houses gracefully embosomed in the fine wood that covers the whole rise. To the left, the landscape is cut as it were by the railway viaduct, consisting of seven beautiful arches, rising upwards of one hundred feet.

The visitor may return to Paris by taking an omnibus at Sèvres, or by the railway at Bellevue, which is half-way down the hill. If by the latter means, he will enter by the *rive gauche* into Paris, at the Boulevard Mont Parnasse, where he will find omnibuses waiting to take him to any part of the city. Near Bellevue Station is the small chapel of *Notre Dame des Flammes,* built to commemorate the frightful railway accident of 1842, when more than 200 passengers were burnt to death, owing to the carriage doors being shut. One of the victims was Admiral Dumont d'Urville; who is buried in the neighbouring *Cemetery of Mont Parnasse,* along with Bishop Gregoire, Orfila the chemist, and others. *Montsouris Park* and reservoir are near this; with an Observatory open Saturday by ticket from the Director. Not far is one of the entrances to the *Catacombs.* These last, which extend 200 acres, and are visible twice a month, were first excavated for building stone, and contain three million skulls, taken for sanitary reasons from the crowded graveyards after 1786, and piled up in the galleries.

SEVENTH DAY.

BIBLIOTHÈQUE NATIONALE—PLACE LOUVOIS—BOURSE—CONSERVATOIRE DES ARTS ET MÉTIERS—ST. DENIS—ENGHIEN—MONTMORENCY—CHURCH OF ST. VINCENT DE PAUL.

THE short trip into the country of the previous day will, we trust, dispose the visitor to accompany us to-day to some of the remaining monuments and public places of Paris which he has not already seen. We will therefore start from the **Bibliothèque Nationale,** in the Rue de Richelieu. This building presents to the street only a large unsightly wall, with blank windows; but on entering the gateway, the visitor finds himself in a vast court, five hundred and forty feet long, in the centre of which is a statue of Charles IX. During the regency of the Duke of Orleans, the royal library proving inadequate for the number of volumes which had accumulated in it, the books were transferred to the present building, a mansion that formerly belonged to Cardinal Mazarin. This library had been formed at an early period, and gradually augmented by successive monarchs, who collected valuable books and manuscripts from different parts of the world. In the reign of Henry II., a decree was issued that a copy of every book printed within the jurisdiction of the king's censor should be placed in it. Its value was also considerably increased by the confiscation of the property of the Constable Bourbon, and by a collection of medals and MSS. bequeathed to it by Catherine de Médicis. At the death of Louis XIV., it is computed that there were no less than seventy thousand volumes in the royal library. During the revolution of 1789, the number was rapidly increased, by the confiscation of all the printed volumes and MSS. belonging to the monasteries and other religious establishments which were then suppressed. The Bibliothèque Nationale now contains upwards of three millions of volumes, including duplicates and pamphlets. It is divided into four departments, viz : Printed Books, Maps (about 80,000), Geological collections, Manuscripts, Engravings, Medals and Antiquities. Here may be seen specimens of bookbinding and printing from the earliest times. An Apocalypse, printed from solid blocks of wood; a Bible printed by Gutenberg, with some of his types; Racine's Sophocles, with his MS. notes; Voltaire's notes on Frederick the Great's letter; Rousseau's music; and a translation of the *Ars Moriendi*, printed by Caxton, are among the chief curiosities. In one of the rooms, two colossal metal globes, nearly twelve feet in diameter, made at Venice, by order of Cardinal d'Estrées, may be seen. The other salons well worth noticing, are the *Cabinets of Medals and Antiquities*; the *Gallery of Ancient Sculpture*, where is the Egyptian Zodiac of Dendarah, and the *Salle des Ancêtres*, a room fitted up after the Egyptian original, and representing the ancestors of Thothmes III.

A spacious hall is fitted up for reading, to which the public are admitted from ten to four every day without any order or impediment. The other parts of the library are shut on Sundays and fête days; open to the public on Tuesdays and Fridays; to students on other days.

The open space in front of the Bibliothèque Nationale is the *Place Louvois*, where formerly stood the French opera house. It was at the entrance of this theatre that the Duke de Berri was assassinated in 1820, and the event made such an impression on the king, that he ordered the building to be demolished, and another erected elsewhere. The theatre was accordingly transferred to the spot behind the Boulevard des Italiens, where the present spacious establishment was erected in the short space of a year. In the centre of the *Place*, an elegant fountain has been erected. The principal figures represent the four principal rivers of France. The design is by the late M. Visconti.

A little further on, towards the boulevards, and turning to the right, is the

Bourse (or Exchange), one of the finest pieces of Grecian architecture in Paris; it is the "Royal Exchange" and "Stock Exchange" in one. It occupies the space once occupied by the convent of the *Daughters of St. Thomas*, and was commenced in 1808, after the designs of Brongniard, the architect; though not finished until 1826. It consists of a rectangular pile, 212 feet long, by 126 feet wide. The whole is surrounded by a gallery supported by sixty-six Corinthian columns, beneath which the merchants walk and discuss their business. A fine flight of steps, running the whole length of the front of the building, gives it a majestic appearance. At the corners are placed statues emblematic of Commerce, Consular Justice, Industry, and Agriculture. At the *Chamber of Commerce*, in Place de la Bourse, is a Commercial Library, open 11 to 4. A fee is now demanded from all persons (not subscribers) who enter the Bourse during business hours, from 12 to 3.

The interior consists of a vast hall, one hundred and sixteen feet long, by seventy-six feet wide, capable of containing two thousand persons. The ceiling is divided into compartments, and embellished with fresco paintings by Abel de Pujol and Meynier, having the effect of bas-reliefs. To the right we see the *Union of the Arts and Commerce giving*

prosperity to the State; on the left, *France receiving the products of the four quarters of the world*; in front, *Paris delivering the Keys to the Genius of Commerce, and inviting Commercial Justice to enter her gates*. A library, called the Bibliothèque du Commerce, principally containing works on commercial subjects, is in connection with the Bourse, and may be seen any day from twelve to four. The hall is always open.

Opposite to the Bourse is the *Théâtre du Vaudeville*, established in 1827; enlarged 1867. It is capable of containing one thousand nine hundred persons. Light dialogues and comedies, relieved by singing, interlarded with quaint sayings in Parisian slang, often of doubtful character (*double entendre*), characterise the performances at this theatre. The prices range from one franc up to eight francs. Performances commence at eight.

The next object of interest we will visit is the *Conservatoire des Arts et Métiers*. It will therefore be necessary to proceed on to the Boulevards de la Rue Vivienne, which runs in front of the Bourse, and pass down by the Boulevards Poissonnière, Bonne Nouvelle, and St. Denis, to the Rue St. Martin. In the Rue St. Martin, before arriving at our destination, we shall observe on our left the *Fontaine St. Martin*, a curious fountain, built against a round and spired tower, which once formed part of the outer walls of the abbey of St Martin des Champs. A few steps more will take us to the

Conservatoire des Arts et Metiers (the useful arts and trades).—This institution was founded on the site of the above-mentioned abbey, by the Convention, under the management of Gregory, Bishop of Blois, in 1794. The object of the institution is the improvement of machinery of every kind, by exhibiting models of the best and most recent inventions for the purpose of stimulating the creative faculty in the minds of other artists and mechanics. Previous to 1798, three repositories of machines existed in Paris, but in this year they were amalgamated into one. In 1810, a gratuitous school of arts was originated, which was re-organised and enlarged several times, until in 1838 it was finally established under its present regulations. No patent for any sort of improvement in machines, or the invention of new ones, is granted until a model of the same has been deposited in this museum; so that instruments, from the simplest tool to the most complicated piece of mechanism, are collected and classified in the salons of this building.

The principal entrance to the Conservatoire is on the west, under a solid archway, richly sculptured, beneath the pediment of which, is inscribed, *"Conservatoire Nationale des Arts et Métiers."* The edifice consists of a part of the old abbey of St. Martin des Champs, and of the chapel belonging to it erected by Pierre de Montereau, the architect of the Sainte Chapelle. The style is Gothic. The museums are held in spacious saloons, communicating with lecture rooms of modern construction. The Library, in the Abbey Refectory, which contains upwards of 20,000 volumes, on mechanical and mathematical subjects, is most elegantly fitted up. There are also fresco figures of Chemistry, Natural Philosophy. Painting, and the Plastic Art.

On the *ground floor*, are arranged in beautiful order, weighing machines, looms, spinning machines, printing presses, screw-making machines, agricultural implements, such as ploughs, harrows, mills, crushing and winnowing machines, &c. There are also specimens of porcelain, silk, glue, &c. In the vestibule is a bas-relief of Dædalus and Icarus; and, in an adjoining out-house, Tuxford's locomobile engine, which gained the chief medal at the Great Exhibition of 1851, may be seen.

On the *upper storey* are exhibited steam and fire-engines, apparatus for lighting and heating, turning lathes, and amongst them one **that** belonged to Louis XIV. There are, moreover, rooms devoted to geometrical illustrations; to carpentry; to the making of compasses; to specimens of stereotype; furnaces, &c. Also to instruments belonging to the science of natural philosophy or physics: as air-pumps, electric machines, &c., and to clocks and chronometers.

The Museum is open on Tuesdays, Thursdays and Sundays, from ten to four; other days by passport or stamped card, with a fee of 1 fr. to the attendant.

Having seen all that is to be seen here, there will be time to spend the rest of the afternoon in a short trip to the

Abbey of St. Denis. The town itself, which contains about sixteen thousand inhabitants, offers nothing of striking interest, if we except its antiquity—its historical associations—and its beautiful abbey, which enclosed, till 1789, the ashes of nearly all the kings of France, from the time of Clovis to that of Louis XVIII. It is situated about three miles and a-half from Paris, on the right bank of the Seine, and may be reached either by omnibus or railway. The railway station is that of the *Chemin de Fer du Nord, Place Roubaix.* The trains start frequently: 1st class, 80 centimes; 2nd, 60c.; 3rd, 40c. A run of a few minutes takes you to the station at St. Denis. The abbey is a few minutes' walk from the station. Or you can go by omnibus from the Rue d'Enghien, near the Porte St. Denis, for forty centimes, the road partly consisting of the Avenue de Paris, lined with double rows of trees.

A beautiful new church is erected in the town. St. Denis was bombarded by the Germans, and held by them till September, 1871. The Abbey Church shows marks of injury; and some houses were destroyed.

The foundation of this abbey is almost coeval with the establishment of Christianity in France. It is said that St. Denis, who was beheaded on

Montmartre (the Mount of Martyrs) walked, after his execution, with his head under his arm as far as this spot *(Ce n'est que le premier pas qui coûte)*, angels celebrating the miracle as he passed along; where he gave up the ghost, after requesting that he might be buried there. A tomb and chapel rose above his ashes. Ste. Geneviève, the patroness of Paris in 496, was the means of having the chapel enlarged, and in the following century it became the abode of a company of Benedictine Monks. Chilperic, the youngest son of Dagobert, was the first who was laid within its vaults, whilst his father was the first king who shared the same fate. In 754, Pépin le Bref was consecrated in the church, and, as a mark of his gratitude, pulled down the old edifice, and commenced another on a scale of greater magnificence. This building was finished and consecrated in 775, in the reign of Charlemagne.

Only the crypt of this church now remains. It was demolished by Suger, Abbot of St. Denis, in 1140; and in the course of five years another was erected, of which the towers and porch remain. The other parts of the present building were constructed between the years 1231 and 1281, a period of half a century. In the erection of this edifice, not only the most celebrated architects were employed, but the most skilful makers and stainers of glass were sent for, even from distant countries. During the revolution of 1789, this church, the work of so much skill and labour, the mirror of so much beauty and elegance, excited the fury of the people, for containing the tombs of the Kings of France, and suffered accordingly. The richly stained glass was broken, the lead of the roofs melted down to make bullets, the splendid monumental tombs of the kings broken open, and their ashes, which had been quietly inurned there for centuries, either scattered to the winds or buried carelessly in a neighbouring cemetery, from which they were brought back to the church under Napoleon and the consequent reigns. The *Oriflamme*, the consecrated banner of France, was torn to pieces in the Reign of Terror, and a decree was even passed for the entire demolition of the abbey. In 1806, however, Napoleon, who had given back the church to the empire, ordered its restoration and especially the vault of the Bourbons, which he intended henceforth to be the resting-place of his own dynasty.

The building is a splendid specimen of early Gothic, having been restored on the original plan under Louis Philippe. When the alterations and decorations in the interior are complete, it is proposed to transport the body of Napoleon I. from the Invalides hither. The façade, which is the part erected by Suger, is very fine, and contains three portals, consisting of retiring arches, ornamented with angels, &c. Bas-reliefs of *Jesus in the Midst of the Saints*, the *Day of Judgment*, and the *General Resurrection*, grace the centre porch. The bas-relief on the north porch represents *St. Denis and his Companions led to Execution*, and on the south, *A Scene in the Life of the Saint*.

The form of the church is that of a regular cross, and consists of a nave and two aisles. The nave is very splendid, and exhibits those light and elegant forms, which particularly distinguished the architecture of that period. Some of the chapels which surround it are gorgeous in decoration, and all are admirably in keeping, producing the most striking effect. The choir is separated from the nave by a railing of beautiful workmanship. The church is also enriched by paintings of some of the first masters. That which stood over the high altar is by Krayer, a pupil of Rubens, and represents the martyrdom of St. Denis. In the chamfering of the second window is a statue of the Virgin and Child in white marble, the robes of which are interspersed with precious stones. In the Sacristy are ten paintings, illustrating the principal events connected with the history of the Abbey. Amongst them are *Charles V. and Francis the First visiting the Abbey*, by Gros; *St. Louis receiving the Oriflamme*, by Barbier; *the Preaching of St. Denis in Gaul*, by Monsiau, &c. As a large portion of the cathedral, however, is undergoing extensive alterations, the temporary removal of some of these has been necessitated.

But that which will now particularly interest the spectator is the *Tombs of the different Monarchs*. The first to claim his attention as being the most ancient, is the tomb of Dagobert, a work of the thirteenth century. It is a mausoleum with pinnacles, and a richly ornamented canopy, representing the vision of a monk, who dreamed that he saw the king carried off by a legion of devils. The tombs of Louis XII. and Anne of Brittany, beautifully executed in white marble, by Paolo Poncio, and of Henry II. and Catherine de Médicis, should be noticed. The tomb of the latter is adorned with twelve columns of deep blue marble, and twelve of white marble. The two sovereigns are reposing on a couch. Next to this is the tomb of Francis I. and his wife Claude, of France, erected in 1550. Bas-reliefs, representing the battles of Marignan and Cérizoles, ornament the pedestal, which support figures of the king and queen.

In one of the transepts we see a spiral column, raised to the memory of Henry III., who was murdered at St. Cloud by Jacques Clement. Opposite, is a marble pillar raised by the unfortunate Mary Queen of Scots, to the memory of her husband, Francis II. Two other columns, one of marble, to the memory of the Cardinal Bourbon, and the other of porphyry, to the memory of Henry IV., should be noticed. The tombs of Duguesclin, Sancerre, and La Rivière are to be seen in the first chapel, on ascending the south steps of the choir.

In one of the chapels are busts of Henry IV., Diana of France, in a kneeling posture, and Charles de Valois. An urn in front contains the heart of Francis I. Not far from this is a statue of Marie Antoinette kneeling, which is considered to be a most perfect likeness. There are also two colossal figures. This monument is intended as an expiatory souvenir of the memory of the Duke de Berri, who was assassinated in 1820. Between these two is the mausoleum of Louis XVIII.

The old Abbey buildings were set apart for the *Maison Impériale Napoléon*, an institution founded by the first emperor, for the instruction of daughters, sisters, &c., of members of the Legion of Honour; and, after 1855, placed under the special protection of the Empress. None but children of officers above the rank of lieutenant are nominated to St. Denis; but at the branch establishments of St. Germains and Ecouen, those of a lower grade are admitted. Visitors can ascend the *Tower* under the guidance of the attendant. The staircase is of stone, and it is well lighted. From the gallery can be seen the abbey itself, the remains of the ancient abbey, the town of St. Denis, and a vast expanse of country. The dimensions of St. Denis are: width of façade, 103 feet; length of edifice, 333 feet; height of uninjured tower, 179 feet; height of interior to roof, 89 feet.

Should the visitor have time, he could not do better than meet one of the trains leaving Paris, and proceed a little further on to *Enghien* and *Montmorency*.

Enghien is situated about 7 miles from Paris, on the borders of a lake, since 1766 celebrated for its sulphurous waters, which, as well as the prettiness of the situation, has given rise to several thermal establishments, and the construction of several private country villas. On the hill above is

Montmorency—Containing upwards of two thousand inhabitants. It owes its principal importance to the beauty of its position, being seated high amongst the hills, and enjoying a magnificent prospect of the country below, and the woods by which it is surrounded. A multitude of country seats may be seen dotting the valley, over which the eye runs, whilst to the left the outline of Paris may be traced in the distance. The air here is pure and fresh, and the fruits that grow on the sides of the hills early ripen, and acquire an exquisite flavour. But Montmorency owes its principal attractions for the visitor to its *Hermitage*, which was formerly the residence of Jean Jacques Rousseau, and the spot where he composed his *Emile* and finished his *Nouvelle Héloise*. It was afterwards occupied by Grétry, the composer, who died here 1813.

Returning to the railway station, half-an-hour's run will bring us again into Paris and the Rue Lafayette. In this street is the fine **Church of St. Vincent de Paul**, which is well worthy of inspection, and may be almost said to rival the Madeleine in the gorgeousness of its decorations. It is of modern construction, being commenced in 1824, and finished in 1844. A graceful flight of steps, intersected by a carriage drive, leads from the Place Lafayette up to its elegant portico. Two lofty square towers containing two clocks, one for telling the hour of the day, the other the days of the month, flank the façade. The interior of the church consists of a nave and four aisles, separated by rows of Ionic pillars. Richly gilt bronze railings divide the aisles into chapels, whilst a semi-circle of fourteen columns of the same order, supporting a semi-cupola, enclose the choir. Over the altar is a bas-relief of the Last Supper. The church contains fine specimens of stained glass, and the windows where St. Vincent de Paul is represented, surrounded by the Sisters of Charity, are remarkably beautiful. A splendid organ surmounts the southern portal.

The visitor may descend to the Boulevards, either by taking the Rue Hauteville, which is opposite the church, or by the Rue du Faubourg Poissonnière, which is at the end of the Rue Lafayette. In Rue Buffault, near Avenue de l' Opéra, is a new Synagogue. The *New York Herald Office* reading-room is in the Avenue, with Tiffany, the jeweller's shop.

EIGHTH DAY.

LE TEMPLE—ARCHIVES NATIONALES—IMPRIMIERIE NATIONALE—PLACE DES VOSGES—BAS-
TILLE—PÈRE LA CHAISE—PLACE DU TRONE—VINCENNES.

As we visited yesterday some of the most interesting places in the northern arrondissement of Paris, to-day will be devoted to some of those lying eastward, even as far as Père la Chaise and Vincennes. But, before we leave the town we will go to some of those places which are most remarkable for their historical associations or peculiar attractions, as they lie in our route. It will, therefore, be best to hasten on as far as the Boulevard du Temple, when descending the street of that name, we shall see the market and the ruins of the palace of that name.

The **Temple**, as its name implies, formerly belonged to the order of the Knights Templar, who possessed extensive domains in this quarter of the city. All that exists of it at present is the Palais du Prior, which, in 1814, was converted into a convent, and appropriated to the Dames Benedictines de l'Adoration du Saint Sacrement, under the direction of Madame la Princesse de Condé, formerly abbess of Remiremont. The façade fronting the court of the Temple is composed of eight Ionic columns, above which are placed allegorical figures of Justice, by Dumont; Hope, by Leseur; Abundance, by Foucon; and Prudence, by Boichot. The portico is composed of six Doric pillars. The façade fronting the street is adorned by two statues representing the Marne and the Seine.

There stood formerly in the Temple a high quadrangular tower, 150 feet in length, which was built in 1222, or perhaps earlier, and flanked by smaller towers. This was the donjon or fortress of the Knights, and sometimes it was even inhabited by the kings of France. During the first revolution it became the prison of the unfortunate Louis XVI. Here also were confined Sir Sidney Smith, Pichegru, Moreau, and Toussaint l'Ouverture, and from it Sir Sidney escaped. It was demolished, however, in 1810, and no vestige of it remains.

In what was anciently the grand enclosure of the Temple has been established a *Market*, (Marché du Vieux Linge) where old clothes, furniture, &c., are sold, under a large and commodious covered hall.

In the Boulevard des Filles du Calvaire, adjoining, stands the *Cirque d'Hiver* (formerly *Cirque Napoleon*), built in 1852. It is only open during a portion of the year. The prices are ½ to 2 francs; and performances begin at eight.

Proceeding down the Rue du Temple until we arrive at the Rue de Bracque, which is on the left of us, we shall have at the further end of the street the

Hôtel des Archives Nationales, the principal entrance of which is from the Rue Paradis. Until 1697 this property belonged to the Dukes of Guise, but in that year it was purchased by François de Rohan, Prince de Soubise, who, in 1706, had the place rebuilt after designs by Lemaire, and gave it the name of Hôtel de Soubise. The principal entrance is adorned by Corinthian columns, trophies, the arms of Rohan and Soubise, and some fine sculptures by Coustou. The vestibule and staircase are painted by Brunetti. At the period when this fine edifice was erected, this quarter was the fashionable part of Paris; and this, as well as several other mansions in the neighbourhood, attest the splendour of the nobles of the early part of the eighteenth century. This splendour, however, has been greatly dimmed by the uses to which these hotels have been put, and, in the present instance, it is not very easy, amidst the masses and heaps of papers that fill every part of it, to realise altogether the stories of its former sumptuousness.

Before 1789 the national documents were scattered about amongst various public offices and religious establishments; but in 1793, by a decree of the Convention, they were collected together and placed in the palace of the Tuileries, where they were separated into two classes, the *Archives Judiciaires* and the *Archives Domaniales*, under the direction of the antiquarian Camus. The latter were, in 1798, transferred by order of Napoleon to the Palais Bourbon, from whence they were subsequently transferred to the Hôtel de Soubise. These archives are divided into six sections, viz.: the ancient *Trésor des Chartes*, or collection of titles and charters from the twelfth century down to the first revolution; eighty volumes of manuscript, containing different acts passed from the time of Philip Augustus to that of Louis XVI.; an infinitude of documents, belonging either to Paris or the provinces; a topographical collection, and an excellent library of 14,000 volumes relating to the history of France, as well as a variety of curiosities and souvenirs, illustrative of the progress of civilisation in France.

The public is admitted on Sundays; or on Thursdays, by ticket, from 9 till 3, to visit the establishment; but a written order is required from the Minister of the Interior to use the manuscripts.

Close by the *Archives Nationales* is the *Imprimerie Nationale*, where all the government papers, and papers referring to state matters, are printed. The entrance to it is in the *Rue Vieille du Temple*. This building, which possesses no great architectural beauty, was formerly called the *Palais Cardinal*, because it belonged to the Cardinal Rohan, whose intriguing spirit made him so conspicuous a figure during the reigns of Louis XV. and XVI. The national printing office was established first at the Louvre by François I., but in 1793 it was transferred to the Hôtel de Thoulouse, since the Bank of France, and from thence, in 1809, to the place it now occupies.

This establishment, as we have said, is principally devoted to the printing of the acts of government and of the legislature. It is one of the most complete in the world, and contains several steam presses, as well as a great number of hand presses. It possesses also fifty-six founts of letters, comprising all the known languages of the nations of Asia, and even the Assyrian cuneiform characters. The kings, queens, and knaves, as well as the ace of clubs, in a pack of cards, are printed here, this being a government monopoly, but the rest of the pack are printed by the card manufacturers themselves. The weight of type in use at this establishment amounts to 7,142 cwt. Besides the printing department, the various operations of binding are done here. When Pius VII. visited the office, the Lord's Prayer in 150 different languages was presented to him, and before he left, the same, bound up in a splendid volume, was placed in his hands.

The public is admitted to view the Imprimerie Nationale at 2 o'clock on Thursdays, by passport.

At the corner of the Rue Franc Bourgeois may be seen an elegant turret, near which the Duke of Orleans was murdered in 1407, by the Duke of Burgundy. This murder acquired a greater degree of importance from the long and bloody feuds which it gave rise to, and which disturbed France for several years, and finally led to the capture of Paris by the English.

Pursuing the Rues Franc Bourgeois and Neuve St. Catherine, we shall arrive on the

Place des Vosges, which was formerly called *Place Royale*. This place, surrounded with buildings of a uniform character, containing galleries of arcades, was built by Henry IV., on the place of the ancient Palais des Tournelles, or Palace of Turrets, so called from the numerous turrets that decorated it. This famous palace was occupied by Louis XII. and Francis I., but was destroyed in 1565 by order of Catherine de Médicis, in consequence of her husband, Henry II., having been killed whilst tilting with the Count of Montgomery in a tournament held in the great court. The present houses were commenced in 1602. The part separated by an iron railing from the street is planted with trees, and adorned with four fine fountains, encircled by prettily arranged flower gardens. In 1639 a bronze equestrian statue of Louis XIII. was erected here by the Cardinal Richelieu, but this, like that of Henry IV. on the Pont Neuf, was destroyed in 1792. During the empire a splendid fountain occupied its site, but, in 1829, the present statue in white marble was placed there.

The *Place des Vosges* derives its name from the circumstance that the government, during the first revolution, to stimulate the payment of taxes throughout the country, decreed that the Department which first paid up its assessments should be honoured by having its name given to one of the public places of Paris. The Department of the Vosges won that honour, and the *Place Royale* was changed into the *Place des Vosges*.

During the revolution of 1848, this place

was the scene of several severe conflicts between the troops and the insurgents.

In Rue des Tournelles, Boulevard Beaumarchais, is a richly ornamented *Synagogue.*

Passing out on the south side by the Rue des Vosges, we enter the eastern end of the Rue St. Antoine, celebrated in every revolution, and see on the left the **Place de la Bastille** and the *Column of July.* On this spot stood formerly the Bastille (or Bastile), in grounds which ran back to the river. On the 14th of July, 1789, the old fortress of the Bastille was taken by the people, and in the following year entirely demolished, when part of its materials were carried off, to assist in the construction of the Pont de la Concorde. The 14th July has ever since been observed as a national fête day. In 1831, it was agreed to erect a monument on this spot to the memory of those who had fallen during the Three Days, 27th, 28th, 29th July, and the present column was begun. It is erected on an archway built over the Canal St. Martin, and rests upon a basement of white marble, supported by blocks of granite.

The **Column of July** is of bronze, and of the Composite order. It is 154 feet high, and 12 feet in diameter. The weight of the metal employed amounts to 1,458 cwt.; the whole cost of erection to 48,000*l.* Upon the shaft are inscribed the names of 615 of those, who fell in the memorable conflict of July. Over the capital is a gilt globe, surmounted by a figure, also gilt, of the *Genius of Liberty.* He is represented standing with one foot on the globe, whilst his wings are outspread, as if ready for flight. The statue is by Dumont, the medallions on the basement by Marbœuf.

During the sanguinary days of June, 1848, the *Place de la Bastille* was the theatre of some of the most desperate struggles between the insurgents and the soldiers. At this end of the Rue St. Antoine the largest barricade was thrown up, and it was in attacking it that General Negrier was killed. It was at this barricade also that Archbishop Affre, who had come on his errand of peace, was struck down by a stray shot 1848. The houses on either side of the Place suffered greatly on the occasion, and were dreadfully riddled with balls. One of them, the *Belle Fermière,* which stood alone at the entrance of the Rue de la Roquette, was reduced to ashes by cannon balls and howitzers. In 1871, the Place was one of the positions of the Communists, and was only taken after a hard fight, 25th May. Vincennes Railway Station and many houses were burnt. The Column was saved from being blown up, for which preparations had been made in the vault below.

Taking an omnibus from the Place de la Bastille for the Barrière de Mont Louis, we shall arrive opposite the entrance of

PÈRE LA CHAISE, or the Cemetery of the East; so called from its being laid out on a piece of ground where formerly stood the house of Father la Chaise, the confessor of Louis XIV.; who is notorious as having persuaded that monarch to revoke the Edict of Nantes. Before his time, however, this spot was called *Champs l'Evêque,* because it belonged to the Bishop of Paris. It afterwards became the property of a wealthy grocer, who built a magnificent mansion on the hill, which was afterwards given to the Jesuits of the Rue St. Antoine, in whose possession it continued until the reign of Louis XIV. It then received the name of Mont Louis, and Père la Chaise was made superintendent of the institution. It was subsequently purchased and repurchased, passing through several hands, until M. Frochot, prefect of the Seine, bought it for the purpose of converting it into a cemetery, which was accordingly effected. In 1804 the ground was consecrated, and on the 21st May of that year the first grave made in it. It then contained 42 acres, but it has since been so considerably augmented that it covers upwards of 150 acres.

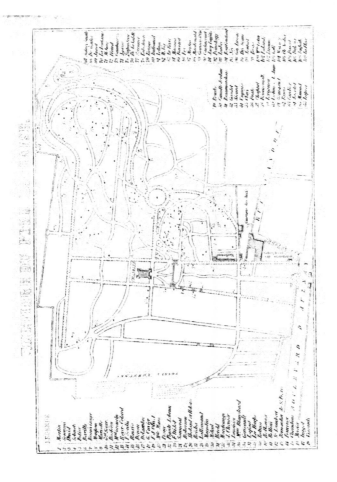

The hill on which Père la Chaise has been formed commands a fine view of Paris and the country beyond, and being tastily arranged and laid out, has become a place of universal attraction. The Communists were driven from a strong position which they held here, 27th May, 1871, when several tombs were injured. Many of the monuments possess great beauty and architectural elegance. The principal to be seen are the tombs of *Abelard and Héloise, Madame Demidoff, Casimir Périer, Lavalette, Boieldieu*, &c. The Cemetery is said to contain more than 50,000 funereal monuments.

The tomb of **Abelard and Heloise** lies to the right on entering. It consists of a rectangular chapel, built of materials brought from the Abbey of the Holy Ghost, which Abelard founded in the twelfth century, and of which Héloise was abbess. The length of it is fourteen feet, the breadth eleven, and the height twenty-four. Fourteen columns, with rich foliaged capitals, support trifoliate arches, surmounted by cornices wrought in flowers. The whole is Gothic. In the chapel is the original tomb built for Abelard by Pierre le Vénérable.

The monument to *Casimir Périer* is erected on a piece of ground given gratuitously by the city, as a mark of respect for their illustrious citizen, and consists of an excellent statue of that statesman placed on a high and profusely decorated pedestal.

The tomb of *Madame Demidoff* is a beautiful structure of white marble, elegantly ornamented, and adorned with ten Corinthian pillars, which support the entablature.

A pyramid of white marble, twenty-one feet high, and a bas-relief portrait of the marshal, point out the resting-place of *Massena*; and a little further on is an iron railing, which encloses the remains of his companion-in-arms, *Marshal Ney.* No other sign indicates the spot. Some passing hand has rudely traced the words, *sta viator, heroem calcas*, on the railing.

It would be impossible to enumerate or point out in these pages the various objects of interest, historical, &c., to be seen in this cemetery. A guide may be had for a small gratuity.

The following list, in addition to those already mentioned, will be found useful to visitors who only seek monuments of most prominent interest :—Arago; Auber; Balzac; Beaumarchais; Boieldieu; Barras, President of the Directory; Bellini, the composer; Béranger; Champollion, the Egyptian scholar; Cherubini, the composer; Gen. Clément-Thomas, shot by the Commune, 1871; Marshal Davoust Caulaincourt; Cambacérès; V. Consin; Cuvier; David d'Angers; Denon; Delille; Delavigne, the poet; General Foy; Madame de Genlis; Godoy, Prince of Peace; Geoffroy St. Hilaire; Marshal Grouchy; Lafontaine; Laplace; Labédoyère; Laffitte; Marshal Lefebvre; Gay Lussac; Molière; A. de Musset; Marshal Ney; Pozzo di Borgo; Garnier-Pagès; St. Pierre, author of "Paul and Virginia;" Racine; the Queen of Oude; Rossini (1868); Ledru Rollin; Abbé Sieyès; Scribe; Abbé Sicard; Admiral Sir Sidney Smith; Talma, the actor; Baron Taylor, aged 93 (1880); Ex-President Thiers, 1877; Visconti, the architect Volney, the philosopher. Madame Rachel, the actress; Rothschild, A. Fould, &c., are buried in the Jews' quarter, near the entrance.

In returning homeward, the visitor passes the *Prison des Jeunes Détenus* (House of Detention for Young Criminals), and the new *Bicêtre*, on opposite sides of the way, in the *Rue de la Roquette*. The latter is designed for convicts; and executions take place in front of it. Here above 60 persons, seized as hostages, including Archbishop Darboy, President Bonjean, and the Curé of the Madeleine, were shot by the Communists, 24-7th May, 1871. Not far from this is the *Abattoir Popincourt*, or Ménilmontant, one of the six or seven large public slaughter-houses with which Paris is supplied. On proceeding in another direction from Père la Chaise, you may go to the

Barrière du Trône and the *Château de Vincennes.* This Barrière constitutes the eastern entrance of Paris, as the Barrière de l'Étoile forms the western entrance. Two handsome Doric columns, nearly two hundred feet high, stand on either side of the gateway, and form a prominent object from any part of Paris. They were commenced in 1788, but remained unfinished until 1847. On the summits of these pillars, two statues, one of *Philippe le Bel*, by Dumont, and the other of St. Louis, by Etex, have been raised. The Barrière derives its name from the fact that, in the August of 1660, a throne was placed there, on which Louis XV. sat whilst he received the homage of the Parisians. Winding stair-cases lead to the galleries at the top of the shafts, from which a good view may be had. A great Gingerbread Fair is held here, two or three miles long.

About three quarters of a mile down the Avenue de Vincennes is the

Château de Vincennes, a fine old feudal fortress, which is well worth a visit, on the east side of Paris. It owes its origin to Philip Augustus, who surrounded the wood of Vincennes with thick walls, and built at this extremity a hunting seat. Louis IX. often visited this manor, and, at the foot of an oak close by, used to administer justice to those who brought complaints to him. Philip the Bold enlarged the forest by taking in several estates, and defended it by new enclosures. In 1337, however, Philippe de Valois ordered the hunting-seat to be destroyed, and the donjon, or high tower, now standing, to be erected. Charles V., who frequently made i his place of residence, built the Sainte Chapelle within its walls; Louis XI., ever suspicious, jealous, and cruel, turned it into a state prison, where he could delight himself by tormenting his victims, with the additional pleasure of the assurance that they could not easily escape from his hands. From this time till the reign of Charles IX., who came to die there, terror-stricken with remorse for the massacre of St. Bartholomew's Day, it was little frequented by the kings. Marie de Médicis ordered considerable embellishments to be made there, and her son, Louis XIII., continued new constructions at the southern extremity, which, however, were not finished until the reign of Louis XIV.

The Château may be considered as a specimen of the means of defence during the middle ages, as it is constructed on the best principles then known. Unfortunately, however, the nine square towers which flanked the fortress were destroyed in 1818, to place the buildings on the more advanced principles of modern fortification, so that the only one that remains intact is the Donjon. The château is constructed in the form of a parallelogram, of which the length is about a thousand feet, and its breadth six hundred. The donjon is surrounded by a thick wall, and a ditch 40 feet in depth. It is flanked by four turrets, which at each storey, forms a chamber with a fire-place in it. There are five storeys, and on the fourth an external gallery, from which a splendid view of the wood, the hills to the east of Paris, and Paris itself, may be enjoyed. The walls are 16 feet in thickness, and shew not the least sign of decay.

As we have said, the Donjon early became a state-prison, and from that time many illustrious victims have been immured within its walls. Amongst the most illustrious we may mention the Prince de Condé, whom Marie de Médicis seized and placed there, with the hope of thus prolonging her regency; the Marshal Ornano, who died there in 1621; the Duke de Vendôme, who was confined here for some time; Mirabeau, a considerable part of whose unhappy existence was passed here; the Prince Polignac; and lastly, the Duke d'Enghien, whose impolitic seizure and murder will leave a lasting stain on the character of Napoleon.

In the chapel is a monument, erected to the memory of the Duke, and in the eastern foss is a cypress tree, planted on the place where he was shot.

It will interest the English visitor especially to learn that in this donjon the brave and heroic Henry V., after being crowned King of France, died in 1420, and that his unfortunate son resided in it 1431-34. The Château is now one of the principal arsenals of France, and in a gallery on the eastern side is a fine collection of small arms. It was occupied by the Communists, May, 1871. The visitor may obtain admission to see the château by applying to *M. le Ministre de la Guerre*; open Saturday, 12 to 4. The *Asile Nationale de Vincennes*, on the outskirts of the forest, is established for convalescents who leave other hospitals, and for workmen who meet with accidents in erecting public edifices. It was opened in 1857, and sometimes accommodates upwards of 5,000 inmates.

The *Bois de Vincennes* makes part of a public park, of 2,190 acres, the most ancient one in France, and originally a Gaulish forest. Louis VII. surrounded it with a wall on the side of Paris, and built a Corps de Garde, which still remains. Louis XV. completely restored and replanted it, spending above a million livres on it. Under the Second Empire it was again renewed and turned into one of the great public promenades.

The principal objects of interest are :—1. The Lac des Minimes, covering a surface of 20 acres, with 3 islands. 2. The Cascade. 3. The Pelouses. 4. The Ruisseau de Nogent; the Mare; the Ruisseau des Minimes, near the Polygone d' Artillerie ; the *Camp de Saint Maur*, or Champ de Manœuvres ; the Fond de Beauté; the Ferme Napoléon, which is the theatre of new experiments in agriculture; the Lake of Gravelle; the Lake of Saint Maudé; the Artificial River; the Salle d'Escrime ; the Tir National, or National Rifle Ground; the École de Pyrotechnie; the Hippodrome in the Plaine de Gravelle, near the Gravelle and Faisanderie Redoubts. Nogent-sur-Marne, outside the Bois, is a good station for Fort de Nogent and for *Champigny*, where Trochu and Ducrot made a last desperate attempt to break the German line, 30th November and 2nd December, 1870.

The lakes of this wood are supplied by the Marne. The Bois de Vincennes embraces an area of 370 hetares (one hectare equal to two and a half acres) of forest, and 55 in clumps of trees and shrubs; 375 in meadow land, 56 in roads, and 20 in lakes and ornamental waters. The total length of the roads and alleys is 70,033 mètres (mètre=3ft. 3⅜in.), that of the canals 27,160 mètres, and the streams 9,900. About 5,500 metres of water are employed for watering the alleys, &c., and the supply of the ornamental waters.

An omnibus, leaving Vincennes, will take the visitor into the heart of Paris after he has examined the fortress ; or he may return by the branch railway on the Strasbourg line. If the route be by omnibus, *viâ* the Place de la Bastille, the reader will pass the Orphanage founded by the Empress in 1856; and the *Hôpital Ste. Eugénie*, to which she also gave her name—a Military Hospital, facing the Porte de la Tourelle. The former is richly endowed by means of a subscription raised in Paris as a present to the Prince Impérial, as well as by a grant from the late Emperor. The latter institution—a little to the left. in the Rue Charenton—is for sick children. On the route of the great boulevards, further on near the Rue Ménilmontant, is the *Cirque d'Hiver*, or Winter Circus, open from the 1st October to the 1st of April.

I

NINTH DAY.

FONTAINEBLEAU.
Open Daily (except Tuesday), 11 to 4.

STATION.—Chemin de Fer de Lyon, Boulevard Mazas. Trains start frequently throughout the day. Fares: 6fr. 60c.; 4fr. 95c.; 3fr. 65c. Near this station is the *Mazas Prison*, or *Nouvelle Force*, the French Model Prison, on the separate system, like Pentonville. It has undergone several important alterations in internal management (open by Ticket from the Préfect of Police). It superseded La Force, which was demolished in 1852. It is in this quarter also, that 18,000 square mètres of land have been bought by the Government, for building houses for persons of small means, which are afterwards sold to them by auction.

ONE of the most agreeable diversions for the visitor, is an excursion to Fontainebleau; and well does it repay the fatigue of the trip by the variety and beauty of the objects it presents. The town itself, prettily situated in the midst of the forest, is regularly built, with broad and fine streets, and from any point affords a striking picture of neatness and cleanliness. It contains 10,669 inhabitants, and is distant about 35 miles from Paris, up the Seine. It possesses a public library of upwards of 30,000 volumes, and an obelisk, erected in 1786, in commemoration of the birth of the children of Louis XVI. It is a subject of dispute from whence the place derives its name, but it is supposed that it comes from *Fontaine Belle Eau*, which was given to the spot as early as the tenth century, on account of the abundance of good water then found there.

The Château.—The present palace rose at different epochs, and we shall therefore not be surprised to find that it is in some respects irregular and heterogeneous. Louis VII. and Philippe Auguste were amongst the first who took up their abode here, and after them Louis IX. and his successors. The latter greatly enlarged and embellished the palace, but, by the time of Francis I., a part of the primitive building had fallen to ruin. This prince, however, who loved the site, had the Château nearly entirely reconstructed by the first architects of the age, who were even sent for from Italy. Henry IV. is said to have laid out more than two million pounds upon it, whilst Louis XIII. and Louis XIV. made considerable additions. Their successors, down to Napoleon and Louis Philippe, have also left traces of their affection for the spot, by various improvements and decorations.

The Château is full of historical associations, and was the scene of some tragical events. In 1539, Francis I. received the Emperor, Charles V., on his visit to France, in this palace, when great fêtes were given. In 1602 Marshal Biron was arrested here, and sent to the Bastille to be executed. In 1657, Christine, Queen of Sweden, had the Marquis of Monaldeschi assassinated in one of the apartments. Here, in 1685, Louis XIV. signed the Revocation of the Edict of Nantes, and in the following year the great Condé died at the age of sixty-six. Nearly eighty years afterwards died also, in this château, the Dauphin, the only son of Louis XV., and father of Louis XVI.; also Louis XVIII., and Charles X., of an illness supposed to have been caused by poison. In 1808 Charles IV., of Spain, who had been kidnapped by Napoleon was confined here 24 days; and, in 1812, Pope Pius VII. suffered the same fate here for nearly two years, being subjected to many threats and humiliations. In 1809 was pronounced here the declaration of divorce between the Emperor and Josephine; and on the 6th of April, 1814, Napoleon, after he had signed his abdication, bade farewell to his favourite Garde Impériale, in the Cour du Cheval Blanc, which, from that circumstance, has received the name of Cour des Adieux.

The Château of Fontainebleau covers nearly thirteen acres of land, without including the external dependencies, the garden, or the park. It is composed of five courts, the Cour du Cheval Blanc, the Cour de la Fontaine, the Cour du Donjon, the Cour des Princes, and the Cour des Cuisines, or de Henri IV., besides several buildings in different styles. The principal entrance is by the Cour du Cheval Blanc, or des Adieux, which is 300 feet in length by 100 in depth. On the right rises the wing of Louis XV., a long building four stories high; to the left extends the wing of Francis I., only one storey in height, formerly appropriated by the ministers of the court. At the bottom is the grand façade, the work of the architects, Vignole and Serlio. In the centre is the celebrated staircase, known as the Escalier en fer à Cheval, consisting of two flights of steps, and so called because it is in the form of a horse-shoe. It is also called the Escalier d'Honneur, and was built by Lemercier in the reign of Louis XIII. It was on these steps that the Emperor Napoleon stood, when he bade adieu to his faithful soldiers in 1814; and it was in this court that, in the March of the following year, he passed in review the troops he was about to lead to Paris and Waterloo.

The court derives its name of du Cheval Blanc from an equestrian statue in plaster, a copy of the horse of Marcus Aurelius, which was cast at Rome, and brought to this spot in 1650.

Behind the principal body of the building lies the Cour de la Fontaine, surrounded on three sides by the beautiful structures of Serlio, and containing a double staircase leading up to the Salle de Spectacle. In the middle is a basin, into which four grotesque heads pour water. From this court the visitor enters into the gardens, from which he sees the beautiful pavilion of Louis XIV. The Cour du Donjon follows immediately after, and is so called from the heavy and massive donjon built by Louis IX., which stands at one extremity of the court. Forty-five columns of grey freestone, with capitals quaintly sculptured, support the external balcony. The court is enclosed by a peristyle, pierced by a gateway, designed by Vignole, and surmounted by the graceful baptistery of Louis XIII., by Debrosses. Crossing the fosse on the other side, we arrive at the Cour des Cuisines, a vast and regular area of buildings, constructed in 1590 by Jamin, for the offices of Henry IV. The Cour des Princes is the smallest of the courts, and abutting upon it are the apartments formerly occupied by the Queen Christina. A Chinese Museum is to be seen here.

Having given a description of the plan of the Château, we will now enter its principal saloons, and point out whatever may be most interesting and curious for the visitor to notice. Entering then the Wing of Louis XV. from the Cour du Cheval Blanc the visitor passes through a suite of apartments formerly occupied by the sister of Napoleon, and afterwards by the Duchess de Nemours, and arrives at the Galerie des Assiettes or des Fresques, so called from 88 beautiful plates of Sèvres porcelain inserted in the walls, representing the principal objects connected with the history of Fontainebleau. It is also celebrated for the fine frescoes painted by Ambroise Dubois, which adorn its ceilings and wainscot. From this gallery a passage leads to the *Appartements de la Duchesse d'Orléans* (generally called *des Reines Mères*), the first salon of which was fitted up as an oratory by Pius VII., during his imprisonment in the palace: a small porcelain cabinet in a room belonging to the suite represents the arrival, reception, and marriage, of the Duchess with the late Duke of Orleans. Adjoining is the *Appartement d'Anne d'Autriche* (also styled *des Reines Mères*), composed of seven rooms richly decorated. On the ceiling of one of them, the gods of Olympus are represented in relief on gilt wood. In it Charles V. slept during his visit to Francis I., in 1539. The Grand Salon is remarkable for the profusion of arabesque ornament with which it is decorated. Passing by the *Salle du Billard*, we arrive at the vestibule, at the foot of the horse-shoe staircase, from which a door leads into the *Chapelle de la Sainte Trinité*, in which the marriages of Louis XV. and the late Duke of Orléans was celebrated. It was built after the designs of Vignole, in the reign of Francis I., on the site of the chapel erected there by St. Louis; but the decorations were not finished till the reign of Louis XIII. The fine paintings on the vault are by Freminet. The high altar is by Bourdonne. The six statues are by Germain Pilon; the Descent from the Cross by Jean Dubois.

Galerie de Francois I.—The gallery was embellished by order of the prince, whose name it bears, in 1530, and displays the richness of his taste. It is situated on the first floor, at the bottom of the Cour de la Fontaine. The ceilings and wainscoats are of oak and walnut, profusely sculptured and gilded. Fourteen large frescoes by Rosso and Primaticcio, surrounded by bas-reliefs in stucco, adorn the walls. The apartments occupied by Napoleon, and where he signed his abdication the 5th of April, 1814, are entered from the landing-place of the chapel by a staircase. There also is kept a fac-simile of the document, and the table on which it was signed. The bed-room of the emperor is in nearly the same condition as he left it. Passing through the *Salle du Consul* and the *Grand Chambre du Roi* the visitor is ushered into the *Appartements de la Reine*, consisting of four rooms, facing the garden of Diana. The *Chambre de la Reine* is most beautifully decorated, and was successively occupied by Marie de Médicis, Anne d'Autriche, Marie Antoinette, Marie Louise, the ex-queen of the French, Marie Amelie, and the Empress Eugénie.

The visitor will now be ushered into the *Galerie de Diane*, built by Henry IV., and decorated with some fine frescoes by Ambroise Dubois. It was nearly destroyed by the fall of the roof at the beginning of the present century, but in 1807 the rebuilding of it was commenced, after designs by Heurtant, and completed during the reign of Louis XVIII. The paintings on the ceilings are by Abel de Pujol and Blondel. From this gallery we pass on into the *Salons de Réception*, which are nine in number, decorated with a profusion of gilding and painting. These rooms are in the donjon or keep of the château, and form the oldest part of the building. It will be impossible to give a detailed description of them all: the principal of them to be observed are the *Salon des Tapisseries*, containing some fine old Flanders tapestry; the three *Salons de Francois I.*, with a beautiful chimney-piece attributed to Benvenuto Cellini; the *Chamber de Henri IV.*, decorated by Ambroise Dubois and Paul Bril; and the *Salle de Louis XIII.*, once occupied by that monarch, but since that time greatly altered. The ceiling is one of the most beautiful specimens of the kind. Adjoining this *appartement* is the *Salle de Spectacle*, established as a theatre by Louis XV., and capable of containing 600 spectators. It is sometimes used for concerts given by the garrison.

Returning to the *Escalier du Roi*, we shall enter the *Appartements de Madame de Maintenon*, fitted up for that celebrated personage by Louis XIV. In one of them the *Grand Cabinet*, the king signed the Revocation of the Edict of Nantes, and accepted the crown of Spain for his grandson from the Spanish deputies, an act which caused the long and bloody War of the Succession. After this comes the *Galerie de Henry II.*, built by Francis I., but decorated by Henry II., with great magnificence. This gallery which is the most splendid room in the château, is 120 feet long by 30 in width, and as many in height. It serves as a state ball-room. The champfering of the windows is nine feet in thickness. The walls are painted in frescoes by Primaticcio and Nicole, which were restored in 1835 by Alaux. Its beautiful chimney-piece is the work of the sculptor, Bondelet. This room, from the luxurious splendour of its fittings up, may be regarded as the finest in the palace.

Having visited the *Library*, formerly the *Haute Chapelle*, we descend to the *Chapelle de St. Saturnin* between the Donjon and the gardens, which has a peculiar interest for the English visitor, as having been consecrated by Thomas à Becket during his temporary exile in France. It has, however, been frequently restored and ornamented since its consecration in 1169. The subjects of the stained glass windows were designed by the late Princess Marie, daughter of Louis Philippe. From this we pass on to the *Galerie des Colonnes*, a vast salon built under the Galerie de Henri II., and corresponding with it. It is so called from the enormous columns of stucco by which it is ornamented. It was here that the religious part of the ceremony of the marriage of the Duchess of Orléans, according to the Protestant ritual, took place in 1837. Passing through the *Porte Dorée*, a gateway richly ornamented by Rosso and Primaticcio, we arrive at the *Vestibule de St. Louis*, which contains statues of the monarchs who mainly contributed to embellish or enlarge the château, from Louis VII. down to Henri IV., from which we enter twelve rooms called the *Petits Appartements*, in one of which is a painting representing the murder of Monaldeschi. An inscription under the window records the deed as having taken place near the spot. The visitor will now find himself, after quitting these apartments, in the *Vestibule de la Sainte Trinité*, with the *Cour du Cheval Blanc* once more before him.

Having made the round of the interior of the château, it will be expedient to lose no time in visiting the gardens. The *Jardin Anglais*, designed and planted by Heurtant, extends along the front of the château. Here the fine Chasselas Grapes are grown on long frames. There is also another garden laid out by Lenôtre, in the old fashioned style of gardening. Across the sward winds a little stream, which takes its source at the Fontaine Belle Eau, and falls into a pond, covering an area of eight acres, to the south of the Cour de la Fontaine. Beyond this is the *Park*, containing a great number of pleasant alleys and walks, and a magnificent cascade, which feeds a canal up, wards of a mile in length. In the waters of the garden are some fine fish, especially carp, which are kept until they become of an enormous size. But that which the visitor will probably be most anxious to see is the magnificent wood, or

Forêt de Fontainebleau.—The surest and most expeditious way is to hire a vehicle, a number of which are always ready, and to penetrate, under the guidance of the driver, into the heart of the forest. However, to those who would prefer it, there are always saddled horses at hand, and the advantage of these is, that paths may be pursued which it is impossible to follow on wheels. Whichever course the visitor adopts, expedition is necessary. The spots most frequented are the *Hermitage de Franchard*, where was formerly a large monastery, and near which is the *Roche qui pleure*, the waters of which were supposed to have miraculous powers of healing; the *Gorge de Franchard*, a wild and romantic place, consisting of a huge amphitheatre, covered with woods and rocks; the *Gorge d'Apremont*, more magnificent still, inasmuch as it is more extensive, and commands a fine view; the *Caverne des Brigands*, which is situated at the top of the gorge, and was dug about a century and a half ago by robbers, who infested the country.

and made this place, then almost inaccessible their retreat; and the *Valley of La Solle*, near which is the *Cliff of St. Germain*. The view from this spot is very beautiful, and of a softer character than that on the other side of the forest. Standing at the head of the valley, the eye ranges over a fine amphitheatre, covered with oaks and beech, and enclosing a plain, dotted with picturesque villages. The landscape is bounded by a long line of hills, far away beyond the hills that form this beautiful amphitheatre. At the *Cliff of St. Germain*, the stones are nearly all crystalised. One good point of view is at the Fort de l'Empereur. There are other places of great beauty to be seen,

but as it would be impossible to traverse every part of a forest containing nearly fifty-five thousand acres in one day, we have pointed out those spots which the visitor may request his guide to take him to. Half-way between Fontainebleau and the Gorge of Apremont, is a *carrefour* in the Forest from which several alleys branch off. It is remarkable for the height of the trees that surround it. One oak is especially worth noticing. It rises nearly eighty feet before throwing off a branch.

We will now suppose the visitor returned to Fontainebleau, where he may have an excellent repast at the Hôtel de Lyon, or at the Hôtel de Londres, and will only warn him that the last train for Paris usually leaves about 9 p.m.

TENTH DAY.

RUE ST. ANTOINE—ST. PIERRE ET ST. PAUL—FONTAINE ST. ANTOINE—HÔTEL DE SULLY—TEMPLE PROTESTANT—ARSENAL—GRENIER DE RÉSERVE—PONT D'AUSTERLITZ—JARDIN DES PLANTES—HALLE AUX VINS—MANUFACTURE DES GOBELINS.

WE wish this day, the tenth and last that we shall have especially to direct his steps, to guide the visitor to a part of the city he has not yet visited, and to two objects of considerable interest, the *Jardin des Plantes*, and the *Manufacture des Tapisseries des Gobelins*, which he has not yet seen. It will, therefore, be advisable for him to make his way to the Hôtel de Ville, behind which and the Caserne Napoléon, is the Rue St. Antoine. This street, besides possessing some fine specimens of domestic architecture of the middle ages, acquires great interest, from the political events of which it has been the theatre. It is also the centre of the Protestant quarter of Paris, and contains a large number both of Lutherans and Calvinists

On the right, as he descends, the visitor will see the *Lycée Charlemagne*, a college established on the site of an old Jesuit college, which was founded in 1582, and suppressed during the first revolution. Next to this is the Church of *St. Pierre et St Paul*, begun in 1627, and finished in 1641, in which year Cardinal Richelieu consecrated it in presence of Louis XIII. and his court. It is built on an elevated platform, approached by a flight of steps. The façade is decorated with three orders of architecture, placed one above the other, of which, the two lowest are Corinthian, and the upper Composite. The interior is embellished with architectural ornaments and sculpture, and the dome is fine.

Further, on at No. 143, is the *Hôtel de Sully*,

the mansion occupied formerly by that celebrated minister. It is a fine specimen of the time in which it was built, as it is still in good preservation. Proceeding further up the street, the visitor will come upon the *Temple Protestant*, or chapel belonging to the French Protestants, of the Calvinistic persuasion. It was built formerly by Mansard, for the Dames de la Visitation, whose convent was destroyed in 1789. Service is performed here every Sunday, in French, at half-past twelve.

Passing down the Rue Petit Musc, which is the first to the west of the *Temple Protestant*, we shall arrive at the *Rue de Sully*, in which is

The Arsenal.—On this site, the city of Paris established a depôt for artillery and munitions of war, in 1396, which afterwards became national property; but a fearful explosion having taken place in 1563, the building was reconstructed on a larger scale. Henri IV. also had it enlarged, and added a garden, and created the office of grand-master of the artillery, which he bestowed on Sully. Louis XIV. transferred the casting of cannon to the frontiers of his kingdom, so that the only use to which the present establishment was put, was that of casting statues for the gardens of Versailles, &c. It suffered from the Communists 1871.

It possesses, however, a very rich library, called the *Bibliothèque de l'Arsenal*, to which the public is admitted every day (Sundays and Fête days excepted), from ten to three. This library contains about two hundred thousand printed volumes, and six thousand three hundred manuscripts. The works are chiefly on history, foreign literature, and poetry, and it is especially valuable for its collection of Italian authors. It was formerly called Bibliothèque de Paulmy; being originally formed by the Marquis de Paulmy. Afterwards it was named *Bibliothèque de Monsieur*, having been purchased by Charles X., whilst Count of Artois; but since 1830 it has received the name of Bibliothèque de l'Arsenal.

The rooms in which Sully was accustomed to receive Henry IV. are still shewn. Apply with passport, to the director, at the bureau.

Passing down the Rue Morny (now Rue Pierre Charron), we arrive at the *Grenier de Reserve*, a building commenced by Napoleon, in 1807 His object in constructing this immense building, which is two thousand one hundred and sixty feet in length, was to have collected there a sufficient quantity of grain and flour to provide Paris for four months against the contingency of want. It was to have had five stories, besides cellars and attics. However, in 1814, the original plan being abandoned, it was divided into three stories. Four water channels, for turning mills, were also cut underneath the cellars. The government requires every baker to keep constantly twenty full-sized sacks of flour in this storehouse. The building is capable of containing one hundred thousand sacks. Its great usefulness was tested during the famine caused by the siege of 1870-71, but it was half ruined by the Communists in May, 1871. Appli- cation for admission must be made at the bureau, in the *Place de l'Arsenal*. Continuing down the Rue Crillon, towards the river, and taking the left, we arrive at the

Pont d'Austerlitz—a fine stone bridge, consisting of five very fine elliptical arches, supported by piers and abutments of stone, placed on piles. It was begun in 1801, and finished in 1807, at a cost of one hundred and twenty thousand pounds. Length, four hundred feet; breadth fifty-six feet. Its construction was undertaken by a company, who were to keep it in repair for seventy years, and receive toll during the same time. In 1848, however, the bridge was thrown open, free to foot passengers. From this bridge, looking westward, a fine view of the back of Notre Dame, the Hôtel de Ville, the Panthéon, and different parts of the city may be obtained. Looking up the river the eye follows it through Bercy, nearly to where the Seine joins the Marne. Opposite the Pont d'Austerlitz, is the principal entrance into the

Jardin des Plantes.—This botanical and horticultural garden was established by Louis XIII., in 1635, at the instigation of his physician, Guy de la Brosse, and contained then only seventy acres. Buffon, who was named superintendent of it in 1729, devoted himself to it, and enriched it by valuable additions. He collected here, from all parts, the most varied productions of nature, and established its museums, its galleries, and its hot-houses. All the dispositions of the gardens were his work. But, after him, the place languished until Bonaparte gave it a new impulse, and filled its flower-beds and museums with collections despotically brought from other countries. These were, however, restored in 1814, and the support of the gardens has been since provided for by an annual grant of the government. Here may be seen specimens of flowers, and shrubs, and trees, native or exotic, from the smallest bush to the gigantic cedar of Lebanon; besides a variety of birds, beasts, and fishes, which represent the different species of the animal kingdom. Some were killed for food in 1870-71, and the collection suffered.

Besides these gardens and collection of living animals, there are also museums of geology, botany, comparative anatomy, anthropology, and zoology; a fine scientific library, laboratories, and an amphitheatre, where lectures upon the different branches of natural history are delivered to the students of the University, or others whose tastes may induce them to pursue either of these studies. Everything is complete for the development of that science to which Buffon and Cuvier so largely contributed.

In the centre of the garden is a conical mound, on the summit of which is a pavilion, made of bronze, from which a fine view of this part of Paris, and the eastern environs, may be had. All the prominent objects which as seen from the Arc de l'Etoile were indistinct, now become clearly visible; and the columns at the Barrière du Trône, the towers and wood of Vincennes, the heights of Belleville, and the landscape towards Sceaux and Fontenay-aux-Roses, may easily be distinguished. On one of the pillars of the pavilion is a sun-dial, above which is inscribed the motto—"*Horas non numero nisi serenas.*" Half-way up the ascent, is the fine cedar brought from Lebanon by an English physician, and planted where it now stands, in 1734. The gardens are open every day from morning till sunset, but the animals can only be seen from eleven to three. The *Musée de l'Histoire Naturelle*, the *Musée de Mineralogie*, and the *Musée d'Anatomie*, are only to be seen on Tuesdays, Thursdays, and Saturdays, by the public. The bureau for tickets is near the *Musée d'Anatomie Comparative*. At the corner of Rue Cuvier is *Fontaine Cuvier*.

To the west of the Jardin des Plantes, is the **Halle-aux-Vins**, an extensive market for Wines and Brandies, covering above 100 acres. It was commenced by the order of Napoleon, in 1803, on the site of the ancient Abbey of S. Victor. The interior is composed of five large masses of building, divided into streets, called after the names of different wines, as Rue de Languedoc, Rue de Bordeaux, Rue de Bourgogne, &c. These buildings serve for magazines, cellars, and halls. It is estimated that the *Halle* may contain four hundred and fifty thousand casks, and sometimes as many as one thousand five hundred casks enter in one day.

One of the most interesting objects to be seen of its kind in Paris, and which we have left unavoidably to the last, is the

Manufacture des Tapisseries de Gobelins, Rue Mouffetard, No. 254, the reputation of which has long been universal. Much of it was burnt by the Communists, 25th May, 1871, and above seventy fine works were destroyd. What remains is open free, on Wednesday and Saturday, from 1 to 4; catalogue, 50c. The best way to reach it from the Jardin des Plantes s by taking the Rues

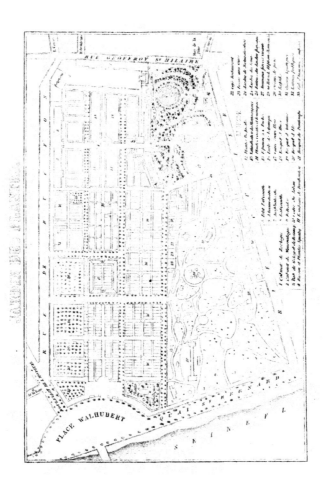

Geoffroy St. Hilaire, and Censier, the first of which runs at the back of the gardens. This manufactory was originated by John Gobelin, in 1450, who established here a celebrated dyeing factory. Afterwards his successors brought from Flanders the art of making tapestry—and in 1655 M. Gluck introduced the art of dyeing wool and cloths of a scarlet colour. Under Louis XIV. it received still greater development—the establishment became a *royal manufactory*, and the direction of it was given by the great Colbert to the celebrated painter Lebrun: from that time it has attained a very high degree of perfection. Lately the *Savonnerie*, so renowned for the richness and variety of its products in carpets, and originally founded by Catherine de Médicis, has formed part of the establishment.

On entering, the visitor is introduced into rooms which when complete were six in number, containing 25 looms. It is scarcely possible to conceive how, by the simple process of weaving, the effects of painting, with all its purity and fineness of colouring, may be reproduced, with almost perfect exactness. The carpets take sometimes from five to ten years in making, and cost from one thousand four hundred to six thousand pounds. The largest carpet ever made measured one thousand three hundred feet, and consisted of sixty-two pieces. Not more than six hundred and twenty workmen are employed in this manufactory, who earn from sixty to one hundred pounds a-year. When they are disabled by age and infirmities, they are allowed to retire on a pension of from twenty-four to forty pounds a-year.

In the same Rue Mouffetard is *St. Médard*, a church of the 15th and 16th centuries.

An omnibus will always be found outside the manufactory, which, by correspondence, will take the visitor to any part of Paris he may wish.

SUPPLEMENTARY DAY (A).

The Races of Paris.

MANY visitors to Paris who have a taste for sport or military pageants and illuminations will be pleased to have additional information relating to these matters.

Races and Steeplechases.—These have attracted much attention of late years in France, and received a great push from the Jockey Club, and the success of Count de Lagrange and Gladiateur.

The principal races are at the end of May and beginning of June. Three prizes are awarded by the Government, the best being reserved for the Autumn Meeting. The Great Paris Prize (Grand Prix) of 100,000fr. is given to the Spring Meeting. They are held at Longchamp, in the Bois de Boulogne, and Chantilly, beside a few other places.

Longchamp is only a short cab drive from Paris. Prices of seats:—Pavilion, 5fr.; interior of weighing house (enceinte du pésage) 20fr.; admission of pedestrians to ring, 1fr. The Circus of Longchamp has two courses, 92 feet wide; length, 6,175 feet. The display of fashion and toilettes on the grand stand in May is dazzling.

Chantilly.—40 kilomètres from Paris, Station in Paris, Place Roubaix. Trains, race-days, every 12 minutes.

Hotels at Chantilly: Swan; Lion; Grand Cerf, &c. Furnished rooms. Racecourse, 2,000 mètres. Prices: Pavilion, 5fr.; interior of weighing house (enceinte du pésage), 20fr.; Pedestrian admission to raceground, 1fr.

Chantilly is a beautiful spot in the heart of a great forest, and has several racing studs; St. Peter's English Church; and the seat of the Duke d'Aumale, at the *Petit Château*, a mediæval house, which stands on a lake, and contains a picture gallery, chapel, &c. Extensive gardens, well laid out, surround the house. All that remains of the *Grand Château*, in which Condé lived, is the fine stables, large enough for 180 horses. The rest was destroyed at the Revolution, 1789. Twelve roads branch from the Table Ronde in the forest. Races in May (Grand Prix) and October, when the French Derby and St. Leger are run.

Steeplechases are held at **La Marche,** near Ville d'Avray (rail to Versailles, Rive Droite). Course, 13,852 feet, broken with 24 obstacles. Admission for carriages to course: 20 to 15fr.; 5fr. for a horseman; 3fr. for pedestrians. Other Races are held at Auteuil, on Whit-Monday; at Le Vesinet, near St. Germains; and at Fontainebleau, in June and September.

One of the most amusing features of these steeplechases is the road, as on the Derby day near London. Those who do not care to go to La Marche should see the turns-out along the Avenue de l'Imperatrice (now Avenue Uhrich) going there, or returning thence at 5 or 6 p.m. The rope harnesses and bells with old-fashioned French postillions, mixed with smart English drags, are very amusing.

SUPPLEMENTARY DAY (B).

IF the visitor has a spare day, there are certain points of prominent interest in Paris that he should by no means overlook. The Institute, the Observatory, the Polytechnic School, and other scientific and literary institutions of the capital, are well entitled to attention in themselves, from their history, and the great men attached to them.

The charities of Paris are so noble and admirable that they ought not to be passed over. For surely the trophies of a pacific and humanitarian spirit are as well entitled to study and admiration as those that relate to a ruder, lower order of society, now fast passing away, in which war was the dominant idea and motive, and all that pertains to it matter of first interest.

The **Institute** (noticed page 48) is unique in Europe, from admitting into membership celebrities of all classes in literature and science. It is the senate of the combined wisdom of the republic of letters and science. The building of the Institute (Palais) was that erected with money left by Cardinal Mazarin, 1660, on the site of the Tour de Nesle, of infamous memory. It contains the *Bibliothèque Mazarine,* or Mazarine Library, containing 200,000 vols. and 4,000 MSS.; open 10 to 4, except Sundays. Napoleon I. was a member of the Institute, and fond of attending its sittings. One of its principal branches is the new *Académie Française,* of forty members, masters of style and eloquence. Its chief functions are the discussion of literary excellence, and the distribution of prizes in poetry, history, eloquence, and acts of virtue. The income of the Academy is 88,000f. Napoleon III., in 1860, gave the prize of 20,000f. to the most useful work. The Academy voted it to M. Thiers for his *History of the Empire,* and M. Thiers gave

the same back to the Academy. Open 12 to 4, except Sundays. For the Observatory, see page 51, and the Sorbonne, page 54.

The **Polytechnic School** is just behind the Church of St. Etienne du Mont, in a building given to it, 1805 (The College de Navarre). The school was founded 1795. A donation of 72,000fr. a year was made to it. The pupils were to pay 500fr. a year, and be subject to military discipline. The prescribed course of study is two years, but the preparatory years to fit one to enter amount to five. The examination for entry is difficult, and the professors are scientific celebrities.

The **Charities** of Paris are as numerous as its demands. The gay capital could not suffer the public eye to be saddened with the sight of public misery and distress, as in London. La Mendicité is forbidden in the department. In London it has the workhouse; in Paris, the prison. Yet private and public charities have done much to alleviate misery in the French metropolis.

A visit to *Charenton Lunatic Asylum* is instructive and impressive. The management is admirable, and the celebrated soirées of the lunatics are quite a feature of the institution. In Paris there are 40,056 households, or 101,570 persons, succoured by charity. The sum devoted to charity by the Budget de l'Assistance Publique is above twenty million francs.

Almost all the French hospitals are served by nuns of three orders: Les Sœurs Augustins, Hôtel Dieu, de la Charité, de Saint Louis; the Sœurs Jansenistes, la Pitié, Beaujon and Ste. Antoine; the Sœurs de la Charité, Ste. Eugénie, Necker, and les Enfants Assistés. The following table will show the number of those assisted in 1864 in the principal Paris hospitals:—

	Admitted	Died.
Hôtel Dieu	11,968	1,419
Pitié	8,735	1,065
Charité	7,079	730
Saint Antoine	9,953	1,188
Necker	5,647	746
Cochin	1,569	175
Beaujon	6,590	633
Lariboissière	9,796	1,228

The **Hospitals** of Paris are divided into two classes, general and special. Of the latter class, are the Accouchement, Rue Port Royal; Incurables (Femmes), Rue de Sèvres, 42; Incurables (Hommes), Rue Popincourt. Hospice (or Refuge) de la Vieillesse (Femmes), or *La Salpêtrière*, Boulevard de l'Hôpital; and a similar one for men, or the *Bicêtre*. The Salpêtrière (on a site of a Saltpeter factory), was founded 1656; and is a collection of 45 houses, 1,680 feet long, with room for 5,200 women, including lunatics. The Bicêtre, also founded 1656, is at Gentilly, near Fort Bicêtre, and occupies a square, 900 feet each way, with room for above 2,000 old men. Some other charitable institutions were founded at the following dates: Charenton Lunatic Asylum, by Sebastian Leblanc, 1641; the Accouchement was founded by the Convention, 1795; La Pitié, founded in 1612; Hôtel Dieu, the greatest of all, behind Notre Dame, and the oldest in Paris, said to have been founded in the seventh century, by Bishop Landry; La Charité, by Mary of Médicis, 1602. *Blind Institution* (Institution Nationale des Jeunes Aveugles) 56, Boulevard des Invalides; for 200 to 300 children; open on Wednesdays and Saturdays, 1-30 to 5; or by application to Director. It has a printing office, sale room, and chapel. Founded 1784, by V. Hauy.

Deaf and Dumb Institution (Institution des Sourds-Muets), 224, Rue St. Jacques, near the Luxembourg. Founded 1720, by the Abbé de l'Epée, whose bust is here. It contains about 200 boys and girls.

At Porte Maillot is the new *Hertford Hospital* for English patients, founded by the benevolent Sir R. Wallace, Bart., as a memorial of the late Marquis of Hertford, who bequeathed to him a large fortune.

At 77, Avenue Wagram, is *Miss Leigh's Mission Home for Young Englishwomen*, containing nearly 80 beds; with a Sanitorium, and a Crèche for infants, as well as a Soup Kitchen (at No. 79) for the poor, which is open in winter. Connected with these is a *Free Reading Room and Young Women's Christian Association*, for English girls employed in Paris, at 88, Faubourg St. Honoré. Also an *English Orphanage*, at 35, Boulevard Bineau, Neuilly, for poor English left orphans, the gift of Mr. Galignani, 1876; open 2 to 4. Hon. Physician to both Homes, Dr. Bishop, 99, Rue de Mornay. Near the Orphanage is *Christ Church*, a new building which holds about 500 persons, with Schools attached. Service at 11 and 3-30.

The suburb of Levallois-Perret (now built over) in this quarter, between Neuilly and Clichy, takes name from M. Levallois, who erected the first house here, in Rue de Courcelles.

In Rue Montmatre is a *Young Men's Christian Association*.

Miss Broen's Mission is at Belleville, 21, Rue Piat.

Baron Haussmann, the famous Prefect of the Seine, opened, in 1866, an admirable institution for the reception of lunatics, and the industrial treatment of imbeciles. It is the *Asile Clinique*, near the Boulevard St. Jacques, with accommodation for 500 lunatics, occupied in agricultural work. Nothing can be better than the organisation of this establishment. The bathing arrangements are quite a model. In Rue Bodier is the *Museum of Aerostation* (Baloons); open on Thursdays, 2 to 6, free.

ENVIRONS OF PARIS.

To make the work more useful, we subjoin a few of those spots in the neighbourhood o Paris, which, if the stranger have time, will amply repay a visit. To each belongs its peculiar feature of attraction.

Asnières.—This place is situated on the left bank of the Seine, about five miles from Paris, and contains about 6,000 inhabitants. It is the summer residence of many wealthy Parisians. The park of Asnières is celebrated for its gay amusements, fireworks, illuminations, concerts and balls, on Sundays and fête-days. Boat-racing, a sport which is becoming much in vogue with the French people, also takes place here. It is reached by the Chemin-de-fer de St. Germain, Place du Havre. It suffered in the war of 1870-1. The sewage of the City is discharged into the river near this spot, but there is a project for transporting it to the great plain of Jeuneville.

Belleville.—This place, situated on the hills to the north-east of Paris, is much frequented on Sundays. From it may be obtained a fine view of the city. It lies just outside the barrier-walls. Omnibuses will take you there. It was the head-quarters of the Red party and the supporters of the Commune, 1871. Here is the *Park of Les Buttes-Chaumont*, a creation of the last few years, by which an unhealthy corner of Paris has been converted into an agreeable place of recreation. The stranger visiting Paris, and wishing to see it, must go from the centre of Paris towards the Porte St. Martin, and follow the Faubourg St. Martin; cross the Boulevard de la Villette, and follow the Rue Puebla, which will take him direct to one of the principal gates of the Park.

The area of the Park is estimated at 24 hectares, about equal to that of the Tuileries. Its gates, six in number, are open at 7 a.m. and shut at night. The principal gates are—1. At La Petite Villette, near the Protestant Church. 2. Rue Fessard (Petite Villette). 3. Rue Puebla, near Rue Pradier, Belleville. 4. Boulevard A (opposite Rue Fessard), Belleville. 5. Rue de Crimeé. 6. Rue de Meaux.

The Park is under the care of gardiens in uniform.

On entering the Park by the Port of Rue Puebla the visitor soon reaches an eminence, Mont Puebla (the highest in the Park), commanding an extensive view of Paris and its Monuments, of the Canal de l'Ourcq, St. Denis, and a distant horizon.

The Park is under the care of gardiens in uniform; and is intersected by a number of alleys winding among flower-beds, arranged with the taste peculiar to the French, and among lawns of green turf, covering what was lately an unsightly waste. Nor are trees wanting, some of considerable size, Parisians having the art of transplanting full-grown trees in the most successful manner. M. Alphand was the principal engineer by whose designs these happy results have been achieved. One of the principal attractions of the Park is a Lake, enlivened by the presence of a number of waterfowl, and by a cascade, and adorned with a Sibyl's Temple on an island.

Excellent carriage roads lead all round the Park, and the Paris *Metropolitan Railway*, or Chemin de Fer de Ceinture, has a station close to the lake.

This line has only one class of carriages, with one price according to distance.

The precincts of the Park were formerly occupied by knackers' yards, depôts of night-soil, reservoirs of urate, where desiccated night-soil was prepared to be delivered over to farmers and agriculturists. The late Emperor did much in reclaiming and transforming it.

The finest point of view in the Park is enjoyed from the Terrasse (aux Mamelons), with a balustrade of 60 pillars and a length of nearly 400 feet. This place commands a very extensive prospect. Close at hand, and underneath you, are the Lake, the Sibyl's Temple, and the whole Park. Further off are Paris, with its numerous buildings; La Petite Villette and its Protestant Church, and La Grande Villette; the large *Abattoir* (Slaughter House) of *La Villette*, on a space of 67 acres; the Paris *Cattle Market*, ⅜ mile square, on the plan of the City of London; and the *Entrepôt des Blés* (Granaries). These adjoin the Canal de l'Ourcq and its basins Beyond, are Montmartre; and Saint Denis and its Cathedral.

Further in the distance appear numerous towns, villages, military forts, châteaux, and hamlets, woods, and forests, and lastly ranges of hills forming the horizon, which extend from right to left over a space of 30 miles, in five or six different Departments.

Bois de Colombes is a pretty little village near Asnières, near a railway station (de l'Ouest). There are some lovely walks. A fête is held every year, commencing about the 5th of June, and lasting a fortnight.

Bougival, situated on a hill rising above the Seine, in a romantic spot. The road leading from Bougival to Louveciennes is very picturesque, and on either side may be seen numerous country seats, amongst them the Château of Madame Du Barry, the Château of the Count Hocquart, and the Château de la Jonction. It is 7 miles from Paris, and contains 1,400 inhabitants. Route—Chemin-de-Fer de St. Germain.

Compiegne, 53 miles from Paris, by the Northern Rail. An old château, near the Forest, containing a *Musée Cambodgien* (of Buddhist remains), a Gallo-Roman Museum, pictures and furniture. Open, 11 to 4. *Pierrefonds Castle*, a fine restored mediæval work, is 9 miles distant.

Enghien —About the same distance from Paris as Bougival, reached by the Northern Rail. It is situated on the borders of a lake, whose mineral waters have long been celebrated. This lake is very beautiful, and surrounded with pretty cottages and bowers. Route—Chemin-de-Fer du Nord. Close to Enghien, on a hill, is the favourite resort of Montmorency.

Fontainebleau—page 74.

St. Germain-en-Laye or **St. Germain's.**—Down the river, 15 miles from Paris, by rail. Pop., 14,283. It would be a great omission to fail in visiting this town, so celebrated as it is for its historical associations, and the beauty of the scenery. Before the eleventh century there was no other habitation in the vast Forest that covered this spot than a small chapel, dedicated to St. Germain. This was enlarged into a monastery, and in the 12th century, Louis le Gros erected a château near it. This château was destroyed by the English, in 1346. It was rebuilt, but several times plundered by the English and Armagnacs, after which, it was left neglected until Francis I., taking a fancy to the spot, repaired the château, and celebrated his marriage there. Henry II., however, laid the foundation of a new château, to which Charles IX. and his Court retired from the religious disturbances of the city. Henry IV. and Marie de Médicis took up their residences in the new building, whilst the old was repaired and fitted up, by the king's orders, for the beautiful Gabrielle d'Estrées. The magnificent Terrace, from whence so extensive a prospect may be obtained, was laid out during this reign. Louis XIII. used St. Germain as his favourite residence, as did, likewise, Louis XIV., until the Château of Versailles was ready for his reception. After this, the Palace found an occupant in the dethroned King James II., to whom it was allotted by his generous patron. During the revolution of 1789 it was divided into the residences of private individuals, and during the first empire became a cavalry barrack; after the restoration it was occupied by a company of the life-guards; it is now used as a *Museum* of Gallo-Roman antiquities; open Sundays, Tuesdays, and Thursdays; 11 to 4.

The *Terrace*, celebrated for the magnificence of its view, is nearly three miles long, and looks down upon the winding Seine. Behind this commences the noble Forest of St. Germain. The only remains of the Château Neuf, as it is called, is a tower in which Louis XIV. was born, now converted into a restaurant, under the name of the *Pavillon of Henry IV*. In the church, on the *Place de Château*, is a monument erected by the late King George IV., to the memory of James II. It stands in a small chapel near the doorway, to the right on entering, which has been restored by Queen Victoria. The Theatre, in Place du Théâtre, was fitted up by Alexander Dumas.

M. Thiers died at St. Germains, 1877. It was occupied by the Germans in 1870. A part of the railway from Pecq to St. Germain is on the atmospheric principle. Station, Place du Havre. At *Vésinet* Station is a pretty Park, with a Working Men's Hospital, or *Asile de Vésinet*, on a site of 100 acres, founded by Napoleon III.

Joinville.—Situated about six miles from Paris, and commanding a fine view of the Marne. The road to it lies through Vincennes and the woods of Vincennes and Joinville. Omnibuses from the Place de la Bastille.

Montmartre.—Montmartre, or Buttes de Montmartre, is now a part of Paris, within the new barrière. It derives its name Montmartre, or Mons Martyrum, from the execution of St. Denis and his companions, which took place here. Its great height above the city makes it a favourable point from which to obtain a *coup d'œil* of the streets and public buildings of Paris. Here the Communists began the rising against the Government by taking the cannon, 18th March, 1871, when the 88th regiment fraternised with them, and after killing Generals Thomas and Lecomte. A large monumental Church is in progress at this point. In a valley to the west of the hill is situated the *Cemetery of Montmartre*, which may rival in the beauty of its position the Cemetery of Père la Chaise. It contains, too, the remains of several celebrated personages. An auxiliary Cemetery is open at Méry-sur-Oise, 15 miles by rail.

Neuilly.—About a mile and a half beyond the Barrière de l'Etoile stands the village of Neuilly, on the left bank of the Seine. It is elegantly built, and of rather modern date. From the bridge which crosses the river, a fine view may be had of its islands, and the country seats that line its banks. The principal object, however, to be seen is the Château de Neuilly, situated in a beautiful park, sometime the residence of Louis Philippe and his family. The palace was built in the reign of Louis XV., when, and until the revolution, it belonged to private individuals. After that time it passed to M. Talleyrand; then to the Prince Murat and the Princess Borghese; and finally to Louis Philippe. In February, 1848, it was nearly destroyed by a mob, who left Paris, and breaking into it, gave themselves up to all kinds of riot, and drunkenness. Many houses were destroyed in 1870.

About half a mile from the Arc de l'Étoile, on the road to Neuilly, near the Porte Maillot, is the chapel *St. Ferdinand*, erected by the late King of the French to the memory of the Duke of Orleans; not far from the spot where that unfortunate prince was accidentally killed July, 1842, by being thrown out of his carriage, when the horses took fright. The room in which he died is now the sacristy. Opposite the door is Jacquand's picture of the Duke on his Death-bed, surrounded by his relatives and friends. Amongst the group of statuary are two figures, beautifully executed in marble, by Marie, the lamented sister of the duke.

St. Ouen, situated 5½ miles from Paris, by omnibus, on the right bank of the Seine, which is spanned by a bridge, erected 1857. It was here that King Dagobert is supposed to have fixed his residence. In 1482, Louis XI. annexed the royal property here to the Abbey of St. Denis, that its monks might pray for a prolongation of his life. It should be observed that the superstitious monarch died the next day. The château, from this time, passed through various hands, until it became the residence of Madame de Pompadour, who expended considerable sums in embellishing it. In 1814, Louis XVIII. sojourned here the evening before his entry into Paris, and signed the declaration called the Declaration of St. Ouen. An ice-house, with large storehouses for corn, is established in this town.

Close by is another château, formerly the property of M. Necker, where his daughter, the celebrated Madame de Stael, was born.

Rueil.—About 10 miles from Paris, by rail. It is situated at the foot of a hill, covered with vines and fruit trees. It was here that Cardinal Richelieu had his residence during the stormiest period of his political career. Near to Rueil is the palace of *Malmaison*, so closely and dearly associated with the name of Josephine. In the Norman church of this village (where a beautiful monument is erected to her memory) the empress lies buried. The church also contains Napoleon III.'s monument to his mother, Queen Hortense.

Sceaux.—By rail. Sceaux (pron. "So)"

offers few of the attractions it did formerly. A Château was built here by the celebrated Colbert, embellished with sculptures by Pujet and Girardon, and surrounded by a garden laid out by Lenôtre. This château was purchased in 1700 by the Duke de Maine, who enlarged and adorned it at an immense cost. As he and his son were men of enlightenment and taste, this château became the resort of the most distinguished literary men of the age, as well as of the most fashionable society of Paris. The revolution of 1798 put an end, however, to the splendour and magnificence of this establishment, the building was destroyed, and the grounds suffered to run to waste. Recently the Maire of the place has purchased the park for the use of the inhabitants, and here several fêtes and festivals are held. It was the residence of Florian, the novelist, who is buried here; and has a Cattle Market and glass factory.

The railway from Paris to Sceaux is an experimental one. The object is to ascertain in how small a curve, and up how steep an ascent, a train may be conducted. The visitor will, therefore, be surprised to find himself winding up a steep hill, and turning very sharp angles, but he need be under no apprehension, as though the result has not been satisfactory for general purposes, the transit has been proved to be safe.

About a mile beyond Sceaux is a restaurant situated in a wood, called *Robinson*. To this place vast numbers of the Parisians flock. The principal attraction is a Chestnut Tree sufficiently large to hold two pavilions, and upwards of 15 or 16 persons. From these pavilions, in which the visitor may dine, an extensive view of Paris and the intervening country may be had. Throughout the gardens numerous bowers and seats are distributed.

Route. Chemin-de-Fer de Sceaux, Barrière d'Enfer.

CONTINENTAL HOTELS, &c.

AIGLE.

GRAND HOTEL DES BAINS D'AIGLE.
CANTON DE VAUD (Switz).

SITUATED 20 minutes from the Station, at the entrance of the "Vallée des Ormonts," healthy position, large Park and charming Promenades and Environs. Baths of all kinds. Moderate charges. Omnibus at the Station. **E. MESNER** Manager.

AIX-LA-CHAPELLE.

HOTEL DU GRAND MONARQUE.
DREMEL'S HOTEL.

THIS Magnificent and Large Hotel for Families and Single Travellers, continue to maintain its European reputation for being the favoured residence of Travellers of all nations. The Proprietor, Mr. FRITZ DREMEL, obtained this unusual patronage by the extreme cleanliness and the comfort of his apartments, the richness and excellence of the viands and Wines, added to the attention and civility of the attendants. Table d'Hôte at 2 and 6 o'clock.

Hotel Nuellens.—Proprietor, Mr. G. F. DREMEL, opposite the fountain Elisa, and situated in the most fashionable part of the City, has great attractions to Tourists and Travellers. This House possesses excellent accommodation for single persons or large Families, and the Cuisine department will afford satisfaction to the most fastidious taste. *Extract from the 18th Edition of Murray's Handbook.*—"This Hotel, in the best situation, is recommended as capital." Table d'Hôte at 6 o'clock.

Kaiserbad Hotel.—Bains de l'Empereur. This new and splendid Bath establishment has been recently fitted up in the most comfortable and elegant manner. The principal spring of Aix rises in the Hotel itself.

The Neubad Hotel.—(New Bath attached to the Hotel also belongs to Mr. DREMEL; it has extensive accommodation, 1879).

Mr. DREMEL, the well-known Landlord of the "**Grand Monarque,**" "Neubad," and "Nuellens" Hotels, is also Proprietor of the "Kaiserbad Hotel," and personally superintends the Management of the four establishments. Mr. DREMEL spares no expense or efforts to render the accommodation of these superior first-class Hotels preferable to all others. The combination in one hand of four Establishments of such magnitude, enables the Proprietor to afford suitable accommodation **at all Prices.**" These establishments are especially arranged for Winter Cures.

HOTEL DU DRAGON D'OR, CARL ROHMER, Proprietor.—This large and well-known Establishment, close to the Kursaal, and opposite the principal Bath Houses, has an excellent reputation for its general comfort, cleanliness, superior accommodation, and very moderate charges. The Proprietor lived several years in England. Table d'Hôte at 1 and 5 o'clock. Carriages at the Hotel. Arrangements for the Winter season from the 1st October.

HOTEL DU NORD.
Just Opposite the Rhenish Railway Station.
EXTREMELY CLEAN AND COMFORTABLE. EXCELLENT COOKING. Moderate Charges. English Newspapers.
(The Proprietor lived many years in England.)

AIX-LES-BAINS.

GRAND HOTEL D'AIX, kept by M. GUIBERT.—First-rate establishment, admirably situated near the Casino, the Public Garden and the Thermal Establishment, **Omnibuses at the Railway Station.**

ANTWERP.

NOTICE TO TRAVELLERS ON THE CONTINENT.
HOTEL DE L'EUROPE, PLACE VERTE.
FIRST-CLASS HOTEL. Central Situation. Excellent Table d'Hôte. Wines of the best Vintages. Great attention paid to Visitors. Moderate charges. Baths.

HOTEL ST. ANTOINE.
SPACIOUS HOUSE OF FIRST ORDER, UNDER NEW MANAGEMENT,
PLACE VERTE.
COACH-HOUSE AND STABLING.

HOTEL DE HOLLANDE (STROOBANT'S), Rue de l'Etuve, close to the London and Hull Steamboat Wharf. This Hotel, being now entirely under a new management, and being newly fitted-up with great comfort, is recommended to English travellers, who will find every convenience Choice Wines of the best Vintages. English daily and weekly newspapers. Every attention is paid to travellers by the landlord. Mr. STROOBANT, who speaks English. and being well acquainted with the Continent, can furnish every information required. Table d'Hôte at half-past twelve and five o'clock. Private dinners at any hour.

HOTEL DE LA PAIX, Rue des Menuisiers,
Opened the 1st May, 1869.
THIS HOTEL, formerly the HOTEL DES PAYS BAS, has been entirely re-built and newly furnished.

HOTEL DU COMMERCE,
Rue de la Bourse, close to the Exchange and Place de Meir.
E. COLLIN, Proprietor.
Second-Class Hotel, entirely re-built and newly furnished.

ARNHEIM, HOLLAND.

GRAND HOTEL DU SOLEIL.
THIS magnificent well known First-class Establishment, situated in the most delightful part of the Town, is highly recommended to English and American Travellers.

HOTEL DE BELLE VUE.
ONE of the finest Hotels in Holland, situated near the Railway Station, and the banks of the Rhine. Table d'Hôte. Baths. Good Stabling.

ARONA.

HOTEL D'ITALIE, AND DES POSTES.
THIS Hotel is not very large, but beautifully situated opposite the Lake. The proprietors, Messrs. ZANETTA, are very civil and obliging. Moderate charges.

BLOIS.

GRAND HOTEL DE BLOIS.

Very comfortable Table d'Hote and private Dinners.

APARTMENTS FOR FAMILIES.

Close to the Castle of Blois. Comfortable Carriages for visiting Chambord and the Environs.

BOLOGNA.

GRAND HOTEL BRUN,

W. WELLER & CO., Proprietors.

First-rate accommodation for Families and single Gentlemen.
THE GRAND HOTEL FEDER, TURIN, is kept by the same Proprietors.

GRAND HOTEL D'ITALIE.

FIRST-CLASS Establishment, newly re-fitted up. All the attendants speak English and French. Baths.

GIUSEPPE NICOLA, Proprietor.

HOTEL PELLEGRINO.

GOOD Second-Class Hotel, in a central situation. Recommended to Single Gentlemen and Families who desire to combine economy with good accommodation. Omnibus to all Trains.

BONN.

THE GOLDEN STAR HOTEL.

THIS first-rate and unrivalled Hotel, patronised by the English Royal Family, the English Nobility and Gentry, is the nearest Hotel to the Railway Terminus, and to the landing-places of the Rhine Steamboats. The Proprietor, Mr. J. SCHMIDT, begs leave to recommend his Hotel to English Tourists. The Apartments are furnished and carpeted throughout in the best English style, and the charges are moderate. Apartments during the Winter at moderate prices. The London *Times* and *New York Herald* taken in during the whole year. Six excellent Pianos to be found in the different Sitting-rooms.

GRAND HOTEL ROYAL.—This excellent Hotel, one of the best on the Continent, patronised by H.M. the King Leopold of Belgium, and by the Royal Family of England, is admirably situated on the banks of the Rhine, and commands the most beautiful view of the Seven Mountains.

H. ERMEKIEL, Proprietor.

BREMEN.

HOTEL DE L'EUROPE.—C. A. Schulze, Proprietor.   One of the best
Hotels in the north of Germany, on the Boulevards, close to the Station, Post-office, and
Exchange.
                    Omnibus to and from every Train.

BRUCKENAU.

15 Kilometres from Tossa Station (Elm-Gemuenden Line), 3¾ Miles from the Baths of Kissingen.

CASTEL HOTEL (Schosshotel).

FIRST-CLASS ESTABLISHMENT, with a beautiful view of the Rhone.
                    Well lighted and airy Bedrooms.

BRUGES.

HOTEL DE FLANDRE.—The established reputation of this old Hotel is
the best guarantee to the travelling public.

                    ROSZMANN-SCHUPP, Proprietors.

GRAND HOTEL DU COMMERCE, near the Grande Place and the
Railway Station. This first-class Establishment, the largest and oldest in the town, offers to
Families very good accommodation, excellent cooking, and good wines.

                    Proprietor, Mr. VANDENBERGHE.

BRUSSELS.

HOTEL DE L'EUROPE,
PLACE ROYALE, BRUSSELS,
IN A FINE, OPEN, AND HEALTHY SITUATION,
FOR FAMILIES AND GENTLEMEN.

Excellent accommodation and moderate charges, civility and attention, recommend this
Hotel to the esteemed patronage of English and American visitors. Most of the rooms
overlook the Place Royale and the Park. Families or Gentlemen can pre-engage rooms
by letter or telegram.

Table d'Hote at 6 o'clock.   Dinners at any Hour.
ENGLISH SPOKEN.

CANNES Continued.

CARLSRUHE.

HOTEL GERMANIA.

SITUATED a few minutes from the Railway Station, on the Public Gardens. First-Class Hotel.

JOSEF LEERS, Proprietor.

CASTELLAMMARE.

HOTEL QUISISANA.
NICOLA SOLDINI, Proprietor.

BEAUTIFULLY situated in its own grounds on the Hill in front of the Royal Palace of Qui-si-sana (here is health) ov rlooking Vesuvius and the Bay. Full South. First-Class House, highly recommended by English and American families for its **pure air.** Best centre for excursions to Vesuvius, Pompeii, Capri, Amalfi, Paestum, and Sorrento. Carriages, saddle Horses, Donkeys, and Guides attached to the Hotel. English Newspapers, and Billiard Room. Arrangements for Families. Winter Pension from 8 frs. a day.

(The Hotel d'Angleterre, Sorrento, belongs to the same Proprietor.)

CHALONS-SUR-MARNE.

HOTEL DE LA CLOCHE D'OR.—Kept by E. JAUNAUX ERNEST, Proprietor and Director. This Hotel has always been recommended for its great comfort. Table d'Hôte and Restaurant.

CHAMBERY.

HOTEL DE L'EUROPE.
17, RUE D'ITALIE, 17.

FIRST-CLASS HOTEL, entirely re-furnished, patronised principally by Families and Tourists. Great facilities for visiting the "Grande Chartreuse."

CHAMOUNIX (Mont Blanc).

HOTEL AND PENSION DES ALPES.
J. KLOTZ, Proprietor.

MAGNIFICENT View of the whole Chain of Mont Blanc. Landlord and Landlady both speak English, French, and German.

CHAUMONT (near Neuchatel, Switzerland).

HOTEL AND PENSION DE CHAUMONT, PRES NEUCHATEL (SUISSE). Kept by C. RITZMANN, Proprietor of Hotel Suisse, Cannes. Beautiful spot for a Summer séjour, situated 1000 mét. above the level of the Sea. Milk cures.

COLOGNE.

HOTEL DISCH,

IN BRIDGE STREET.

THIS first-class well-known Hotel is most centrally situated close to the
Cathedral, the Central Railway Station for Berlin, Paris, Brussels, Calais, and Bonn Railways,
the Quay of the Rhine Steamers, the new Tubular Bridge over the Rhine, &c. Superior accommodation
and comfort will be found here for Families, Tourists, and Gentlemen passing through
Cologne, *en route* to or returning from the Rhine, the North of Germany, &c. Messrs. DISCH
and CAPELLAN keep a large assortment of the best stock of Rhine and Moselle Wines for wholesale.

The Hotel Omnibus conveys passengers to and from the Railway Stations.

HOTEL DU NORD.

FIRST CLASS HOTEL, near the Cathedral, on the Rhine.
Railway Tickets and Booking Office for Luggage in the Hotel.

GRAND HOTEL VICTORIA, COLOGNE.—This first-class Hotel is, with-
out exception, one of the handsomest and most elegant hotels of Germany. It is situated on
the "*Heumarkt,*" opposite the New Monument of King Frederic William the Third, near the
landing-place of the Rhine Steamers, the new Bridges, the Cathedral, and Railway Stations.
Excellent *Cuisine.* Table d'Hôte. Choice Wines. Carriages and Omnibuses at the Hotel. Fixed
and moderate prices.—F. W. LUGENBUHL, Proprietor.

CONSTANTINOPLE.

HOTEL ROYAL.

FIRST CLASS FAMILY HOTEL in every respect, well situated, close to the British Embassy.

CONSTANCE.

HOTEL AND PENSION CONSTANZERHOF.

SWIMMING BATHS ON THE LAKE BELONGING TO THE HOTEL.

PENSION.

HOTEL DU BROCHET (Hecht Hotel).
FIRST-CLASS ESTABLISHMENT.

SITUATED opposite the Harbour, and commanding a beautiful view over the
Lake. Excellent *Pension.* Table d'Hôte at 1 and 5 o'clock. Spacious House, exceedingly
clean, quiet, and newly re-furnished with great comfort. The Proprietor has the sole right of fishing
in the Rhine and Lake. Boats and all appliances in the House. Prices very moderate. French and
English Papers.

HOTEL DE L'EUROPE.
LANG HOUTSTRAAT.

THIS large and commodious first-class Hotel, situated in the centre of the principal objects of attraction, offers to visitors most excellent accommodation at moderate charges.

HOTEL DU VIEUX DOELEN.—Proprietor J. J. VAN SANTEEN, TOURNOOIVELD, 5.—This first-rate Hotel, patronised by the high class of society, is delightfully situated in the vicinity of the Royal Park and public buildings. Table d'Hôte. Beautiful garden.

HAMBURG.

ENGLISH HOTEL,
2, Admirattat Strasse.

Well situated Hotel, near the Exchange and the Harbour.   English spoken.

HOTEL ST. PETERSBURG.

THIS first-class Hotel is most advantageously situated in the principal prome-nades, immediately facing the Alster Bassin, and contains large and small elegantly fur-nished apartments for Families and single Gentlemen.

G. REUTER, Proprietor.

HOTEL DU BELVEDERE. Well appointed first-class Hotel, advantageously situated on the Alster Bassin. Charges moderate. N.B.—Lights and Service not charged.

L. HENER, Proprietor.

HOTEL DE L'EUROPE.—First-Class Family Hotel, situated on the Alster Bassin, the fashionable quarter of the Town. Table d'Hôte. Restaurant "a la Carte." Hydraulic Lift. Terms moderate. English Newspapers. Recommended.

HANOVER.

UNION HOTEL.—This well-known, first-class, and favourite Hotel, for Private Families and Gentlemen, is beautifully and cheerfully situated right opposite the Railway Station. Fixed prices. No charge for light or attendance. Terms for Pension: from 6 to 10 francs der day. Table d'Hôte. Baths.

HOTEL ROYAL, immediately opposite the General Railway Station for Bremen, Berlin, Brunswick, Cologne, Hamburg, &c., admirably situated in the best part of the city. The Cuisine and Wines are of first-rate quality, and the accommodation excellent for families or single travellers. The Reading-room is well supplied with Newspapers and Periodicals. A beautiful garden for the use of visitors. Table d'Hôte at 1 and 4 o'clock, and private dinners to order. Private Carriages. Baths. English and French spoken.

HAVRE.

HOTEL DE L'EUROPE, Rue de Paris.

THE situation of this well-known and old-established Hotel is central and convenient. Table d'Hôte. Restaurant à la Carte. Omnibuses to and from the Railway Station and Steamers.

GRAND HOTEL ET BAINS FRASCATI.

FIRST-CLASS Establishment; entirely re-built in 1871. The only Hotel in Havre situated on the banks of the sea. Moderate charges. Open all the year.

Mr. J. DESCLEVES, Manager.

GRAND HOTEL DE NORMANDIE,
RUE DE PARIS.

FIRST-CLASS Hotel, exceedingly well situated in the centre of the Town. Apartments for Families. Music and Conversation Saloons. "Table d'Hôte." Restaurant à la Carte. English and German spoken.

M. DESCLOS, Proprietor.

HOTEL D'ANGLETERRE, Rue de Paris, 124 and 126.—Exceedingly well situated in the best quarter of the town, opposite the Town Hall, is recommended for its comfort and moderate charges. English spoken.

HEIDELBERG.

HOTEL EUROPE, HEIDELBERG.

THE above is the most beautiful and best situated Hotel in Heidelberg, standing in its own extensive Gardens, which are free for the use of Visitors. Fine Reading Room. Omnibus of the Hotel at the Station. Terms strictly moderate.

HAEFELI GUJER, Proprietor.

Mr. H. G. exports, at wholesale prices, Wines and Swiss Alpine Honey.

Railway Tickets are issued in the Hotel.

CASTLE HOTEL.

FIRST-CLASS Establishment, beautifully situated in the middle of the Park Schloss, commanding a most splendid view. It is fitted up with all the comfort of the present time; So splendid Apartments elegantly furnished, 21 Balconies, magnificent Dining-rooms with outlers on four superb platforms. Terrasses. Three Tables d'Hôte every day. Private Dinners, Reading-room and Smoking-room. English and Foreign Newspapers. Pension all the year at moderate charges. English, French, and Italian spoken. Omnibuses from the Station to the Hotel, 1 mark. Imperial Telegraph and Post Station in the house.

Proprietor: H. Albert, formerly proprietor of the H. de l'Europe, Mannheim.

HEIDELBERG—Continued.

HOTEL DU PRINCE CHARLES,

SOMMER and ELLMER, Proprietors.

Considerably enlarged by a new building, containing a splendid Dining Room, Breakfast Room, Reading Room, and Smoking Room.

The nearest to the Castle, and commanding a fine view of the Ruins.

THIS Hotel, patronised by their Royal Highnesses the Prince of Wales and Prince Alfred, is without question the best situated and most frequented in the town; it possesses an excellent Cuisine, and is favourably known for its clean and airy bedrooms, good attendance, and very reasonable prices. Reading Room supplied with the London Times, Galignani's Messenger, and American papers, &c. Superior Tables d'Hôte at 1 and 5 o'clock. Mr. Sommer exports Wines to England at moderate prices. Baths in the Hotel. Arrangements can be made for a protracted stay. Omnibuses to and from the station.

Railway Tickets issued and Luggage registered in the Hotel.

KRALL'S HOTEL DE DARMSTADT.

FOUR MINUTES FROM THE STATION.

THIS Hotel is beautifully situated on the Bismark Square, with a view on the Neckar and the new Bridge. English and French Newspapers. Pension. Moderate charges.

HOTEL DE HOLLANDE.

QUIET and delightfully situated on the banks of the Neckar, and commanding a fine view of the opposite romantic mountain scenery.

HOMBURG, OR HOMBURG LES BAINS.

BATHS OF HOMBURG,

Half-an-hour from Frankfort-on-the-Maine.

MINERAL Springs very salutary in diseases of the STOMACH and the LIVER, &c. Magnificent Kurhouse open all the year round. Vast park. Comfortable hotels. Moderate charges.

ROYAL VICTORIA HOTEL.—Has been patronised by His Royal Highness the PRINCE OF WALES, and several other Royal Personages. First-rate for families and single gentlemen, close to the Springs and the Kursaal; one of the finest and best situated Hotels in the town. Newly enlarged. All the attendants speak English. Best French and English cooking. Excellent Wines. Moderate charges. Best Stag shooting from August the 1st till November the 1st. Roebuck shooting, Hare and Partridge shooting, as well as good Trout fishing, free for the guests of the Hotel.

GUSTAVE WEIGAND, Proprietor.

HOTEL DE RUSSIE,

FIRST-CLASS HOTEL, one of the best in the town, commanding a magnificent view. Favourably known for its elegance, cleanliness, and kind attendance.

F. A. LAYDIG, Proprietor.

HYÈRES Continued.

HOTEL ET PENSION DE L'ERMITAGE.

Beautifully situated in the Pine Forest, well sheltered, and commanding magnificent view of the
Mediterranean and the Iles of Hyères.

HOTEL DES AMBASSADEURS.

AUGTE. SUZANNE, Proprietor.

First-class Establishment, newly re-built, in a position one of the warmest and best sheltered
of Hyères. View on the Sea.

HESPERIDES HOTEL AND PENSION.—One of the most comfortable
and economical Hotels in the South of France. English House, highly recommended.
Situated in one of the healthiest parts of Hyères. First-class accommodation. English Newspapers
taken in.

INNSBRUCK.

HOTEL DU TYROL.

FIRST-CLASS ESTABLISHMENT, close to the Railway Station, opened
three years ago by the Proprietor of the now closed Hotel d'Autriche. This splendid building
commands the most beautiful view over the valley and mountains, from all sides of the house, and
contains over 150 Bed-rooms and Saloons. Reading and Smoking-rooms, Breakfast, Restaurant, and
Table d'Hôte Saloons, &c. All modern comfort, combined with moderate charges. Special arrangements made for protracted stay. **CARL LANDSEE, Proprietor,** formerly manager of the
"Hotel du Parc," Lugano.

HOTEL DE L'EUROPE.

KEPT BY J. REINHART.

A new and well-furnished Hotel, conveniently situated, just facing the splendid
valley of the Inn, opposite the Railway Station. English spoken.

INTERLACHEN.

HOTEL AND PENSION BEAU RIVAGE.

NEWLY AND ELEGANTLY BUILT.

IN A DELIGHTFUL OPEN POSITION ON THE HOHEWEG, WITH A SPLENDID VIEW
OF THE JUNGFRAU.
Table d'Hote twice a day. Dinners a la Carte. English comfort.

HOTEL DES ALPES.

This Hotel is surrounded by the Largest Shady Garden,
commanding a full view of the Glaciers.

MARSEILLES Continued.

GRAND HOTEL DE MARSEILLE. Cannebiere Prolongee.—Rue de Noailles, 2. Hotel de 1er ordre et le plus près de la gare parmi les grands hôtels.
ASCENSOR, or LIFT, leading to the floors.

GRAND HOTEL BEAUVAN.
The only First-Class Hotel overlooking the Sea. Full South.
PENSION : 8 francs per day and upwards, according to the Apartments.
OMNIBUS TO ALL TRAINS. TIESSIER, Proprietor.

MAISON DOREE.
FIRST-CLASS CAFE RESTAURANT.

5, Rue Noailles, Cannebiere Prolongee
SPECIALITY: BOUELLABAISSE.

MARTIGNY.

HOTEL DE LA TOUR.—T. LUGON, Proprietor. Beautiful situation. Comfortable Apartments. Very good Cooking. Bath Establishment, with a Doctor attached to it, contiguous to the Hotel. Four Languages spoken.

MAYENCE.

HOTEL D'ANGLETERRE, GUSTAVE HUMBERT, of Frankfort-on-Main, Proprietor, Wine Merchant and Grower.—This elegant, first-rate Hotel, much frequented by Families and Gentlemen, situated in front of the Rhine bridge, is the nearest Hotel to the landing-place of the steamboats, and close to the stations of the Frankfort, Wiesbaden, Bavarian, Cologne, Bale, and Paris railways. It affords from its balconies and rooms extensive and picturesque views of the Rhine and mountains. English comfort. Table d'Hôte. This Hotel is reputed for its superior Rhenish wines, sparkling Hock, which Mr. G. Humbert exports to England at wholesale prices. English Times and Illustrated News. French and German newspapers.

RHEINISCHER HOF.—The Rhine Hotel.—This well-known and favourite first-class Hotel is most conveniently and admirably situated near the Railway Terminus, and the Landing-Place of the Rhine Steamers. Moderate charges.

HOTEL DE HOLLANDE, KLEEBLATT and STOECKICHT, Proprietors.— Successors to F. BUDINGEN. This first-class and well-known Hotel, much frequented by English families and tourists, has been greatly enlarged and improved. English newspapers.

MEIRINGEN.
HOTEL DU SAUVAGE.
FIRST-CLASS HOTEL. Beautiful situation. Large garden, with the finest view on the snow-mountains Wellhorn, Dossenhorn, and Engelshörner, Rosonlani glacier, Alpbach and Reichenbach Falls. Illumination of the Alpbach Falls by Bengal lights every evening during the season. Delightful effect. To be seen from the balconies of the Hotel. Most excellent French cooking. Greatest cleanliness and good attendance. Reduced prices of Pension until the 15th of July and after the 1st of September. Recommended.

MILAN Continued.

GRAND HOTEL MANIN.

THE Proprietors of the above Hotel have the honour to inform English travellers that they have fitted up 40 extra rooms, in the most modern English style.

GRAND HOTEL MILAN.

CORSO ALESSANDRO MANZONI.

FIRST-CLASS HOTEL.   THE ONLY HOTEL IN MILAN WITH LIFT.

Hotel de la Grande Bretagne and Riechmann.

This Hotel has been greatly enlarged and entirely re-furnished.

SEVERAL LANGUAGES SPOKEN.

HOTEL DE FRANCE.

19, COURS VICTOR EMANUEL.

THIS Hotel, centrally situated, enjoys a good reputation for its comfort, cleanliness, and moderate charges. Pension from 8 francs a day. Large and small apartments for Families and single Gentlemen. English, French, and German spoken. The Omnibus of the Hotel meets all trains.

MONTE CARLO.

HOTEL DES ANGLAIS.

FIRST-CLASS HOTEL, especially arranged for a Family Hotel. Lift, with latest improvements. N.B.—Omnibus at Monte Carlo Station.

MONT-DORE (NEAR CLERMONT-FERRAND).

GRAND HOTEL DU MONT-DORE, first established by the late Mr. Tache.*— This Hotel is beautifully situated, and surrounded with Ruins and celebrated Geological Phenomena. Mont-Dore is but five hours distant from Clermont-Ferrand.

MONTREUX.

THE ALPINE MADEIRA.—ENGLISH HOME CIRCLE. CLOS DU LAC CLARENS. Temporary or Permanent residents are received in a very large and beautiful Mansion, equally suitable as Summer or Winter residence. Terms moderate.

MOSCOW.

MOSCOW EXHIBITION—The largest and most comfortable Hotel, situate in the centre of Moscow, with all modern improvements. Hot and cold baths. First-class attendance. Charges moderate. All European languages spoken. Tverskoy street (late Schsvaldisheff).

M. GROVSHETSKY, Proprietor.

OSTEND Continued.

HOTEL FONTAINE.

THIS Hotel is situated in the Longue Rue, near the King's Palace, the Kursaal, and Casino, nearest to the sea. It is patronised by the nobility and gentry, and frequently has the honour of receiving Princely visitors. This Hotel is one of the finest establishments in the country. It remains open all the Winter Season.

HOTEL CIRCLE DU PHARE AND RESTAURANT.

THIS FIRST-CLASS HOTEL is situated in the best quarter of the Town, facing the Digue and Bathing. The Proprietor, who is an Englishman, spares no trouble to make his Visitors as comfortable as possible. Table d'Hôte at 5. Restaurant "a la Carte." Terms from 10 frs. a day upwards. Arrangements made for Families. Splendid view from terrace of Hotel. Special terms for Winter. English and American papers taken in. Proprietor, FINCH.

MERTIAN'S NEW FAMILY HOTEL AND PENSION.

SITUATED Rue d'Ouest, close to the Kursaal and Bathing place. First-class Hotel, recommended for its comfort and moderate fixed prices.

Open all the year round.

GREAT OCEAN HOTEL.

OPEN FROM 1st JUNE TILL 1st NOVEMBER.

MAGNIFICENT First-class Hotel, unrivalled for its splendid situation, facing the Sea and the Baths, close to the new Kursaal and the Royal Family's residence.

HOTEL ROYAL DE PRUSSE.—H. HILLEBRAND, Proprietor. First-class Hotel, about 50 yards from the sea dyke. Table d'Hôte at 5 o'clock. Omnibus at the station and landing place.

Under the same management—

GRAND HOTEL DU LITTORAL.—This first-class Hotel, facing the sea, and nearest to the new Kursaal. Dinners at any hour.

HOTEL DU GRAND CAFÉ.

THIS well-known, old-established Hotel, situated on the Place d'Armes. Good Table d'Hôte, and excellent Wines. Good attendance. The Hotel is open all the year. Omnibuses to and from each train.

HOTEL DE RUSSIE.

THIS first-class new Hotel is situated on the Digue, adjoining the Cursaal. Newly furnished throughout. Omnibus to the Station.

GRAND HOTEL MARION.

FIRST-CLASS Hotel, open all the year round. The largest of the town. 150 Rooms. Much frequented by English Tourists. Central situation. Renowned for comfort. Advantageous terms made with families. Beds, light, and attendance from 3s. per day. From 4s. and upwards, good dinners, including half a bottle of Claret. Table d'Hôte. Reading, Smoking, and Sitting Rooms, Pianos, &c. Omnibus at Trains and Steamers. Garden. Stables and Coach-houses. Excellent cheap Wines and Spirits of JOHN MARION & Co., Proprietors, wholesale merchants, opposite the Hotel.

GRAND HOTEL DU LOUVRE

700 ROOMS AND SALOONS.

164 and 168, Rue de Rivoli, and Place du Palais Royal.

TABLE D'HOTE at Six o'clock.

HOTEL DE LA PLACE PALAIS ROYAL,
170, RUE DE RIVOLI, 170.

First-rate Table d'Hôte.

PENSION AT MODERATE PRICES

Fronting the Place du Palais Royal, opposite the Louvre. This Hotel is beautifully situated, and the most comfortable in Paris. Highly recommended to English Families. Rooms from 3 frs.

ASCENSOR LEADING TO EACH FLOOR.

HOTEL DE RUSSIE (à Grossir),

2, BOULEVARD DES ITALIENS, 1, RUE DROUOT.

First-class Hotel. Rooms and Apartments from 2 to 25 frs. per day. Pension and Table d'Hôte.

HOTEL DE RIVOLI, 202, RUE DE RIVOLI.—J. STOLLE, Proprietor. This Hotel, delightfully situated, just opposite the Gardens at the Tuileries, in the vicinity of the Palais Royal and the fine Promenade of the Champs Elysées, offers to travellers of all countries every advantage and comfort requisite in a first-class Hotel. Large and Small Apartments, elegantly furnished. Single Rooms, 3 frs. and upwards. Meals served in the Apartments, either à la carte or à prix fixe. Baths in the Hotel. Terms moderate. All languages spoken.

PARIS Continued.

PARIS Continued.

GRAND HOTEL ANGLO-AMERICAIN, 113—Rue St. Lazare—113. Opposite the St. Lazare Station, most central position, near the Grand Opera and the Madeleine Church. All modern comforts combined with moderate prices. Board at 7s. per day. Arrangements for families.

H. BELLE, Proprietor.

PERFUMER.

GUERLAIN—15, Rue de la Paix, 15, à Paris.

"PARFUMERIE DE LUXE."

OPTICIAN.

THE oldest and most celebrated house of "Chevalier," Engineer, only exists in the Palais Royal, 158, Galerie de Valois, has been carried on since 1760 by the same family. (It was first established Quai de l'Horloge.)

ARTHUR CHEVALIER, o * * Master in Sciences.

Specially for Microscopes, Opera Glasses, Navy Telescopes, Mathematical, Physical, and Meteorological Instruments, &c. 20 Medals. ARTHUR CHEVALIER, grandson and son of Vincent and Charles Chevalier.

Ingeneer STROPÉ, Optician,

Member of the Royal Academy. Purveyor to the Royal Court of England.

24, PALAIS ROYAL, 24.

Old and sole family carrying on the same business since 1785.

Manufacturer of Opera Glasses, Telescopes, Microscopes, and all instruments required for Physic, and for Natural Science. First Class Medal, Paris International Exhibition, 1879.

BOOTMAKER.

ROCHE,
16, RUE VIVIENNE, 16.

ENGLISH SPOKEN.

PAU.

PAU, a Winter Resort, renowned for the numerous cures which a residence has effected, particularly in cases of Affections of the Chest, Heart, Larynx, and Throat. Villas, houses, and furnished apartments to let, at various prices. For all particulars, which will be sent gratuitously, address Mr. LE BARON DE BRAUNEKER-BERIDEZ, Directeur Gérant de l'Union Syndicale, 7, Rue des Cordeliers, Pau.

GRAND HOTEL GASSION, LAFOURCADE BROTHERS.—First-class Establishment, of a monumental construction, situated on the Boulevard du Midi, near the "Chateau Henri IV.," with a splendid panoramic view. English and all other languages spoken.

PAU—Continued.

HOTEL DE FRANCE, Mr. GARDERES, Proprietor.—This First-class
Hotel, situated on the Place Royale, commands the most splendid view of the whole chain
of the Pyrenees.

GRAND HOTEL BEAU SEJOUR.

FIRST-CLASS HOTEL, recommended for its comfort and its beautiful
situation, commanding an extensive and magnificent panorama. Large and small well-furnished Apartments for Families, overlooking the Pyrenees and the Valley of the Gave. A large
garden surrounds the Hotel. American and English Family Hotel. Moderate charges.

HOTEL DE LA POSTE, Place Grammont.—First-class Hotel, situated near
the Castle. Large Apartments for Families. *Restaurant à la Carte. Table d'Hôte.* South
aspect. English and Spanish spoken.

MAISON COLBERT.—This First-Class Pension, with a large Garden
and Tennis Lawn, is kept by the daughters of an English Physician. It is highly recommended for its healthy situation, full South aspect, comfortable Rooms, Good Table, and Moderate
charges. Apply to the Proprietors, Pension Colbert, 39, Rue Montpensier, PAU.

ENGLISH BOARDING HOUSE, Maison Etchebest, 2, Passage Raymond-
Piante, 2. Established for 19 years, in a central but quiet quarter, conducted by an English
Lady. Detached House. South aspect. Meals at general table. Apply to the Proprietor.

SARDA'S PRIVATE HOTEL,
31, RUE PORTE NEUVE.

THE Proprietor, JEAN SARDA (Courier), has the honour to inform visitors
to Pau, that his house has been entirely re-furnished, and offers every comfort of an English
home. The house is well situated in the best part of the Town, and commands a fine view of the
Pyrenees in the South; each floor is fitted up with a balcony, which is very suitable to invalids.
Charges as follows:—Board 6 frs. per day, three meals, Breakfast, Luncheon, and Dinner. Rooms
from 1 to 4 frs. a day. Public Drawing Room, with piano. Smoking Room. English and French
Newspapers. Arrangements can be made by the Season. English, Spanish, and Italian spoken.

Pension Hattersley, Rue Porte Neuve, 27.

KEPT by the wife of an English Clergyman, and combining, as far as
possible, the comfort of an English home, with the advantages of a Continental residence.
For terms, apply to Mrs. HATTERSLEY, 27, Rue Porte Neuve.

Pension Barbey, Rue Montpensier, 36.

THIS Establishment, adjoining the English, Scotch, and Roman Catholic
Churches, is recommended for its tranquil situation, its comfort, and its excellent Cooking.
Moderate charges.

PAU Continued.

JOHN JARVIS,
ENGLISH AND FRENCH CHEMIST,
BY EXAMINATION IN ENGLAND AND FRANCE.

Associate of the Pharmaceutical Society of Great Britain. **4, RUE SERVIEZ, 4.**

PEGLI (Italy).

GRAND HOTEL, PEGLI, kept by Landry and Girard. This First-Class Hotel has all desirable comfort. Large and small Apartments. Drawing-rooms. Reading and Ball-rooms. Billiard-room. Hot and Cold Baths. Excellent place for sketching and botanizing. English service in the chapel on the grounds of the Hotel. Boarding at moderate prices.

PISA.

HOTEL GRANDE BRETAGNE. The best Hotel in the Town. Beautifully situated full South, adjoining the English Church.

POITIERS.

GRAND HOTEL DU PALAIS.
FIRST-CLASS HOTEL, recommended to Families en route to the South of France.

Le Presse. ## POSCHIAVO (Lake).

GRAND HOTEL AND PENSION LE PRESSE.
NEAR the Lake Poschiavo, at the foot of the Bernina, and in proximity of the Engadin. This Hotel offers every desirable comfort. English Chapel. Post and Telegraph Offices. Carriages for excursions, &c.

PRAGUE.

HOTEL D'ANGLETERRE (Englischer Hof).—Proprietor, Mr. F. HUTTIG. This first-rate Establishment is much frequented by English Travellers for its moderate charges, comfort, and cleanliness. Table d'Hôte 4 o'clock. English Newspapers. English and French spoken.

HOTEL GOLDEN ANGEL (ZUM GOLDENEN ENGEL),
Zeltnerstreet (Old Town).—F. STICKEL, Proprietor.
THIS Hotel is situated at no great distance from the Terminus of the Railway to Dresden and Vienna, the Post and Telegraph Offices, the Custom-house, the Theatre, and other public buildings. Warm and Cold Baths. English and French Newspapers.

RHEIMS.

HOTEL DU LION D'OR.—This excellent Establishment, very well situated, just opposite the Cathedral, is conducted by the Proprietor himself, Mr. DISANT, junior, and deserves, in every respect, the patronage of English travellers. Table d'Hôte. English, German, and Italian spoken.

RIVA (on the Lago di Garda).

HOTEL ET PENSION DU LAC.—Ten minutes' walk from the town, commanding a splendid view of the Lake and Mountains, most agreeable for families who wish to make a long stay in this country. Baths. Table d'Hôte. English and French spoken.

ROME.

Grand Hotel du Quirinal,
ROME.

HOTEL COSTANZI.

THIS first-class Hotel contains 350 sleeping rooms and Saloons, all elegantly furnished. Lift. Fine Gardens.

GRAND HOTEL DE RUSSIE, ET DES ILES BRITANIQUES.

This First-class Establishment possesses the advantage of a beautiful Garden, and is situated near the English and American Churches; the principal apartments facing the South, and the entire Hotel being warmed by calorifères, the whole arrangements and moderate prices give universal satisfaction.

G. MAZZERI, Proprietor.

CONTINENTAL HOTEL.
Proprietors, LUGANI & PRESEUZINI,
THE SAME PROPRIETORS
Of the Hotel d'Allemagne in Rome, and the Hotel de Turin in Menton.

ROTTERDAM.

VICTORIA HOTEL.—This Hotel, opened in May, 1869, and built expressly for an English Hotel, is situated in the centre of the town (West End), on the most fashionable Promenade of Rotterdam, just opposite the landing-place of all the Steamers to and from England. Combined civil attendance and moderate charges. Table d'Hôte. Choice Wines. English News-papers. English, French, and German spoken.

SPEZIA.

GRAND HOTEL D'ITALIE.

PIERRE PERNIGOTTI, the new Proprietor, offers a comfortable home and first-rate Cuisine at moderate charges. The only Hotel in Spezia that has an Establishment of Hot and Cold Baths.

HOTEL ROYAL DE LA CROIX DE MALTE.

SOLE HOTEL of the name at Spezia, and kept always by the same Proprietors, LENZI BROTHERS. Every Sunday, English Divine Service in the Hotel.

GRAND HOTEL SPEZIA.

SPLENDID situation. First-class Hotel with large and small Apartments. Two Villas adjoin the Hotel. Varied Promenades and Drives. Winter Station.

MENETREY-HAUSER, Proprietor.

ST. GERMAIN EN LAY.

SUMMER SEASON. **PAVILLON LOUIS XIV,** SUMMER SEASON.

HOTEL RESTAURANT, with a large Garden, at the entrance of the Park Place Pontoise. Winter Season, Hotel Du Louvre, at Nice, renowned for its good French cooking and fine situation. STIKELMANN LARCHER, Proprietor.

ST. MORITZ (ENGADIN SUISSE).

Season, from 1st June to 15th Sept. **HOTEL DU LAC.** Season from 1st June to 15th Sept.

First-class Hotel, richly furnished. Recommended for its beautiful position.

STRASBOURG.

HOTEL DE PARIS.

FIRST-CLASS HOTEL, magnificently situated near the Cathedral, in the most beautiful part of the town. Table d'Hôte and Restaurant. Moderate charges.

HOTEL DE LA MAISON-ROUGE, Grand Place, kept by Mr. FREYSZ. This old-established Hotel will be found equally desirable for Families and single Travellers, in consequence of its central situation, excellent accommodation, and moderate charges. Table d'Hôte twice a day. Excellent Wines. Omnibuses at the Station and Steamboats,

GRAND HOTEL TIVOLLIER.—A newly-built and elegantly-furnished Hotel, in the best and healthiest part of Toulouse. Replete with every comfort. Baths in the Hotel, and Lifts to all the floors. The Proprietor, Mr. TIVOLLIER, has been celebrated for his first-rate cooking.

TOURS.

GRAND HOTEL DE L'UNIVERS,

ON THE BOULEVARD, NEAR THE STATION.

Highly recommended in all the French and Foreign Guide Books.

HOTEL DE LA BOULE D'OR,

RUE ROYALE.

MOST comfortable establishment, situated in the best part of the town. Table d'Hôte. Private Service. English spoken. Moderate charges.

Grand Hotel de Bordeaux.

FIRST-CLASS HOTEL, opposite the Station, on the Boulevard, recommended for the comfort and cleanliness of its Apartments. Mr. FLEURY, Proprietor. English spoken.

TARRAGONA.

HOTEL DE PARIS.

FIRST-CLASS HOTEL, containing large and small well-furnished apartments. Baths. Carriages. Omnibus to and from every train. Terms moderate. Interpreter

GRAND HOTEL DU FAISAN.

17, RUE ROYALE.

FIRST-CLASS Establishment, situated in the best part of the town. Well furnished Apartments, overlooking a garden, in full South. Recommended to families.

TRINT.

GRAND HOTEL TRENTO.

THIS House, situated close to the Railway Station, built for a Hotel, is elegantly furnished, and fitted up with all modern improvements. Large and small apartments. Dining Room and Smoking Room. Reading Saloon, supplied with English and Foreign newspapers.

TREVES, ON THE MOSELLE.

TRIESTE.

HOTEL DELORME.

TURIN.

HOTEL DE L'EUROPE.

HOTEL FEDER (Palais Sonnaz).

GRAND HOTEL LIGURIE, TURIN.

BAGLIONI'S HOTEL ET PENSION D'ANGLETERRE.

HOTEL TROMBETTA,

TURIN Continued.

KRAFT'S GRAND HOTEL DE TURIN,

Branch of the Bernerhof, at Berne, and Kraft's Hotel de Nice, at Nice.

CLEAN and comfortable FIRST-CLASS HOTEL, conveniently situated, opposite the Central Railway Station (arrival platform). Fixed and reasonable charges. No Omnibus wanted.

N.B.—The Kraft's Grand Hotel de Turin is on the left hand side coming out of the Station.

Grand Hotel Suisse.

ADVANTAGEOUSLY situated opposite the Central Railway Station (arrival platform), in the finest part of the Town, affording all the comfort and requirements of the present times. Charges strictly moderate. **J. PERROTTI, Proprietor.**

N.B.- No Omnibus wanted from the Station to the Hotel.

RESTAURANT DE LA MERIDIENNE,

7, RUE ST. THERESE, 7,

18, RUE DE ROME, 18, "GALERY GIESSER," FORMERLY NATA.

ANTONIO BONFANTE, Proprietor.

French and Italian Cooking. Private Saloons on the first floor, with special service.

ULM.

HOTEL DE RUSSIE (RUSSISCHER HOF).

CARL HEINRICH, Proprietor. This splendid and first-rate Establishment, situated opposite the Post Office, twenty paces from the Railway Station, and close to the Promenade, is elegantly and comfortably furnished. Charges moderate. Arrangements made with Families or Single Persons remaining for a period.

VALENCIA (SPAIN).

HOTEL DE LA VILLE DE MADRID,

KEPT by Mr. CARLOS CANTOVA D'HYOS.—This first-rate Establishment, situated on the Villarroza Square, No. 5, has been entirely re-furnished with every modern comfort and luxury, and now offers the most desirable residence to English travellers visiting this fine climate. Excellent Cuisine and good attendance. Foreign Newspapers. English, French, and Italian spoken. Baths, &c.

VARESE (ITALY).

In direct communication by Rail with Milan and the Lakes Maggiore and Como (English Church).

GRAND HOTEL VARESE, was opened 1st July, 1874.—Beautiful First-class Hotel, offering all the comfort and requirements of the present time.

Dr. DAUBENY, M.D., Resident Doctor in the Hotel.

VENICE.

DANIELI'S ROYAL HOTEL.—This Hotel, so extensively and favourably known for the excellence of its management, accommodation, and attendance, and for its moderate charges, has just been enlarged, repaired, and refitted. Table d'Hôte. Interpreters for all (the European) languages.

GRAND HOTEL (formerly Hotel New York), kept by G. L. BARBIERI & Co., on the Grand Canal.—First-class House, with South aspect: the largest, best appointed, and most richly-furnished Hotel in Venice. Excellent cookery. Private gondolas at the Hotel. English and other Languages spoken.

GRAND HOTEL VICTORIA.

THE largest and finest Hotel in Venice, sumptuously furnished, most conveniently situated near the Piazza San Marco. Baths. Excellent service and Cooking. Charges moderate. Arrangements for Pension.

HOTEL DE L'EUROPE.

OLD Established First-Class Hotel, situated on the Grand Canal. Visitors will find this Hotel very comfortable, well situated, and reasonable in its charges.

HOTEL BEAU RIVAGE (formerly a dependance of Hotel Danieli.—This First-class Hotel is most charmingly situated, overlooking the Lagunes, and commanding the most brilliant panoramic views of Venice.

HOTEL D'ANGLETERRE (formerly Hotel Laguna and Pension).—Opposite the Landing Place for the Peninsular and Oriental Steamers.—This hotel, situated in the full South, Quai des Esclavons, commands a splendid view, and overlooks the Lagune and the surrounding Islands near San Mark's Square. Excellent Cooking. Good Table d'Hôte. Choice Wines and Moderate Prices. English spoken.

Grand Hotel d'Italie and Hotel Bauer.

NEAR St. Mark's Square, on the Grand Canal, facing the Church of St. Maria Salute. Fresh and Salt Water Baths, ready at all hours.

BAUER GRUNWALD, Proprietor.

DR. SALVIATI'S Establishment for Glass and Mosaics, Palazzo Swift, Grand Canal, next to the Grand Hotel.

Dr. SALVIATI is the well-known reviver of Industrial Arts. N.B.—Visitors should be careful not to be misled by the Gondoliers. Branch Houses: 17, Rue de la Paix, Paris; 311, Regent Street, London.

VERONA.

GRAND HOTEL DE LONDRES,

FORMERLY Hotel Tour de Londres.—A. Ceresa, new Proprietor.—The Largest and Finest Hotel in Verona, most central position, near the Roman Amphitheatre and new English Church. All languages spoken. Highly recommended.

VERONA Continued.

GRAND HOTEL ROYAL, BARBESI. Et Des Deux Tours.—This Hotel is the first, the most spacious, and the most convenient in the town. Furnished in the most comfortable manner. Table d'Hôte. Omnibuses to and from the Station. All Languages spoken.

VERVIERS.

HOTEL DU CHEMIN DE FER.—Mr. C. RENSONNET, Proprietor.— Situated immediately facing the Railway Station. The Hotel du Chemin de Fer has been patronized by numerous English families. French, English, German, and Dutch spoken.

VICHY LES BAINS (FRANCE).

GRAND HOTEL,

SITUATED in the Park, facing the Casino and the new Music Kiosk. Recommended for its exceptional position.

GRAND HOTEL DES PRINCES, FAVIER-NAUD, Proprietor.—This Hotel is situated between the two parks, in the rue du Parc, overlooking the Casino and Bath Establishment. It has spacious apartments, with attendance of the best description, and a Table d'Hôte is held daily. It offers all the comfort and advantages of a private house, and has been recommended in Murray's Handbook to English Tourists and Invalids. Omnibus belonging to the Hotel conveys travellers to and from the railway terminus at every train.

GRAND HOTEL DES AMBASSADEURS, situated on the Park. This magnificent Hotel is now one of the first in the town. It is managed in the same style as the largest and best hotels on the Continent. By its exceptional situation, the house presents three fronts, from which most beautiful views are to be had. English and Spanish spoken. Interpreter.

GERMOT-GRAND HOTEL DU PARC,
FACING THE BATHS AND THE PARK.

AS Paris, Lyons, and Marseilles, Vichy has its Grand Hotel. The GRAND HOTEL DU PARC, at Vichy, for its comfort and elegance, leaves nothing to be desired. Carriages and Omnibuses at each train.

GRAND HOTEL MOMBRUN & DU CASINO.

FIRST-CLASS HOTEL, situated in the Park, facing the Casino, the new Kiosque, in the centre of the "Sources" and thermal establishments. Table d'Hôte. "Restaurant." Moderate charges. Several languages spoken.

VIENNA.

JOHN FROHNER'S HOTEL "IMPERIAL," formerly the Palace of the Duke of Wurtemburg.—This magnificent first-class Hotel commands splendid views out of four street frontages, and is in close proximity to the Music Vereins Hall, the Kunstlerhaus, the Grand Opera, the Town Theatre, the City Park, and the Schwarzenberg Platz. English and French cooking. N.B.—An advantage which will surely be appreciated, is that *English Divine Service* is held in the *Gothic Chapel* of the Hotel.

WILDBAD.

HOTEL KLUMPP,

Formerly HOTEL DE L'OURS.

Mr. Wm. KLUMPP, Proprietor.

THIS First-Class Hotel, containing 45 Saloons and 235 Bedrooms, with a separate Breakfast and new Reading and Conversation Rooms, as well as a Smoking Saloon, and a very extensive and elegant Dining Room, an artificial garden over the river, is situated opposite the Bath and Conversation House, and in the immediate vicinity of the Promenade. It is celebrated for its elegant and comfortable Apartments, good *Cuisine* and Cellar, and deserves its wide-spread reputation as an excellent Hotel. Table d'Hôte at 1 and 5 o'clock. Breakfasts and Suppers *à la carte*. Exchange Office. Correspondent of the principal Banking-houses of London, for the payment of Circular Notes and Letters of Credit. Omnibuses of the Hotel to and from each Train. Fine Private Carriages when requested. Warm and Cold Baths in the Hotel. Lift to every floor. Excellent accommodation.

HOTEL BELLE VUE,

BY MR. STOCKINGER.

THIS First-Class Hotel, beautifully situated at the entrance of the Promenade, within one minute from the Baths, and three minutes from the new English Church, is much patronised by the Nobility, Clergy, and Gentry, and is frequently honoured with the visit of Princes. It is celebrated for its cleanliness, good attendance, and moderate charges. The *Cuisine* department, as well as the qualities of the Wines, will offer satisfaction to the most fastidious taste. Excellent Sitting and Bed Rooms, furnished with English comfort; Conversation and Reading Rooms; Smoking Rooms; Ladies' Music Room. Warm and Cold Baths in a separate building, newly added to the Hotel. "Times" and other foreign papers taken in. An Omnibus of the Hotel meets every train during the season.

The nearest to the New Trinkhalle, opened June 1873.

WORMS.

HOTEL OLD EMPEROR.—A. KIRSCHHOFER, Proprietor.— First-class Establishment, strongly recommended to travellers on the Rhine. The House is well supplied with every modern convenience and improvement for the reception of visitors. It is situated in the centre of the town, opposite the Cathedral, and near the new monument to Luther. Omnibuses to every train. Private Carriages. Hot and Cold Baths. English Papers. English and French spoken.

WURZBURG.

KRONPRINZ HOTEL.—T. AMMON, Proprietor. Honoured by the presence of his Imperial Majesty the Emperor of Germany, on the occasion of his recent visit to this Town. This First-class Hotel is particularly recommended for its large and airy Apartments. Baths, &c. Newspapers and Books, Periodicals in different languages. Moderate Charges. No extra Charge for Service or Candles.

ZURICH.

HOTEL DE BELLE VUE AU LAC.

Proprietor, F. A. POHL.

THIS well conducted establishment, situated on the shore of the Lake, commands, by its charming position, the best view of the Lake and the Alps. Pension arrangements made for Families. *Pension.*

BRADSHAW'S
NEW, LARGE, AND SPLENDID

RAILWAY MAP OF GREAT BRITAIN
(Size—6 Feet 2 Inches, by 5 Feet 1 Inch):

Exhibiting at one view all the Railways, Railway Junctions, and Railway Stations; the Lines of the Electric Telegraph; the Canals, Navigable Rivers, and the Mineral Districts, with their Geological Distinctions; clearly and accurately Defined from the latest and most Approved Authorities, reduced from the Ordnance Survey.

PRICES.

	£	s.	d.
Handsomely Mounted on Mahogany Rollers, and Varnished	4	0	0
In Handsome Morocco Case, for the Library	4	4	0
In Sheets, Coloured	2	10	0

BRADSHAW'S RAILWAY MAP OF GREAT BRITAIN:
Showing the Lines completed and in progress; Size—4 feet 6 inches, by 3 feet.

PRICES.

	£	s.	d.
Mounted on Rollers and Varnished	1	5	0
Cloth Case	1	0	0
In Sheets	0	12	6

The GRAND HOTEL, Trafalgar Square, LONDON

Occupies the FINEST SITE in the CENTRE of the METROPOLIS.

THE GRAND HOTEL

TRAFALGAR SQUARE, LONDON.

This Hotel combines the Elegance and Luxury of the most important and attractive Hotels in Europe and America, with the Repose and Domestic Comfort which are essentially English.

[Lo.-19

Lightning Source UK Ltd.
Milton Keynes UK
UKHW012317210621
385916UK00003B/1138

9 789354 488177